Up in Smoke

Up in Smoke

From Legislation to Litigation in Tobacco Politics

Third Edition

Martha A. Derthick

University of Virginia

Los Angeles | London | New Delhi
Singapore | Washington DC

CQ Press
2300 N Street, NW, Suite 800
Washington, DC 20037

Phone: 202-729-1900; toll-free, 1-866-4CQ-PRESS (1-866-427-7737)

Web: www.cqpress.com

Cover design: Malcolm McGaughy
Cover photos: Photos.com
Composition: C&M Digitals (P) Ltd.

☺ The paper used in this publication exceeds the requirements of the American National Standard for Information Sciences—Permanence of Paper for Printed Library Materials, ANSI Z39.48–1992.

Printed and bound in the United States of America

15   14   13   12   11   1   2   3   4   5

Library of Congress Cataloging-in-Publication Data

Derthick, Martha.
  Up in smoke : from legislation to litigation in tobacco politics/Martha A. Derthick. — 3rd ed.
       p. cm.
  Includes bibliographical references and index.
  ISBN 978-1-4522-0223-5 (pbk.: alk. paper)
  1. Tobacco—Law and legislation—United States. 2. Tobacco—Government policy—United States. 3. Products liability—Tobacco—United States—History. I. Title.

  KF3894.T63D47 2011
  338.4'767970973—dc23

                                                                    2011025063

Contents

Preface

This book has two origins—one intellectual, the other practical. Intellectually, it began with my teaching an undergraduate course in public policy. I was looking for interesting case-study material and thought I detected some in the tobacco wars. I had developed the practice of staging mock hearings on a major policy issue. Most of the time, I used the future of Social Security, but tobacco control also had possibilities. The one mock hearing that we held in Government 438 at the University of Virginia went very well, with numerous engaging roles for the students to play. Because it was Virginia, I was not surprised to have one student, the granddaughter of tobacco farmers, defend the farmers' interests. It was more surprising to have some of the best students in the class play effectively the roles of tobacco company executives.

To the best of my recollection, what first caught my attention was a story in the *Washington Post* saying that the Tobacco Institute had been abolished in response to action by the state governments. Whoa, I said to myself. When did the governments of the United States get the right to abolish lobbies? What country am I living in? Granted, tobacco is bad for smokers' health; even so, our constitutional traditions of free speech and limited government were not founded just for the protection of benign and popular causes.

Beyond that, as a professor it struck me that tobacco was a rich story, engaging questions of constitutionalism, separation of powers, and federalism; the roles of bureaucracy, interest groups, and the legal profession; issue and agenda development; elite versus mass opinion; the influence of money in politics and of moralism on public policy; and government regulation versus individual responsibility. Almost any question a political scientist might want to raise with undergraduates in introductory courses could be teased out of the tobacco wars. I have tried to capture this richness while organizing the story around the central theme of legislation versus litigation as a mode of policymaking. I like that, too, because I think there is no more important question for students of American institutions and policy processes to examine today.

After a brief introduction (chapter 1), the book opens by recounting the history of legislation and tort litigation under what I call a regime of "ordinary politics." Explained in chapters 2 and 3, this regime prevailed between 1964, when a report of an advisory committee to the U.S. surgeon general initiated the modern campaign against tobacco use, and 1993. I then describe in chapters 4 through 6 the dramatic changes that took place starting in 1994, when Commissioner David A. Kessler of the Food and Drug Administration (FDA) opened a drive to reinterpret federal law and subject the cigarette industry to FDA regulation. Later that year, the attorneys general of the state governments, led by Mississippi's Mike Moore, began filing lawsuits against the industry to recover Medicaid costs that they alleged were attributable to smoking. I analyze the fate of these initiatives in chapters 7 and 8. Kessler's attempt at regulation was defeated in the courts. The suits filed by the attorneys general led first (in June 1997) to an attempt at settlement that failed when Congress declined to incorporate it in legislation, but subsequently (in November 1998) culminated in a "master settlement agreement" that is summarized in chapter 9. The book closes with an analysis of the consequences of the settlement, chapter 10, which I updated in 2004 and again in 2010; a new chapter 11, which gives an account of Congress's return to legislation in 2009 with passage of a law regulating tobacco products; and a concluding chapter 12, which is not new but which has been shortened and sharpened in light of events since 2005.

Although the book is about how policy is made rather than what tobacco policy ought to be, how a reader reacts to this long and complicated story is likely to depend on what he or she believes both about tobacco use and about the relation between government and its citizens. How far ought government to go in protecting citizens against their vices, and how far in regulating manufacturers of harmful products? At one extreme, governments in the United States might do nothing about tobacco, which historically was a staple crop of the South, helping to sustain the economy of a desperately poor region. At the other extreme, they could prohibit its growth, manufacture and use. After the danger of tobacco use was scientifically established and officially publicized in the mid-sixties, governments in the United States generally sought to discourage tobacco consumption by occupying a middle ground, relying on taxation, warning labels and other public admonitions, limitations on place of use, prohibition of radio and TV advertising, and prohibition of sales to minors, a prohibition that until the 1990s was not well enforced. Until recently, Congress has implicitly preferred inaction to action.

Critics of tobacco are critics also of tobacco politics, and regard the historic path of compromise as proof of the excessive power of cigarette producers in legislative politics. Many Americans appear to be skeptical of legislatures' ability to do their work well, partly because members receive large campaign contributions from corporate donors such as cigarette manufacturers. No one could claim that elected legislatures are ideal instruments of policymaking. The question raised here is how they compare with litigation-centered alternatives to which Americans have an increasing propensity to resort. Many readers will receive my findings skeptically. They should perhaps take note of the fact that among all of the industries in the United States, including finance and real estate, pharmaceuticals and tobacco, the largest contributors to election campaigns are lawyers and law firms. Even if not convinced by my conclusions, I promise that the reader who stays with the story will get a penetrating look at politics and government as they are practiced in the United States today.

· Acknowledgments ·

As a practical matter, the book began when Charisse M. Kiino, an acquisitions editor for CQ Press, knocked on my office door and asked what CQ should be publishing. I advised a case study on tobacco politics, and she replied by suggesting that I do it. I said I did not know enough about the subject, was not sure whether at retirement age I could muster the passion needed for another book, had a garden to tend, had other academic commitments, and so on. She coaxed me, as did various colleagues thirty or more years younger than I who insisted that of course I could summon the energy for a book, and had confidence that it would be worth reading. Foremost among these were Gerard Alexander, Gareth Davies, John Dinan, Eric Patashnik, and Steven Teles.

The staff of CQ Press has throughout been efficient, supportive, and altogether a pleasure to work with. I am much indebted to Ms. Kiino, who was unfazed when reviews of an early prospectus confirmed my claim that I did not know much about the subject, and whose editorial advice at critical moments improved the result. For more than a decade, she has remained steadfast in support of this work. I also thank Christopher M. Karlsten, who edited the completed manuscript for the first edition; Talia Greenberg, who ably substituted for him when he was on vacation; Katharine Miller, who edited the manuscript for the second edition in 2004; and Joan Gossett, who was in charge of producing it. For the third edition, Sarah Fell, who was in charge of production, and Shannon Kelly, as editor, maintained the high professional standards and good nature of their predecessors.

CQ engaged several reviewers of the prospectus and several more of the first draft of the manuscript, including Juliet Gainsborough of the University of Miami; Evan Gerstmann of Loyola Marymount University; Donald P. Haider-Markel of the University of Kansas; Trey Hood of the University of Georgia; Michael J. Licari of the University of Northern Iowa; Lynn Mather of the University of Buffalo Law School, SUNY; Raymond Tatalovich of Loyola University Chicago; and Stephen Wirls of Rhodes College. Collectively they were responsible for many improvements and also for alerting me to just how controversial the subject of tobacco is. I am grateful also to Mary Graham, who read the first draft; Richard Drew, who read the final one; and Shep Melnick, who read both. Each provided helpful suggestions for the first edition.

I was helped also by the opportunity to present the emerging argument in seminars at the Miller Center of Public Affairs of the University of Virginia, Harvard University, and Claremont McKenna College. For these invitations, I thank, Kenneth W. Thompson; Shep Melnick, the late Delba Winthrop, and Harvey Mansfield; and Charles Kesler, respectively. It was Professor Kesler, searching for a title for my Claremont talk, who suggested "Up in Smoke." At the Miller Center and beyond, Professor Matthew Holden asked pointed and helpful questions, particularly about the role of the attorneys general. At Harvard, several members of the seminar challenged me, including Tom Burke, Robert Faulkner, Meg Jacobs, Morton Keller, Kim Kosman, Marc Landy, Paul Pierson, and Theda Skocpol. At Claremont, faculty members Joseph Bessette and Peter Skerry, as well as Professor Kesler, did the same. I appreciate their encouragement and interest. As I was nearing the end of the manuscript for the first edition, I had the opportunity to present seminars at Cambridge University and Oxford University, thanks to Anthony J. Badger, Gareth Davies, and Daniel Walker Howe. Discussion in those forums yielded several improvements.

In seeking to understand the economics and politics of growing tobacco, subjects that were treated more fully in the second edition, I benefited from the excellent Web sites of the Economic Research Service (ERS) of the U.S. Department of Agriculture, Professor Will Snell of the University of Kentucky, and Professor A. Blake Brown of North Carolina State University. In addition, Thomas C. Capehart Jr., an economist at the ERS, kindly answered many questions that I addressed to him by e-mail.

Professor Joseph White of Case Western Reserve University supplied a large number of detailed comments on the first edition, for which I thank him. Richard J. Bonnie of the University of Virginia Law School, the late Judy Wilkenfeld and Eric Lindblom of the Campaign for Tobacco-Free Kids, Michael S. Greve of the American Enterprise Institute, Christine Hall and Hans Bader of the Competitive Enterprise Institute, and Margaret A. Little all contributed helpfully to my research for the second edition. Ms. Hall and Mr. Bader continued to give assistance as the third edition was prepared.

When I proposed to CQ Press a third edition, Ms. Kiino solicited reactions anonymously from several users of the book, who responded with warm endorsements, for which I thank them even if I don't know who they are. This edition benefited from the opportunity to present a paper at the 32nd annual research conference of the Association for Public Policy Analysis and Management, held in Boston in the fall of 2010. I am indebted to Eric Patashnik for that opportunity and to Rogan Kersh for comments and encouragement on that occasion. As always, I received a great deal of useful advice from John Dinan. Shep Melnick, making a repeat appearance in these acknowledgements, and Sidney Milkis, appearing for the first time, also helped.

Some of the analysis has been published separately in articles, including "Federalism and the Politics of Tobacco," in *Publius: The Journal of Federalism* (winter 2001); "The Lawyers Did It: The Cigarette Manufacturers' Policy Toward Smoking and Health," in *Legality and Community: On the Intellectual Legacy of Philip Selznick* (Berkeley Public Policy Press and Rowman and Littlefield, 2002), edited by Robert A. Kagan, Martin Krygier, and Kenneth Winston; a review of David A. Kessler's book, *A Question of Intent,* in the *Claremont Review of Books* (spring 2001); and "Lawyers' Ethics in Decline," in Carole L. Jurkiewicz, ed., *The Foundations of Organizational Evil* (forthcoming from M. E. Sharpe).

I thank Vince Willmore of the National Center for Tobacco-Free Kids for permission to reproduce an advertisement. I owe a special debt to the staff of the Alderman Library of the University of Virginia, which gives superb service to the faculty, including, I now know, retired faculty. The library staff was prompt and generous with help in tracking down sources, in print and on the Web. Kent Olson, reference librarian at the law school, was also helpful.

To a degree unprecedented in my career, I have written this book by synthesizing secondary and primary sources available through libraries and Web databases. I barely left Charlottesville—indeed, barely left my house. I am a bit uneasy about that. No doubt there are points at which the book would be better had I done interviews, but the source material from books, newspapers, and Web sources was so abundant and so readily available that I settled for relying on them. I relied in particular on the news stories of Gordon Fairclough, Milo

Geyelin, Vanessa O'Connell, and David Kesmodel of the *Wall Street Journal,* and those of Barry Meier and Duff Wilson of the *New York Times.* My debt to them will be evident from the citations. I am, of course, responsible for the use I made of these sources.

Martha A. Derthick
Charlottesville, Virginia
April 2011

CHAPTER ONE

A New Way of Regulating Tobacco

CIGARETTE PRICES IN THE UNITED STATES vary a great deal with the quality of the brand and the state in which the sale occurs, but the price of leading brands shot up everywhere beginning in the late 1990s. In 1997 premium-brand cigarettes were selling at around $1.90 per pack, but over the next five years major manufacturers raised the wholesale price of cigarettes fourteen times.[1] By fall 2003 the price was approximately $3.60 a pack, and it was much higher in states with steep excise taxes, such as California, Maine, Massachusetts, Michigan, New Jersey, New York, Rhode Island, and Washington.

The rise was not accounted for by an increase in the price of tobacco. Although tobacco has historically been a very profitable crop for the farmers who grow it, yielding more income than other crops, only a tiny fraction of the cost of a cigarette—less than 1 percent—was traceable to the manufacturers' tobacco purchases.[2] Nor was the rise accounted for by increases in production costs, which are relatively low because tobacco manufacturing is highly mechanized.

The place to hunt for an explanation of the rising prices is not in the realm of economics but that of politics and law. Rather than searching in tobacco fields and factories, one should look to government offices, law firms, and courtrooms. Approximately 50 cents of the price increase was attributable to legal fees, plus the costs of a legal settlement the major cigarette manufacturers reached late in 1998 with state governments that had brought suit against them between 1994 and 1997, charging consumer fraud and unjust enrichment, among other offenses. This so-called Master Settlement Agreement (MSA) with forty-six states, along with settlements previously reached individually with Florida, Minnesota, Mississippi, and Texas, obliged the companies to pay an estimated $246 billion to the state governments between 2000 and 2025. By the end of 2003, the forty-six MSA states had received more than $29 billion.[3]

In effect, the settlement costs were an addition to the excise taxes on cigarettes that the state governments levy through legislation.

And while the settlement costs were driving the price of cigarettes up, so were rises in both federal and state excise taxes. The federal excise tax per pack rose in 2000 from 24 to 34 cents, and in 2002 to 39 cents. The average state tax at the beginning of 2002 was approximately 44 cents, and in the following two years more than thirty states enacted increases.[4]

Of course, the companies also increased prices to sustain their profits, and some industry analysts believe that these price increases exceeded what was necessary to meet the extraordinary new legal costs. The companies had reason to believe—mistakenly, as it turned out—that the terms of their settlement with the state governments had protected them against price competition and hence a loss of market share.

· Shift in Policymaking Strategy ·

How all this happened is the subject of this book, which analyzes a dramatic shift in the way governments made policy toward the tobacco industry. Between 1964 and 1993, governments practiced what I call "ordinary politics," by which I mean that the principal arena of policy-making was elected legislatures, where the outcomes typically were compromises between contending interests—public health advocates opposed to tobacco use on one side and the industry, consisting of manufacturers and growers, on the other side. Retailers and the broadcasting and advertising industries were sometimes allied with the latter. Litigation against the manufacturers was limited to individual cases and had little influence on public policy. Then the politics of tobacco suddenly underwent a fundamental change, in which policymaking was, at least for a time, largely removed from legislatures and instead made the subject of litigation.

The attorneys general of the state governments initiated the change. Starting with the attorney general of Mississippi, Mike Moore, they began filing suit in the summer of 1994. These suits were in general carried on without public appropriations, and their results, negotiated settlements between legal adversaries, were touted by the attorneys general as having advantages that could not be obtained through other means, including legislation. To finance them, nearly all attorneys general circumvented legislatures by signing contingency-fee contracts with private tort lawyers. Newly enriched with winnings from asbestos and other class-action suits against product manufacturers, these tort lawyers were able to invest some of their wealth in the suits against tobacco in the hope that they would win and be still further enriched. The suits also benefited from legislative support. The legislatures of at least three states, Florida, Maryland, and Vermont, changed state law to ensure that their attorneys general would defeat the industry in the states' courts. What was sacrificed was not policymaking by legislatures but respect for law as an institution.

· Master Settlement Agreement ·

The initial attempt by the state attorneys general and the major cigarette manufacturers to settle the lawsuits and create a new regulatory regime for tobacco was submitted to Congress for action. Completed in June 1997, this potential settlement alluded somewhat disingenuously to the inefficiencies of the many lawsuits, private as well as public, against cigarette manufacturers: "All of these civil actions are complex, slow moving, expensive and burdensome, not only for the litigants but also for the nation's state and federal judiciaries. . . . Only national legislation offers the prospect of a swift, fair, equitable and consistent result that would serve the public interest."[5] National legislation, however, was not forthcoming. The Senate debated a bill but did not act, and the contending litigants resumed negotiations in June 1998.

The document they arrived at, the Master Settlement Agreement of November 1998, besides requiring the billions of dollars in payments to state governments, contained many prohibitions on marketing. It banned transit and outdoor advertising, including billboards and signs or placards larger than a poster in arenas, stadiums, shopping malls, and video game arcades. It banned cartoon characters in advertising, promotion, and packaging, putting an end to the infamous Joe Camel, a hip character that the R. J. Reynolds Company had created and popularized in the late 1980s. It banned the distribution and sale of nontobacco merchandise with brand logos, such as caps, T-shirts, and backpacks, except at tobacco-sponsored events. It also limited brand-name sponsorship of concerts, events with a significant youth audience, and team sports (football, basketball, baseball, hockey, and soccer) to one per year.

The agreement also contained restrictions on the industry's political activity that were little remarked upon in journalistic accounts but are at odds with American political traditions. It disbanded the Tobacco Institute, the industry's lobbying organization. It prohibited the cigarette companies from lobbying against any of the terms of the MSA or challenging their constitutionality. It prohibited them from seeking bankruptcy. It also barred them from lobbying against various state and local legislative proposals, such as those limiting youth access to vending machines or penalizing youths for possession of tobacco.

• FDA Campaign •

The state governments' lawsuits were not the only attempts in the late 1990s at bypassing legislatures to expand the scope of tobacco regulation. Another was a campaign by David A. Kessler, commissioner of the federal Food and Drug Administration (FDA) from 1990 to 1997, to assert jurisdiction over the regulation of tobacco. Under Kessler, the FDA, which earlier had denied that it had such authority, reinterpreted the law and in 1996 issued regulations with the backing of the Bill Clinton White House. This action was overturned in the courts, although only by the narrowest of margins (5–4) in the Supreme Court, which ruled in spring 2000 that the FDA's historic interpretation was correct—it lacked statutory authority to regulate cigarettes.

Kessler's campaign gained momentum after the Republican capture of the House of Representatives in the 1994 midterm elections. It won crucial support within the Clinton administration precisely because it offered a way to pursue health policy objectives without legislation. Defeated in the courts, this campaign in the short run was less significant than the litigation brought by the state attorneys general, but both substantively and tactically the two efforts complemented each other. This book therefore treats both of them, exploring in detail their origins and outcomes, including the failure of Congress to enact the terms of the 1997 settlement between the cigarette companies and the state governments.

• Tobacco and Adversarial Legalism •

Before exploring the rise of extralegislative policymaking, this book describes the legislation and litigation that took place in the years 1964–1993. It begins with the assumption that policymaking by elected, representative legislatures is preferable to litigation as a matter of constitutional principle. Self-government is at the core of the United States Constitution: Here the people rule. Officeholders acquire the right to make decisions on behalf of citizens either by being elected or by being accountable to those who are elected. However, big governments, burdened with many responsibilities, test the principle of self-government.

As a practical matter, legislatures must make broad delegations of rulemaking authority to executive agencies. When these delegations are clear and agency rules fall within their bounds, such rulemaking fits more or less comfortably under my rubric of "ordinary politics." Agency rulemaking in U.S. government is long established, voluminous, heavily regulated by statutory law, and constantly subject to judicial scrutiny. On the other hand, statutory delegations are often vague and contestable, and the American system of separated powers, with a government in which the executive and legislative branches are independently constituted and often controlled by rival political parties, invites entrepreneurship by agency heads. The story told here of David Kessler's enterprise shows both how far a determined agency head can go in mounting initiatives without congressional sanction and how judicial review can restrain such conduct.

Policymaking through litigation, engaging as contestants the parties principally at interest, is more deeply problematic than agency rulemaking, especially when, as in the cases recounted here, out-of-court settlements are reached so neither judges nor juries bring judgments to bear. Negotiations between the contending parties—a typical way of concluding lawsuits—do not feature public deliberation, as legislation ordinarily does in a democracy (even if legislative procedures are often less than transparent).

Since the late 1960s, policymaking through litigation has become entrenched in the United States, rivaling so-called ordinary politics. Always legalistic, the society has grown more combatively so. Always disproportionately led and influenced by lawyers, who have usually accounted for about half of the members of Congress, the society has ceded even greater weight to them. Whereas the United States had just under three hundred thousand lawyers in 1960, it had over a million in 2000, one for every 264 persons.[6] According to the Center for Responsive Politics, which tracks political campaign contributions for industries and interest groups, lawyers and law firms have topped all contributors in every election cycle since 1990 except for 2008, when they were surpassed by retirees.[7]

Political scientist Robert Kagan has given the name "adversarial legalism" to the practice of policymaking, policy implementation, and dispute resolution through lawsuits. According to Kagan, the method is characterized by formal legal contestation and by litigant activism—"a style of legal contestation in which the assertion of claims, the search for controlling legal arguments, and the gathering and submission of evidence are dominated not by judges or government officials but by disputing parties or interests, acting primarily through lawyers."[8]

The practice is distinctive to the United States. According to Kagan, other countries rely more heavily on bureaucratic administration, discretionary judgments by experts or political authorities, or a judge-dominated style of litigation.[9] As the practice is distinctive to the United States, so is the legal profession on which such conduct depends. In no other country are lawyers so entrepreneurial in seeking out new kinds of business and advancing unprecedented legal claims. American lawyers exalt adversarial legalism also by pursuing a zealous advocacy of clients' causes. They are aggressive.[10] The tone of legal contestation over tobacco is captured in a story told by Allan M. Brandt, a Harvard historian who was an expert witness for the U.S. government when it prosecuted the tobacco industry between 1999 and 2006. Prior to his appearance in court, the government's lead attorney asked if he understood what would happen on cross-examination. He said he knew that the industry's lawyers would try to make him look as bad as possible. "No," she responded. "That's not it. They want to destroy you and leave you in a pool of blood."[11]

Note the emphasis on litigants and lawyers rather than judges. Landmark decisions of the U.S. Supreme Court in the late twentieth century, particularly in regard to school desegregation and abortion, have accustomed people to thinking of what happens in the legal system as the product of judges' decisions. In the modern study of American government, they loom as powerful figures—though just how powerful has been a subject of scholarly dispute. For decades there has been a great deal of political debate and scholarly writing about "judicial activism," as well as bitter partisan contests in Congress over appointments to all levels of the federal bench and in state governments when judges are chosen in elections. Judges are not without an ability to shape their own agendas, yet the fact remains that what judges do, particularly at the initial (trial) level, depends very much on what litigants bring to them.[12] And litigants often choose to settle without reaching either a judge or jury.

Activist judges have sometimes surfaced in tobacco policymaking. In the late 1980s and early 1990s, there was H. Lee Sarokin, a federal district judge in New Jersey who the industry repeatedly tried to remove from *Cipillone v. Liggett Group, Philip Morris and Loews*. When Sarokin wrote that "the tobacco industry may be the king of concealment and disinformation," the Third Circuit at last concluded that he had gone too far and removed him from pending tobacco litigation.[13] Much later, in 2006, another famously active federal district judge, Jack B. Weinstein of Brooklyn, certified an $800 billion class action against the tobacco companies for using such terms as "light" and "low-tar" in ways alleged to be misleading. The Second Circuit disallowed the class action.[14] On the whole, however, judges have been circumspect in tobacco litigation, particularly in their reluctance to certify class actions, and they are not the central figures in the following story. Litigants and lawyers are.

Arguably, this makes tobacco a quintessential case of adversarial legalism, but there are so many and such varied cases of policymaking through litigation in the United States that one would hesitate to single out any one as representative. Played for high monetary stakes and for issues of life and death, tobacco has been more dramatic than most litigation and also more extreme in its principal result, the Master Settlement Agreement. It is distinctive and important that the key initiators of the litigation were *public* officials—the attorneys general of state governments. This gave them a critical advantage in relation to their opponents, the private corporations that manufacture cigarettes. State attorneys general are frequent litigators on a wide variety of subjects; as such, they merit study in their own right. Nonetheless, they neither invented the practice of adversarial legalism nor do they monopolize it.[15]

· Notes ·

1. Pat Stith, "Upstart Brands Hurt Big Tobacco," *Raleigh News & Observer,* January 4, 2004, www.mooregop.org/nando_1-4-2004_upstart_brands_hurt_big_tobac co.html, accessed March 17, 2011.

2. Tara Parker-Pope, *Cigarettes: Anatomy of an Industry from Seed to Smoke* (New York: New Press, 2001), 27. Parker-Pope's source was David Adelman, a tobacco industry analyst for Morgan Stanley Dean Witter, who estimated the breakdown of the cost of a pack of cigarettes purchased in New York City at $3.50.

3. National Association of Attorneys General, "President's Message: Fifth Anniversary of Landmark Tobacco Settlement," www.naag.org/news/presmsg-20031117-tobacco.php, accessed January 8, 2004.

4. Centers for Disease Control, "Cigarette Excise Tax per Pack, February 1, 2002," www.cdc.gov/tobacco/statehi/html_2002/excise.htm, accessed January 5, 2004; Gordon Fairclough, "Politicians Are Hooked on Cigarette Taxes," *Wall Street Journal,* February 20, 2002, A2; and American Heart Association, Campaign for Tobacco-Free Kids, American Cancer Society, and American Lung Association, *A Broken Promise to Our Children: The 1998 State Tobacco Settlement Five Years Later* (November 12, 2003), iv.

5. Carrick Mollenkamp et al., *The People vs. Big Tobacco* (Princeton, N.J.: Bloomberg Press, 1998), 270.

6. Clara N. Carson, "The Lawyer Statistical Report: The U.S. Legal Profession in 2000" (2004), reprinted in Andrew L. Kaufman and David B. Wilkins, *Problems in Professional Responsibility for a Changing Profession* (Durham, N. C.: Carolina Academic Press, 5th ed., 2009), 732–733.

7. Open Secrets.org, "Lawyers/Law Firms: Long-term Contribution Trends," www .opensecrets.org/industries/totals.php?cycle = 2010&ind = K01, accessed August 26, 2010; and Open Secrets.org, Tobacco: Long-term Contribution Trends, www .opensecrets.org/industries/totals.php?cycle = 2010&ind = A02, accessed August 26, 2010. In 2008, lawyers and law firms donated $233,917,242, of which $178,814,187, or 76 percent, went to Democrats; the tobacco industry donated $4,221,186, of which $2,613,548, or 62 percent, went to Republicans.

8. Robert A. Kagan, *Adversarial Legalism: The American Way of Law* (Cambridge, MA: Harvard University Press, 2001), 9.

9. *Ibid.*, 3.

10. *Ibid.*, 55–58.

11. Allan M. Brandt, *The Cigarette Century: The Rise, Fall, and Deadly Persistence of the Product That Defined America* (New York: Basic Books, 2007), 500–501.

12. The literature on what courts do is immense. For a masterful introduction to the subject, see Martin Shapiro, "Judicial Activism," in *The Third Century: America as a Post-Industrial Society*, ed. Seymour Martin Lipset (Stanford, CT: Hoover Institution Press, 1979), 109–131.

13. Richard Kluger, *Ashes to Ashes* (New York: Random House, Vintage Books, 1997), 676.

14. David Cay Johnston and Melanie Warner, "Tobacco Makers Lose Key Ruling on Latest Suits," *New York Times*, September 26, 2006, A1; Stephanie Saul, "Appeals Court Panel Throws Out Class Action Over Light Cigarettes," *New York Times*, April 4, 2008, C1.

15. It is true that within the very broad universe of adversarial legalism, the attorneys general with their tobacco lawsuits inaugurated a new type of litigation—mass tort suits filed by state and local governments on behalf of citizens against manufacturers of products that have harmed the public's health. See Donald G. Gifford, *Suing the Tobacco and Lead Pigment Industries: Government Litigation as Health Prescription* (Ann Arbor: University of Michigan Press, 2010). Using the two cases of tobacco and lead pigment, with additional attention to a third (handguns), Gifford evaluates the effectiveness of this particular genre of litigation. His conclusions are similar to mine. Ending with the famous remark of Winston Churchill that democracy is the worst form of government except all others, he adds: "The wave of recent attempts by state attorneys general and judges to replace the programs adopted by democratically elected legislatures with regimes established through . . . litigation, however well intended, is no exception." (229)

CHAPTER TWO

The Ordinary Politics of Legislation

OFFICIAL OPPOSITION TO TOBACCO USE is as old as the use itself. A sultan of Turkey and a czar of Russia put people to death for smoking, thus beating tobacco to the punch. The first known American crusader against smoking was a signer of the Declaration of Independence, Dr. Benjamin Rush of Philadelphia, who was followed not much later by one of the founders of the University of Virginia, John Hartwell Cocke.[1] Horace Greeley, publisher of the *New York Tribune* in the nineteenth century, coined or popularized the saying that a cigar was "a fire at one end and a fool at the other."[2] Late in the nineteenth century or early in the twentieth, nearly all state governments in the United States enacted laws restricting tobacco. At their extreme, these laws forbade manufacture, sale, and possession. The milder, more typical ones applied only to minors. By 1920 minors could legally buy cigarettes only in Virginia and Rhode Island. Although a number of lower courts held that anticigarette laws were unconstitutional, the Supreme Court affirmed their validity in a Tennessee case at the turn of the century.[3]

Despite early efforts at control, tobacco use in the United States rose steadily during the twentieth century, receiving sharp boosts during the two world wars. Gen. John J. Pershing, who commanded U.S. troops in France in World War I, cabled Washington, "Tobacco is as indispensable as the daily ration; we must have thousands of tons of it without delay."[4] G. I. Joe fought the Axis powers in World War II with a cigarette dangling from his mouth. G. I. Joe's commander in chief, President Franklin D. Roosevelt, smoked his with a jaunty, stylish holder. Tobacco farmers stayed at home, excused from the draft, because their crop was judged essential to the war effort.[5]

The popularity of cigarettes continued to grow after the war. Movie stars and athletes smoked. In New York's Times Square a famous billboard, two stories high and stretching half a block along Broadway, blew smoke rings twenty-four hours a day. Smoke filled buses and trains, offices and homes, hotel rooms and bars. Ashtrays overflowed. Butts littered sidewalks and subway platforms. Clothing and upholstery bore holes from cigarette burns. Cigarette lighters and cases made good holiday gifts. Midcentury America was in thrall to tobacco.

The fact that cigarette smoking took hold so widely, at a time when the public did not expect government to protect it from the ordinary hazards of life, helps explain why politicians were reluctant to stamp it out in response to appeals from the public health professions. As a very old and entrenched product, cigarettes benefited from the politicians' instinct to accept whatever is customary. Yet even as this country's tobacco-laden troops were leaving for foreign combat in the 1940s, the scientific case against smoking was building.

· Smoking Linked to Cancer ·

The first scientific reports that smoking caused cancer were published at the turn of the nineteenth century. Scattered reports appeared in the 1930s but were inadequately substantiated. By the 1950s such reports were taking a more credible form. The *Journal of the American Medical Association* carried two articles in 1950 reporting that the incidence of lung cancer was higher among smokers than among nonsmokers, and that the longer and more heavily one smoked, the greater was the risk of the disease. Several different research teams in this country, the United Kingdom, and Germany produced such findings. One of these teams, consisting of Dr. Evarts A. Graham, a chest surgeon at Barnes Hospital in St. Louis, and Ernst L. Wynder, a student at Washington University School of Medicine and later a staff member at the Sloan-Kettering Institute in New York, produced skin cancer in laboratory mice by painting tar on their backs. Graham and Wynder published their results in late 1953.[6]

These scientific findings quickly found their way into mass circulation newspapers and magazines such as the *New York Times* and *Reader's Digest*, giving rise to a "cancer scare" and a temporary drop in the incidence of smoking. Frightened executives of the cigarette industry hired a public relations firm, Hill and Knowlton, to help them devise a response. In 1954 they placed a full-page advertisement, gratuitously entitled "A Frank Statement," in more than four hundred newspapers throughout the country. The ad said that they accepted "an interest in people's health as a basic responsibility, paramount to every other consideration in our business." They also changed their products by lowering levels of tar and nicotine and introducing filters and mentholated brands, in a round of competition known as the "tar derby." Without any evidence on which to rest the claim, advertising implied that these cigarettes were safer than those they were replacing. Seemingly reassured, the public bought the new products and smoked more than ever. In 1960 per capita annual consumption of cigarettes for all Americans age eighteen and over reached a record 4,171, or eleven and a half cigarettes for every person every day.[7] By 1963 it had risen further, to a new peak of 4,345.[8]

· Birth of the Antismoking Movement ·

The movement against smoking began in earnest in January 1964 with the report of the U.S. Surgeon General's Advisory Committee on Smoking and Health, a group of ten experts appointed by Surgeon General Luther Terry in 1962 to analyze evidence about the health effects of smoking. It had met nine times over the course of thirteen months, working as well through subcommittees, specially convened conferences and seminars, and many reports commissioned from consultants. Released on a Saturday (when the stock market would be closed) to two hundred members of the press shut in the State Department auditorium, the report was long, cautious yet compelling, and abundantly documented. By then thousands of articles had been published on smoking and disease. The purpose of the committee was not to introduce new findings but to summarize what existed—and to do so under the weighty auspices of the U.S. government.

The central conclusion was that "cigarette smoking is a health hazard of sufficient importance in the United States to warrant appropriate remedial action." The report said that "in view of the continuing and mounting evidence from many sources, it is the judgment of the Committee that cigarette smoking contributes substantially to mortality from certain specific diseases and to the overall death rate." The committee further concluded that "cigarette smoking is causally related to lung cancer in men" and that "the magnitude of the effect of cigarette smoking far outweighs all other factors." It found that "the risk of developing lung cancer increases with duration of smoking and the number of cigarettes smoked per day, and is diminished by discontinuing smoking." It said that the data for women, though less extensive than those for men, pointed in the same direction. The panel reported that cigarette smoking is the most important cause of chronic bronchitis and could lead to laryngeal cancer. It also reported statistically significant, and possibly causal, associations between smoking and esophageal cancer, bladder cancer, coronary artery disease, emphysema, peptic ulcers, and low birth weight. It said that men who smoked were, on average, about ten times as likely to die of lung cancer as those who did not smoke.[9]

The report was a milestone. Since its release in 1964, the politics of smoking and tobacco has consisted of a struggle to define and pursue the "appropriate remedial action" that it called for. The struggle has been fought on a widening array of fronts and with escalating conceptions of what "appropriate" action would be. Until 1994 legislatures dominated policymaking at the federal, state, and local levels of government.

• Congress as National Policymaker •

Between the mid-1960s, when serious efforts at tobacco control began with the report to the surgeon general, and 1994, when FDA commissioner Kessler made his regulatory démarche, Congress kept control of tobacco policymaking at the national level in its own hands. Beginning in 1965 with a compromise enactment that was more favorable than not to the industry, it slowly became more receptive to the pleas of anti-tobacco activists. Its position changed as its internal composition changed and as antitobacco activists gained in organized strength and skill.

The report to the surgeon general was a summons. When its authors referred to "remedial action," they presumably had in mind mainly the government rather than smokers. In effect, the report invited a response from Congress, the nation's lawmaker, and from the regulatory agencies of the federal government.

Warning Labels and the 1965 Law

The first to respond was the Federal Trade Commission (FTC), which began proceedings to require health warnings on all cigarette packages and in all advertisements just seven days after the report was released. The FTC is one of the numerous "independent regulatory commissions" in the federal government. The members of these multimember bodies, created by acts of Congress, are appointed by the president for fixed and overlapping terms but are not removable by him (hence their "independence"). So swift was the FTC's response that it had obviously been prepared in advance. A liaison from the commission had attended most of the open meetings of the committee, and several months before the surgeon general was to issue the report, the FTC organized a staff task force on cigarettes, consisting of physicians, economists, and lawyers. Thus, the FTC was ready to act immediately.

The FTC had been created in 1914, during the administration of Woodrow Wilson, to check the power of big business. It was originally designed to strengthen antitrust regulation, with jurisdiction over such practices as price fixing. In 1938, during Franklin Roosevelt's New Deal, the Wheeler-Lea Act was passed, empowering it as well to regulate "unfair or deceptive acts or practices in commerce." Thereafter, it would concentrate more on deceptive advertising than on antitrust actions. Armed with this authority, the FTC in the 1940s and 1950s had sought to remove health claims from cigarette advertising. It issued guidelines and brought a number of actions (ten to twenty) against individual companies for false or misleading advertising. For example, in 1942 it prevented the Brown & Williamson Tobacco Company, maker of Kools, from claiming that their cigarettes would keep one's head clear or protect against colds.

As late as 1950, the FTC justified one such action against a cigarette company by arguing that no manufacturer was entitled to claim health superiority because all brands were equally safe: "The record shows . . . that the smoking of cigarettes, including Camel cigarettes [the target of the FTC's action in this case] in moderation by individuals . . . who are accustomed to smoking and who are in normal good health . . . is not appreciably harmful." This rationale was soon abandoned, of course, and by the beginning of the next decade the FTC was prohibiting the industry from publishing tar and nicotine levels in its advertisements and claiming health benefits from filters, the advertising of which had fueled the "tar derby."[10]

Emboldened by the new report to the surgeon general, and without consulting Congress, the FTC in spring 1964 opened three days of hearings on a rule that would require a health warning. The cigarette industry did not appear but was represented by an attorney, H. Thomas Austern, from the elite Washington firm of Covington and Burling. Austern argued that the FTC lacked the necessary rulemaking authority and that, in any case, the issue was too important to be decided by an appointed regulatory commission. A legislature elected by the people should decide whether to require health warnings. The FTC proceeded to publish its proposed rule in the *Federal Register,* taking a step required prior to formal adoption, but the rule never took effect. The commission's chairman deferred to a request from the chairman of the House Interstate and Foreign Commerce Committee that action be postponed while Congress took up the subject.[11]

In summer 1965 Congress enacted the Federal Cigarette Labeling and Advertising Act, which required cigarette cartons and packs to carry this warning: "Caution: Cigarette Smoking May Be Hazardous to Your Health." One might think that opponents of smoking would have welcomed the act as a victory, but instead they denounced the law in the most vehement terms. Philip Elman, a liberal member of the FTC, called it "one of the dirtiest pieces of legislation ever."[12] The *New York Times* condemned it as "a shocking piece of special interest legislation . . . a bill to protect the economic health of the tobacco industry by freeing it of proper regulation."[13] Michael Pertschuk, who was just getting started as a Capitol Hill staff member working on the cause of public health and who would later serve as chair of the FTC, felt humiliated.

The victory for the cigarette makers lay partly in the fact that the warning was weaker than critics of smoking wanted and applied only to packs and cartons, not to advertising, as the FTC would have required. Beyond that, Congress prohibited the FTC from taking any action regulating cigarette advertising until July 1, 1969, when its own law would expire. The prohibition was an unusual reprimand that presumably stemmed both from Congress's anger at the agency for acting without consultation and from sensitivity to the industry's interests. Also, Congress preempted action by the state governments, some of which, such as those of New York and Massachusetts, were beginning to act. The stratagem of preemption is permitted to Congress under the customs and constitutional law of the U.S. federal system. Congress may occupy a field, such as regulation of cigarette labeling or advertising, to the exclusion of state governments by declaring its intention to do so. Finally, although the industry had initially opposed the requirement of a warning, both cigarette makers and their opponents came to understand that such a requirement would actually serve the industry's interests by protecting it from liability. Thus, the industry's critics in 1965 felt outsmarted and overpowered, even duped. Far from a victory for them, the law of 1965 was in their eyes not even a fair compromise between contending forces. It was a dirty trick pulled off by a foe already detested. They yearned to get even.

The consequences of laws are always hard to detect at the time of enactment, and the 1965 act was more of a victory for the foes of smoking than it seemed or they were prepared to admit. However ambiguous politically, it was a first step down antitobacco road, and it contained requirements that the surgeon general make an annual report on smoking and health and that the FTC make an annual report on cigarette advertising. The annual reports of the surgeon general would become an important vehicle in the campaign against smoking.

Congressional Control

For the next two decades, Congress kept control of the tobacco issue mostly in its own hands and out of the hands of regulatory agencies. To be sure, regulatory agencies were not idle in this period. In 1967 the Federal Communications Commission, another independent regulatory agency, ruled that the fairness doctrine of public broadcasting—which held that both sides of controversial issues should be heard—applied to cigarette advertising, and therefore required that the industry's radio and TV ads be counterbalanced with free media time for warnings against smoking. It stipulated a ratio of one antismoking announcement for every three industry ads. This requirement lasted only three years because in 1970 Congress banned cigarette advertising from TV and radio as of January 1, 1971. This ban was upheld in court.

The Federal Aviation Administration, with jurisdiction over the airline industry, segregated smokers and nonsmokers on airplanes beginning in 1973. The Interstate Commerce Commission, with jurisdiction over ground-based interstate common carriers, confined smokers to the rear 20 percent of buses in 1974 and then banned smoking on buses entirely in 1990; in 1976 it segregated smokers and nonsmokers on trains. The FTC, still the regulatory agency most directly involved, remained mostly under wraps, as Congress extended the moratorium on FTC rulemaking in regard to cigarette advertising until June 1971, and thereafter required that the commission give it six months' notice of any such rules. Congress had not liked having its hand forced in 1964–1965.

Nonetheless, the FTC was not passive. After expiration of the statutory moratorium in the middle of 1971, it threatened to file complaints against cigarette companies for failing to include health warnings in their advertisements. In response the industry agreed to use the standard surgeon general's warning in advertisements as well as on cigarette packs.[14] The commission staff tried some hand forcing once again in 1980–1981 by preparing a major report, more than two hundred pages long, which criticized the industry's advertising practices and recommended a series of rotating warning labels cast in strong language. The report was released in 1981 without the endorsement of commission members. Presidents are authorized to name the FTC chair, and the incoming president, Ronald Reagan, hostile to government regulation of industry, quickly removed the activist Michael Pertschuk, President Jimmy Carter's appointee, and replaced him with a more conservative man.

Most telling about Congress's stance against tobacco regulation by agencies, be they multimember independent commissions or line agencies conventionally placed inside the executive branch, was the frequency with which it explicitly omitted tobacco products from new laws regulating hazardous or toxic substances. The laws so treated included the Fair Packaging and Labeling Act of 1966; the Comprehensive Drug Abuse Prevention and Control Act of 1970; the Consumer Product Safety Act amendments in 1976; the Federal Hazardous Substances Act amendments in 1976; and the Toxic Substances Control Act of 1976. Correspondingly, Congress refused requests from antismoking activists to grant jurisdiction over cigarettes to the Food and Drug Administration.

It would be a mistake, however, to read Congress's record as one of action purely in favor of the industry. Keeping the issue in its own hands, Congress passed a number of cautious, compromised laws that slowly gave ground to the opponents of tobacco. These laws fell into three groups: those designed to discourage tobacco use, excise taxes, and price support amendments. In legislative politics, the last two categories were linked.

Congress twice strengthened the labeling requirement. First, in 1969, it stipulated "Warning: The Surgeon General Has Determined that Cigarette Smoking Is Dangerous to Your Health," a considerable upgrade from the mild "may be hazardous" language of 1965. Then, in 1984, consistent with the recommendations of the FTC staff three years earlier, Congress went further and required that four different warnings be rotated, each preceded by the phrase "SURGEON GENERAL'S WARNING":

- "Smoking Causes Lung Cancer, Heart Disease, Emphysema, and May Complicate Pregnancy."
- "Quitting Smoking Now Greatly Reduces Serious Risks to Your Health."
- "Smoking by Pregnant Women May Result in Fetal Injury, Premature Birth, and Low Birth Weight."
- "Cigarette Smoke Contains Carbon Monoxide."

In 1988 Congress banned smoking on domestic airline flights of two hours or less, and two years later it extended the ban to all domestic flights.

The foregoing measures relied on Congress's power to regulate interstate commerce. A law passed in 1992, called the Synar Amendment after Rep. Mike Synar of Oklahoma, used a different yet equally common technique—the imposition of conditions on grants-in-aid given to state and local governments. When Congress renewed mental health, drug abuse, and alcohol abuse programs, some of which used grants-in-aid, it included language requiring the states to have and enforce laws prohibiting the sale of tobacco to anyone under the age of eighteen. Virtually all of the states restricted sales to minors, but such laws were not being enforced. Now states were threatened with loss of up to 40 percent of their mental health and substance abuse grants if they failed to enforce their laws effectively. Specifically, the law required them to conduct random, unannounced "inspections"—stings, in other words—to test vendors' compliance, and to make annual reports on the progress of enforcement.[15]

Congress is empowered by the Constitution to raise revenue, and one of the "ways and means" it uses are excise taxes, imposed on the sale or manufacture of domestic goods, as distinct from tariffs, which apply to imports. A tax imposed on whiskey in the early years of the Republic provoked so violent a response that Congress has ever since been leery of excise taxes. It made an exception during the Civil War, when virtually all consumer goods were taxed, but after the war the Republican-dominated Congress removed the tax on all goods except alcohol, tobacco, and a few luxury items such as perfumes and cosmetics. By the mid-1890s, excise taxes on alcohol and tobacco were yielding close to half of all federal revenues. As of 1980 federal excise tax receipts from tobacco were a mere $2.4 billion, a minor fraction of the total $517 billion in federal receipts, which in the mid-twentieth century were swollen by payroll tax and income tax returns.[16] But the size of the excise tax was still an issue in tobacco politics, if not in fiscal politics. Opponents of tobacco favored any measure that increased the cost of cigarettes and thereby discouraged consumption.

In 1982 Congress temporarily doubled the per pack tax from 8 cents to 16 cents, enacting the first increase since 1951. In 1986 this increase was made permanent. The tax was further increased in 1990 to 20 cents and, effective in 1993, to 24 cents. Members of Congress from tobacco-growing states acceded to the increasing excise taxes as a quid pro quo for continuing tobacco price supports. Since the Great Depression of the 1930s, the federal government had supported the price of tobacco by setting acreage allotments and crop quotas. Farmers rarely grew more tobacco than they could sell, but when they did, the surplus crop was acquired by farm cooperatives with a loan from the government and ultimately sold, whereupon the government was repaid. The costs to the government were minimal, inasmuch as defaults were rare. Nonetheless, it did not make much sense for a government that wanted to discourage smoking to help farmers grow the product being smoked. The issue of whether to continue price supports was raised by Congress in 1981.

The outcome of the debate over price supports was that the net cost of the price support program to taxpayers would be limited by law to the $15 million a year that it took for the Department of Agriculture to administer the program—a trivial sum by the standards of the federal budget. The tobacco growers agreed to cover the cost of any crop stockpiled by the government under loan and ultimately unsold. At the same time, the Department of Agriculture was authorized to cut the support price for tobacco by a third. This arrangement did not work well. By 1985 federal stockpiles of tobacco and crop loans to growers were rising sharply as cigarette consumption fell and domestic tobacco prices surpassed those of foreign countries such as Brazil and Zimbabwe. Growers were nonetheless being driven to the edge of bankruptcy. A new deal was then struck whereby cigarette manufacturers agreed to share with the growers the costs of stockpiled but unsold tobacco and the loans that went with it. They also agreed to buy, at a discount, the accumulated stockpile and to inform the Department of Agriculture of their buying needs in advance so that it could adjust the farmers' acreage quotas accordingly. This arrangement was expensive for the manufacturers but helped prop up a political alliance with the growers, who enjoyed more support in Congress than the manufacturers and who had been angered by the manufacturers' increasing use of imported tobacco. The deal did not, however, stabilize the domestic growing industry. After one year of the new support program, tobacco acreage had fallen to half of what it had been a decade earlier.[17]

Decline of the Industry's Power

On their face, one can detect in this series of enactments a slow, steady weakening of the manufacturers' position. In politics, the act of 1984 mandating four different warning labels was a turning point. Cigarette manufacturers loathed the new labels both for their content and for their number, and tried hard to defeat them. For the first time, the opponents of smoking came away from a legislative fight feeling triumphant rather than impotent and aggrieved.

The cigarette companies' power waned for numerous reasons. An important one was a change in the composition and structure of Congress, which had never been monolithically supportive of the manufacturers. Seven years before the advisory committee's landmark report to the surgeon general, Rep. John Blatnik, a liberal Democrat from Minnesota and chairman of a subcommittee on government operations, had held four days of hearings designed to expose the inadequacy of the FTC's regulation of cigarette advertising. Blatnik issued a scathing report directed at the FTC as well as the industry, and introduced a bill that would have set limits on the tar and nicotine yields of cigarettes and granted the FTC injunctive powers to prevent deceptive advertising. The bill died—presumably a sign of the industry's power at that time—and Blatnik's subcommittee was dissolved.

In the 1960s the drive against tobacco had substantial support in the Senate. The Commerce Committee under Warren Magnuson of Washington had become the legislative home of the consumer movement, for which smoking was the number one public health issue. Frank Moss of Utah was one outspoken critic of the tobacco industry; another was Maurine Neuberger of Oregon, who had replaced her husband in the

Senate after his death. Among the committee's staff members, having arrived with Neuberger, was Michael Pertschuk, who would rise to be chief counsel of the committee and, after that, chairman of the FTC. Pertschuk, only thirty-two in 1965 when he got whipped in the first round of labeling legislation, would become one of the most effective, enduring, and respected leaders of the antismoking movement and the consumer movement generally.

Still, although Congress had long contained critics of tobacco, until the 1980s the preponderance of power, measured both in the number of sympathetic members and in the committee positions they held, lay with the industry. The Congress of the mid-1980s was different. The post-Watergate election of 1974 and internal reforms had intervened, with the result that the House was more liberal and power more diffused. Chairs of numerous newly created subcommittees had gained power at the expense of party leaders and committee chairs, and junior members had gained power in relation to senior ones. Within the Democratic Party, which ordinarily controlled Congress, this meant that northern liberals had made progress at the expense of southern conservatives, including those from the tobacco-growing regions in Virginia, North Carolina, and Kentucky.

This "new Congress" offered many opportunities for legislative entrepreneurship, and no member was better at taking advantage of them than an enemy of the tobacco industry named Henry Waxman, a liberal Democrat from the Beverly Hills area of southern California. In 1979, after only two terms in Congress, Waxman defeated L. Richardson Preyer of North Carolina for the chairmanship of the Subcommittee on Health and the Environment of the House Commerce Committee. It is hard to imagine a single legislative event that would have been more damaging to Big Tobacco. Whereas Preyer, from Greensboro, was a moderate in politics and a former federal judge, Waxman was liberal, tough, and resourceful. A world in which he was king of the Hill for health legislation was not a friendly one for the makers of cigarettes, and cigarette executives immediately noticed the change in atmosphere. They were accustomed to being treated respectfully in legislative halls, even deferentially, as captains of industry. Now they were treated more like criminals. "What hit me," R. J. Reynolds's Edward Horrigan told a reporter in 1998, was that "there was a huge increase in hostility on the part of the . . . congressmen. They were treating us like we were war criminals in the Nuremberg trials."[18]

As the industry's leading congressional foe, Waxman was the sponsor of the 1984 legislation. He needed collaborators in the Senate and found them in Orrin Hatch of Utah and Robert Packwood of Oregon, whose states had for some years supported senators in opposition to cigarettes. In particular, the Mormon population of Utah could be counted on to disapprove of smoking. Before Hatch took this anti-tobacco position in senatorial politics, his predecessor in office, Frank Moss, had done so.

As the leadership in Congress changed to the detriment of the industry, so did the leadership of the industry's lobby. In the battles of the 1960s its chief lobbyist was Earle Clements, a perfect fit for the job. Clements was a former governor of Kentucky and U.S. senator who had been chief whip of the Senate in the 1950s when Lyndon B. Johnson was majority leader. Defeated for reelection, he stayed in Washington to serve as staff director of the Senate Democratic Campaign Committee, a post from which he engineered an electoral victory for Senate Democrats in 1958. Thus, the Democratic Party in the Senate was deeply in his debt, and he used this power for the benefit of his new employer, the Tobacco Institute. He was also a shrewd tactician, adept at discerning what it would take to win a member's vote or construct a compromise. By the 1980s he had retired and been replaced by Horace Kornegay, who had represented a tobacco-growing district in North Carolina. Kornegay, though liked in Congress, was no Earle Clements. Whereas Clements was shrewd, Kornegay was shrill and not able to command the small army of industry lobbyists that descended on the Hill in 1983–1984, when the labeling bill was being considered. The industry substituted others for him, but they were not effective either, and the tobacco lobby committed a series of blunders, including refusal to compromise, going back on its word, and making false claims about commitments from members of Congress. All of these mistakes are cardinal sins in legislative politics, and they enraged even the industry's best friends. Mike Pertschuk, in an account of these events published soon afterward, concluded that by losing in 1984 the tobacco lobby had sacrificed perhaps its leading asset—the appearance of invincibility. No one in Congress would be afraid of it again. It was "isolated, thrashing about, and running scared."[19]

As the industry was losing lobbying capacity, the opponents of smoking were gaining it. In the early 1980s the "big three" voluntary associations in public health—the American Cancer Society, the American Lung Association, and the American Heart Association—collaborated to form the Coalition on Smoking OR Health. A lobbying organization designed to counter the Tobacco Institute, the coalition created a steering committee made up of the heads of the associations' Washington offices. Although increasingly active themselves in the campaign against smoking, these three Washington representatives concurred that their coalition should have a coordinator, a single advocate who would not be focused on a disease or a body part but on their common enemy, cigarettes. This person would need to be skilled at legislative politics. Their choice, Matthew Myers, would be a central figure in the campaign against tobacco use.

Myers had excellent credentials. A cause lawyer, he had come to the FTC in September 1980 from the American Civil Liberties Union, where he had worked on prison reform, and had taken charge of preparing the commission's lengthy attack on cigarette industry advertising. After it was released he began to promote it on the Hill, so he was no stranger to that terrain, still less to the antismoking cause. He resigned from the FTC, expecting that the Reagan administration's leadership of the commission would find a way to remove or thwart him, and went to work for a small law firm. When the Coalition on Smoking OR Health was formed, he volunteered his services and was instead offered employment as staff director. Skillful while his opponents were self-destructing, he got off to a promising start by engineering the victory of 1984.

Beyond these manifestly damaging changes in the lineup of its friends and foes, the cigarette industry was suffering more subtly, but no less surely, from the declining hold of its product on the American public. Between 1982 and 1983 Americans' consumption of cigarettes dropped by about 30 billion—from 624 billion to 596 billion. A cultural change was under way that was reducing the acceptance of cigarettes in American society and thus the importance of the industry in American commerce. Knowledge of the health hazards of smoking was widespread: in 1981, 83 percent of poll respondents agreed that cigarettes cause cancer.[20] Consciously or subconsciously, members of Congress were bound to be aware of these shifts in the public's attitude and correspondingly more willing than before to impose restrictions on the industry.

After the Synar Amendment in 1992, no more regulatory laws were forthcoming from Congress in the early 1990s, but that did not mean that legislators were idle or without influence, for passing laws is not Congress's only contribution to policymaking. One of the most important parts of the policymaking process is what political scientists call "agenda setting"—that is, calling attention to a subject by publicizing its importance and advancing proposals for action. Even when Congress was preventing it from issuing major rules, the FTC did quite a lot of agenda setting on smoking policy in the mid-1960s and again in the early 1980s. Henry Waxman's subcommittee served as an agenda setter in the early 1990s, approving an antismoking bill that would have banned most sales by vending machines, ended public distribution of free cigarette samples, and forbidden the sale of candy and gum in packages designed to resemble tobacco products. An earlier version of the bill would also have banned cigarette companies' sponsorship of sports and entertainment events, which had become a major advertising medium for them after TV and radio advertising was ended, and would have permitted only "tombstone" advertisements in print media—that is, only black lettering on a white background. These bills did not come close to enactment, yet they foreshadowed restrictions that would come later in the decade through means other than legislative action.[21]

· State and Local Legislation ·

Scholars and the media ordinarily give most of their attention to policymaking at the national level, but Washington is not the only place in which officeholders and interest group representatives come together to make public policy. There are fifty state governments in the United States and many thousands of local governments. Policy changes often begin in states and localities, if only because action on a small scale is easier to achieve. Fewer political actors have to be mobilized, and the seemingly lower stakes and relatively limited publicity may mean that opposition is less likely to form.

Some localities or states set an example, which may spread to others. Once a new policy is embedded at the subnational level, its popularity, desirability, or feasibility may appear to have been demonstrated, improving its chances nationally. Also, an argument can then be made that national action is essential for the sake of fairness, which is often thought (whether reasonably or not) to require national uniformity. If the policy affects the manufacture of industrial products, manufacturers are likely to seek a national rule for the sake of efficiency. Thus, although cigarette manufacturers would have preferred no warning labels at all, they certainly preferred one national requirement to the possibility of fifty different ones.

In the modern development of public policy to discourage smoking, activity at the state and local levels did not so much precede national action as provide an important complement and underpinning to it. The formation of grassroots advocacy groups to promote tobacco control laws, as well as their adoption by state and local legislatures, helped establish the power and credibility of the movement against smoking. In a large country with a federal system of government, political movements gain strength from having a wide geographical base and from multiplying their victories in a variety of political forums. It is a disadvantage if activity is concentrated "inside the Beltway," among Washington elites only, with no one paying attention in the rest of the country.

One would not expect a political movement to be equally powerful in all states. Ordinarily, in the American federal system a few states are leaders in public policy innovation and models for the rest. In the contemporary United States, California often is in the lead. In addition to its enormous size, its culture of political activism and popular participation makes it a breeding ground for a variety of political movements. For anyone trying to form a movement, it is a promising place to start.

It should be no surprise, then, that California was the home of one of the most vigorous grassroots campaigns against smoking. California was distinguished in the first instance by the strength of its citizen activity, which sustained numerous chapters of GASP (Groups Against Smoking Pollution) and led to widespread adoption of local antismoking ordinances, starting with one in Berkeley in 1977. In mid-1983, San Francisco became the first big city to adopt restrictive rules against smoking in workplaces, giving impetus to such efforts nationwide. By 1990, 213 California cities and counties had passed such ordinances.[22]

In general the antismoking movement started earliest and attained greatest strength in the Far West and Upper Midwest, although Massachusetts was also in the forefront. It remained weakest in the Deep South and along the border between North and South. Nonetheless, it tended to gather momentum everywhere in the 1980s, with the formation of grassroots groups that stimulated the passage of legislation.[23]

By 1995 the Centers for Disease Control and Prevention and the National Cancer Institute identified 1,238 state laws that addressed tobacco control. Forty-one states restricted smoking on government work sites. Twenty-six states restricted it in private work sites, and thirty-two states, in restaurants. Forty-five states restricted it in a variety of other locations, such as day care centers, shopping malls, grocery stores, enclosed arenas, vehicles of public transportation, and hospitals.[24]

All states have cigarette excise taxes, having enacted them beginning in the 1920s. Virginia (1960) and North Carolina (1969), as states in which tobacco is both grown and manufactured, came late to this form of revenue raising. As of 1951 all states were collecting less than 10 cents a pack, but by 1995 a wide disparity had emerged. The rates remained nominal in the tobacco states—2.5 cents in Virginia, 3 cents in Kentucky, 5 cents in North Carolina—but climbed to 50 cents or more in Connecticut, Hawaii, Massachusetts, New York, Rhode Island, and Washington. Michigan topped all states with a tax of 75 cents.[25]

Only nine states restricted cigarette advertising as of 1995. Utah, with a significant Mormon population, took the more extreme measure of imposing a complete ban on billboards. Sometimes local governments restricted advertising even when state governments did not—Boston, San Francisco, and many other cities banned tobacco advertising on mass transit systems. In 1994 Baltimore banned cigarette and alcohol billboards. Cincinnati prohibited cigarette advertisements near schools, playgrounds, and parks. Such restrictions would probably have been more common but for Congress's having preempted regulation of cigarette advertising and health warnings in its labeling law of 1965. Broadened in 1969, this preemption cast doubt on the authority of state and local governments to act, but when Baltimore's ban was challenged in federal court, it was upheld.[26]

In the early 1990s legislative restrictions on youth access were increasing rapidly at the state level, with emphasis on vending machine and point-of-sale regulations. This movement gained strength from the 1992 Synar Amendment, with its threat of reduced federal grants for substance abuse programs if states did not enforce laws against sales to youth and conduct annual "sting" operations for that purpose. No state completely banned vending machines, but thirty-two had enacted restrictions by 1995. Thirty-three states had required retail licensing for cigarette vendors, with accompanying penalties for failure to enforce laws against sales to minors. Two scholars who studied tobacco control enforcement in the mid-1990s concluded that the states were taking the requirements of the Synar Amendment seriously. The law

> served as a rallying cry for progressive tobacco control states, such as Minnesota and New York, and has forced the hand of those states that have heretofore shunned responsibility for tobacco control (e.g., Texas and Arizona). In a very real sense, it has changed the tobacco control landscape by, for example, virtually institutionalizing the use of sting operations and placing on the policy agenda the prospect of passing laws that penalize minors for possessing tobacco products.[27]

Excise taxes were also rising. Thirty-five states enacted increases in their cigarette excise taxes between 1990 and 1995, typically through legislation but in several cases by ballot initiatives. Only six states—Georgia, Kentucky, South Carolina, Tennessee, Virginia, and West Virginia—had failed to raise cigarette taxes in the 1980s or 1990s. Local jurisdictions often enact their own taxes on cigarettes. As of June 1994,

450 cities, towns, or counties had levied cigarette taxes that were yielding $184 million in local revenue.[28]

The acts of state legislatures, like the acts of Congress, have often disappointed antitobacco activists because they typically involve compromise. Tobacco lobbyists and antitobacco lobbyists contest with one another, and legislators give something to both sides. Controls are enacted, but they are weaker than what the health care advocates would like. Vending machines are restricted but not banned. Penalties for noncomplying vendors are enacted, but they are relatively mild. Controls are coupled with provisions that prohibit discrimination against smokers. Excise taxes are raised, but not to levels as high as opponents of smoking believe to be necessary to deter consumption of cigarettes.

Often the state laws preempt action by local governments. The tobacco industry favors such preemption, but health care activists object to it because the strongest enactments can usually be obtained locally, where the industry is least active. Even when state laws do not formally preempt local action, however, they dampen it. An unintended effect of the Synar Amendment, meant to strengthen tobacco control, was that the law potentially weakened it by inducing concentration of control at the state level. In American government, states always have authority over local governments, which are their creatures, but they do not invariably choose to exercise it. Sometimes they leave discretion with local governments, but when the federal government gives orders to the states, as it did with the Synar Amendment, they are forced to assert themselves.

* * *

The new tobacco control regime of the late 1990s did not develop in response to a legislative vacuum. Legislatures at the national and state levels had enacted many measures. These were modest, incremental, and, among the states, uneven, but taken as a whole they constituted a substantial body of warnings about cigarettes and restrictions on both their accessibility to youths and their place of use.

Moreover, annual per capita consumption of cigarettes had plummeted during the three decades in which legislatures had dominated public policymaking, going from 4,287 in 1966 to 2,493 in 1994. This reduction does not prove that legislation was effective. Informally, social norms were developing to discourage smoking. Yet it is hard to imagine the norms having developed in the absence of government action, both that of public health officials who articulated the scientific case against tobacco and that of the legislatures that responded with regulation.

· Notes ·

1. Susan Wagner, *Cigarette Country: Tobacco in American History and Politics* (New York: Praeger, 1971), 25–30.
2. Ibid., 31.
3. "Tobacco Legislation," in *Cyclopedia of American Government,* vol. 3, ed. Andrew C. McLaughlin and Albert Bushnell Hart (reprint, Gloucester, Mass.: Peter Smith, 1963), 538–539; and Cassandra Tate, *Cigarette Wars: The Triumph of "The Little White Slaver"* (New York: Oxford University Press, 1999), 4–5, and appendix, 159–160.
4. Jacob Sullum, *For Your Own Good* (New York: Free Press, 1998), 35 (citing Egon C. Corti, *A History of Smoking* [London: George Harrap, 1931], 264).
5. Wagner, *Cigarette Country,* 74.
6. For a summary of the research, see Sullum, *For Your Own Good,* 43–47; and Richard Kluger, *Ashes to Ashes: America's Hundred-Year Cigarette War, the Public Health, and the Unabashed Triumph of Philip Morris* (New York: Knopf, 1996).
7. Kluger, *Ashes to Ashes,* 183–184.
8. Sullum, *For Your Own Good,* 52.
9. Good summaries may be found in Kluger, *Ashes to Ashes,* 242–262; and Sullum, *For Your Own Good,* 40–41.
10. John E. Calfee, "The Ghost of Cigarette Advertising Past," *Regulation* (November/December 1986): 35–45. This article argues that government prohibitions on the advertising of health claims have had the perverse effect of discouraging manufacturers from making safer cigarettes. In 1966 the FTC ended its prohibition against including tar and nicotine levels in cigarette advertising, and in 1970 it completed this reversal by negotiating written pledges from the manufacturers that they would include such measurements. The measurements are done by the FTC, which maintains smoking machines for this purpose. The tar and nicotine data are confined to discreet boxes, however. The advertisements emphasize themes of taste, flavor, and lifestyle, the remaining possibilities when health claims are denied. For the FTC history, see also A. Lee Fritschler, *Smoking and Politics: Policy Making and the Federal Bureaucracy,* 4th ed. (Englewood Cliffs, N.J.: Prentice Hall, 1989), 27–28.
11. See the very detailed and informative account in Fritschler, *Smoking and Politics,* chaps. 6 and 7.
12. Kluger, *Ashes to Ashes,* 291.
13. Cited in Michael Pertschuk, *Giant Killers* (New York: Norton, 1986), 33.
14. Sullum, *For Your Own Good,* 53.
15. 106 Stat. 394; and *Congress and the Nation, 1989–1992,* vol. 8 (Washington, D.C.: Congressional Quarterly Press, 1993), 604–605.
16. W. Elliot Brownlee, "Tax Regimes, National Crisis, and State-building in America," in *Funding the Modern American State, 1941–1995,* ed. W. Elliot Brownlee (Washington, D.C.: Woodrow Wilson International Center for Scholars; and New York: Cambridge University Press, 1996), 44–48.

17. Kluger, *Ashes to Ashes*, 550–552. During the 1980s and 1990s Congress legislated frequently and in detail about tobacco production in an effort to protect growers' incomes while avoiding costs to the taxpayer. See Tom Capehart, "The Tobacco Program: A Summary and Update," http://www.ers.usda.gov/Briefing/Tobacco/program2.htm, accessed January 6, 2004.

18. Frank Tursi, Susan E. White, and Steven McQuilkin, "Lost Empire: The Fall of R. J. Reynolds Tobacco Co.," *Winston-Salem Journal*, chap. 25, part 2, "Tobacco's No. 1 Enemy," on www.journalnow.com. "Lost Empire" ran as a series of thirty-five chapters in the *Winston-Salem Journal* starting on October 24, 1999. It appeared daily for more than two months, and I accessed it on the *Journal*'s home page, www.journalnow.com, between January 4 and January 29, 2000. According to "The Making of Lost Empire," an introduction to the series, the paper's reporting team worked for almost eighteen months and "obtained court transcripts and depositions from a dozen trials and reviewed financial documents from the 1950s forward. They looked at a wide range of government reports, including patent applications, Securities and Exchange Commission investigations, surgeon generals' reports, and the Environmental Protection Agency's report on secondhand smoke. They read diaries from some of the participants and looked through family scrapbooks. . . ." The result is a highly informative recent history of R. J. Reynolds, of which I have made extensive use. Unfortunately, the original sources of quotations are not always identified, nor has the series been published in hard form. As of February 2004 it remained accessible on the *Journal*'s Web site, which maintains a database of the paper's articles since November 1997. My citations are by chapter number and part number and title.

19. Pertschuk, *Giant Killers*, chaps. 2 and 3.

20. Lydia Saad, "A Half-Century of Polling on Tobacco: Most Don't Like Smoking But Tolerate It," *The Public Perspective* (August/September 1998): 3.

21. *Congress and the Nation, 1989–1992*, 591.

22. On California, see Kluger, *Ashes to Ashes*, 552–557; and Stanton A. Glantz and Edith D. Balbach, *Tobacco War: Inside the California Battles* (Berkeley: University of California Press, 2000).

23. U.S. Department of Health and Human Services, *Smoking and Health: A National Status Report*, DHHS Publication No. (CDC) 87-8396, revised 2/90 (Washington, D.C.: 1990), 388–390. On the growing strength of the antitobacco movement at all levels of government in the mid-1980s, see John K. Iglehart, "Health Policy Report: The Campaign Against Smoking Gains Momentum," *New England Journal of Medicine* 314 (17 April 1986): 1059–1064.

24. U.S. Department of Health and Human Services, Centers for Disease Control and Prevention, *CDC Surveillance Summaries*, no. SS-6 (3 November 1995), *Morbidity and Mortality Weekly Report* 44: 1–15.

25. *CDC Surveillance Summaries*, 23.

26. *CDC Surveillance Summaries*, 11, 22; and Peter D. Jacobson and Jeffrey Wasserman, *Tobacco Control Laws: Implementation and Enforcement* (Santa Monica, Calif.: Rand Corporation, 1997), 15. In June 2001 the Supreme Court

struck down regulations promulgated in 1999 by the attorney general of Massachusetts, ruling that they had been preempted by Congress. This ruling cast doubt on the validity of all existing state and local regulation of cigarette advertising, but not on the advertising provisions of the Master Settlement Agreement of 1998.

27. Jacobson and Wasserman, *Tobacco Control Laws*, 62–63. The data on numbers of state laws are again from *CDC Surveillance Summaries*.

28. *CDC Surveillance Summaries*, 26. The original source was a publication of the Tobacco Institute, *The Tax Burden on Tobacco: Historical Compilation* (Washington, D.C.: 1994).

CHAPTER THREE

Ordinary Torts: Litigation before It Was Substituted for Legislation

BEFORE THE MID-1990S, TORT LITIGATION against the cigarette companies proceeded independently of legislative policymaking and in no way substituted for it. The plaintiffs were individuals, and the case outcomes applied to them alone. Nevertheless, the history of this litigation is important for understanding the changes in politics and policymaking that led to a new regime of regulation.

The industry's repeated successes in court whetted the desire of its enemies to defeat it there, while the industry's fear of being destroyed through litigation shaped its internal governance and political strategy in ways that would eventually increase its vulnerability everywhere. Within the companies, lawyers gained the ascendancy and prescribed strategies of evasion and concealment that, when revealed in the later litigation, became powerful ammunition for opponents.

• The Early Cases •

The cancer scare of the early 1950s marked the beginning of a series of suits against the companies by individual victims of lung cancer who sought compensation. The suits came in two clusters, one lasting from the mid-1950s to the late 1960s and the other beginning in the mid-1980s and extending to 1992. In neither period did the cigarette companies pay a cent in compensation. Of 813 cases filed, only 23 were tried.[1] All but two resulted in victory for the companies, and the exceptional two were mixed verdicts rather than unqualified defeats.

The companies' success in court is explained both by their litigating tactics and by the law, as understood by juries. Believing that the industry's very existence was at stake, the companies fought with uncommon ferocity. Lung cancer was attaining epidemic proportions—in 1954 twenty-five thousand deaths from the disease were reported, and the number was rising steadily. Cigarette manufacturers feared that if they lost so much as a single case, a stream of litigation could drive their businesses into bankruptcy. The example of asbestos litigation, gathering momentum after a breakthrough verdict in 1971 and causing Johns-Manville to seek bankruptcy protection in 1982, gave credence to their fears. They entered the courtroom determined neither to lose nor to settle.[2]

Although tort cases usually are settled out of court, the cigarette companies never settled, and if they lost at trial, they appealed. They would pay any price, go any distance, use any litigating tactic, to win. For the most part, they won by exhausting their opponents, who had far less money than they did. Their litigating philosophy was summed up by an official of R. J. Reynolds: "To paraphrase General [George] Patton, the way we won these cases was not by spending all of [Reynolds's money], but by making that other son of a bitch spend all of his."[3]

One sign of the industry's wealth and litigating power was that it hired the country's most expensive and prestigious law firms: Arnold and Porter, Covington and Burling, Davis Polk and Wardwell, King and Spalding, Vinson and Elkins, Jones Day Reavis and Pogue, Chadbourne and Parke, Paul Weiss Rifkind—the list could be extended, representing the who's who of the American legal establishment. One firm, Shook Hardy and Bacon of Kansas City, attained its wealth and prominence mainly by specializing in tobacco litigation. In courtrooms each company would have its own legal team, which was ordinarily paired with local lawyers because either the law or shrewd tactics required it. Bitterly, their opponents referred to this well-tailored multitude as the "wall of flesh."

The industry's lawyers employed every delaying tactic that American legal practice affords—and there are many. They filed pretrial motions, mounted procedural challenges, and took depositions endlessly. One of their opponents described their behavior as follows:

> They have done this by resisting all discovery aimed at them, thus requiring a court hearing and order before plaintiffs can obtain even the most rudimentary discovery. They have done it by getting confidentiality orders attached to the discovery materials they finally produce, thus preventing plaintiffs' counsel from sharing the fruits of discovery and forcing each plaintiff to reinvent the wheel. They have done it by taking exceedingly lengthy oral depositions of plaintiffs, expert witnesses, and by naming multiple experts of their own for each specialty, such as pathology, thereby putting plaintiffs' counsel in the dilemma of taking numerous expensive depositions or

else not knowing what the witness intends to testify at trial. And they have done it by taking dozens and dozens of oral depositions, all across the country, of trivial fact witnesses, particularly in the final days before trial.[4]

Rarely could the industry's opponents withstand this onslaught. The typical personal injury lawyer worked on a contingency basis and had to prepare his or her case with limited or no compensation.

While this explains why so few cases were tried, it is not obvious why the industry should consistently win those that were. The explanation is somewhat different for the two different clusters of cases, inasmuch as tort law evolved in the intervening years.

Filed at a time when product liability law was relatively constrained, the early cases relied on claims of negligence and failure to warn. The plaintiffs' lawyers could argue that the tobacco industry had sufficient information about the possibility of harm to engage in research, publish warnings, and refrain from advertising that implied assurances of safety and good health, but courts held that the risks of cigarette smoking were unknowable in advance. In a leading case, *Lartigue v. R. J. Reynolds Tobacco Co.*, the judge wrote that the manufacturer "is an insurer against foreseeable risks—but not against unknowable risks," "the harmful effects of which no developed skill or foresight can avoid."[5]

Product liability law in this faraway time was not ordinarily invoked against a manufacturer whose product, even if intrinsically harmful, conformed to reasonable standards. For a plaintiff to collect, the product had to be defective—a deviation from the common-sense norm. The loaf of bread, for example, had to contain rat poison. If there were danger in the whole wheat flour or yeast, that would not be grounds for suit.

In the mid-1960s this doctrine was framed authoritatively by the American Law Institute (ALI), an association of lawyers, judges, and law professors, in a new statement on tort law. Addressing the standards of liability for defective products, the ALI said,

> The article sold must be dangerous to an extent beyond that which would be contemplated by the ordinary consumer who purchases it, with the ordinary knowledge common to the community as to its characteristics. Good whiskey is not unreasonably dangerous merely because it will make some people drunk, and is especially dangerous to alcoholics, but bad whiskey, containing a dangerous amount of fusel oil, is unreasonably dangerous. Good tobacco is not unreasonably dangerous merely because the effects of smoking may be harmful; but tobacco containing something like marijuana may be unreasonably dangerous. Good butter is

not unreasonably dangerous merely because, if such be the case, it deposits cholesterol in the arteries and leads to heart attacks; but bad butter, contaminated with poisonous fish oil, is unreasonably dangerous.[6]

Tobacco litigation was virtually moribund for the next twenty years.

• Later Litigation •

By the mid-1980s, when the second set of tobacco cases got under way, the social and legal contexts of litigation had changed drastically. A wave of environmental and consumer protection laws had been enacted. The public's consciousness of risk had been elevated. It also was more alert to litigation as a possible response. Moreover, product liability law had evolved in a way that improved the litigating prospects of lung cancer victims who smoked. Courts were beginning to depart from the ALI doctrine and to entertain the possibility that manufacturers could be held responsible for injury from products that were inherently dangerous, even if they were not defective. This doctrine was called "strict liability," and it relied on a method called "risk-utility analysis." If a manufacturer was sued over a product that was unavoidably unsafe, courts would ask whether the benefits of the product exceeded the risks it posed. Tort lawyers squaring off against the tobacco industry found risk-utility analysis attractive. Deaths from lung cancer were approaching one hundred thousand a year. If smoking were an important cause of these deaths, as almost everyone but the tobacco industry now believed, could it possibly be maintained that the benefits outweighed the harm?[7]

Beyond that, courts were beginning to develop a doctrine of comparative fault to apply to product liability cases. Juries that were unwilling to find the tobacco companies entirely at fault for a smoker's lung disease now had the option of finding them partially at fault.

As in the first set of cases, litigation strategies rather than legal arguments constituted the industry's first line of defense. Its lawyers stalled and stonewalled. As before, most cases stumbled short of the courthouse door. A few did go to trial, however, with what seemed like good prospects of success.

Galbraith v. R. J. Reynolds Tobacco Co. was tried in Santa Barbara, California, and decided at the end of 1985, after Galbraith died and the suit was converted into a wrongful death action on behalf of his survivors. It got attention both because it was the first of the new wave of cases to reach trial and because the plaintiff's lawyer was the flamboyant and nationally famous Melvin Belli, the "king of torts." "I want to catch the sons of bitches," Belli said. "I'd like to get a good case and go after them."[8] *Galbraith,* however, was not a good case. The plaintiff, who had smoked for fifty-five years, had several diseases in addition to lung cancer, was not given an autopsy, and was attended by a physician who could not say that smoking was directly related to his death. A majority of jurors concluded that causation had not been established.

A second case that received national attention was *Nathan Henry Horton v. The American Tobacco Co.,* filed in Holmes County, Mississippi, in 1986. It was the first cigarette liability suit to be filed in the state. Horton died of lung cancer in 1987 at the age of fifty after having smoked Pall Malls for thirty-seven years. When he died, his lawyers converted the suit to a wrongful death action on behalf of his wife and son. An autopsy had been performed. The victim had been poor and black, and the jury would be poor and black as well. Most important, Mississippi had a pure comparative fault law. If American Tobacco was found to be even a little bit to blame for Horton's death, the company could be penalized. In almost all of the other forty states that had comparative fault laws, a plaintiff could not recover damages unless the defendants were found to be more than 50 percent responsible.[9]

Horton's lawyer, Don Barrett, was a fundamentalist Christian and reformed racist who pursued Horton's cause with religious zeal, and with the assistance of two black co-counsels. He was well prepared, rhetorically powerful, and from a family of local notables. The jury deadlocked, and the judge declared a mistrial. The case was then retried in a different place in Mississippi—the university town of Oxford— before a predominantly white jury. That trial lasted three weeks, and the jury deliberated for six hours before rendering a surprising verdict: The American Tobacco Company was liable for Horton's death, but no damages would be awarded. The jury foreman, David Roach, who was head of the University of Mississippi's computer center, recalled later that "most people by far thought [Horton] exercised his own judgment, made his own choices" about smoking; thus, they were not inclined to award compensation. Another juror, who had a master's degree in education and worked as a secretary, said, "I think that we probably all felt that [smoking] caused him to be sick, but he was an adult, he knew what he was doing, there was information at that time." A finding of liability without damages struck the jurors as a reasonable compromise. Tobacco company stocks rose, and a stock analyst told *Newsday* that the verdict would "slow plaintiffs' cases to even less than a trickle."[10]

There was also the case of *Cipollone v. Liggett Group, Inc.,* which went to trial in New Jersey in 1988 after four and a half years of preparation. The jury concluded that Liggett was negligent for its failure before 1966, the year the labeling law went into effect, to warn smokers adequately of the risks of smoking and for using advertising that could be interpreted as a warrant of safety. However, it assigned only 20 percent of the fault for Rose Cipollone's fatal illness to the company, finding her to be preponderantly at fault. Because New Jersey law required that damages could be awarded only if at least 50 percent of responsibility was assigned to the defendant, Mrs. Cipollone's estate received no damages. Somewhat erratically, the jury decided to award $400,000 to Mrs. Cipollone's devoted husband, Tony, who had cared for her, but this award, which lacked a foundation in law, was vacated on appeal. So the industry kept intact its record of paying no damages whatever. The jury also gave the industry a victory in that it found no fraud or intentional tort, despite the effort of the plaintiff's lawyer to establish both.[11]

The second set of cases showed, then, that even with a product liability law much more favorable to plaintiffs, juries remained reluctant to find cigarette companies at fault for smokers' decisions to smoke. They were disposed to hold individuals responsible for their own actions. The companies argued successfully in court that smokers had "assumed the risk" of using their product. The cigarette companies continued to escape without any monetary costs other than legal fees. Nonetheless, their legal fees were rising astronomically, and ambiguity was creeping into the outcomes. The jury verdicts in *Horton* and *Cipollone* were not simple verdicts of "not guilty." The juries said that the companies were at least a little bit guilty.

Most ominous for the defendants was the breakthrough of Marc Edell, Mrs. Cipollone's lawyer, in regard to discovery. Edell was determined to succeed where others had failed in the attempt to get company documents, and with the backing of a sympathetic judge, H. Lee Sarokin, he did so. Not only did Sarokin rule to open up the discovery process beyond the dictates of a magistrate assigned to oversee it, he also approved of Edell's use of the documents in seven other cases that he was by then handling for smokers, and of his sharing them with other litigators and making them public. The industry appealed Sarokin's ruling to the Third Circuit and lost. More than half a million documents were eventually produced for Edell's examination. He ordered copies of one hundred thousand of them and introduced three hundred at trial. The *Cipollone* case, then, is a rough analog in litigation to the 1965 labeling act in statutory law. Neither on its face seemed a victory for the opponents of tobacco, but both were significant as vehicles for the development and release of information—the surgeon general's reports in the case of the law, industry documents in the case of *Cipollone*. "It was like having a great big pile of candy to feast on," Edell recounted.[12]

Before long, the feast would get bigger, and there would be more lawyers at the candy counter.

· The Ascendancy of the Lawyers ·

On the industry's side, when it began to be reported that cigarettes cause cancer, executives turned first to experts in public relations and later to experts in law. Both times, they took a hard line. Their instinct was to deny the reports, but what began as propaganda hardened into policy, with widespread ramifications for the industry's conduct.

More than a decade before the report to the surgeon general, a cancer scare broke out with publication of a two-page article, "Cancer by the Carton," in the *Reader's Digest.* Domestic cigarette consumption fell slightly, and the companies' stock prices dropped. Reacting to the public's fear of illness with a corresponding fear for the future of their industry, a small group of executives met in New York late in 1953 and decided to solicit the services of Hill and Knowlton, a big advertising and public relations agency. This decision was the beginning of a close relationship that would last much of a decade.

Led by Paul Hahn, a former lawyer with Chadbourne and Parke who had become head of American Tobacco—then the industry leader with Lucky Strike cigarettes—the executives had in mind creating a "Tobacco Industry Committee for Public Information." They did not believe that cigarettes caused cancer and were "confident that they can supply . . . comprehensive and authoritative scientific material which completely refutes the health charges," according to Hill and Knowlton's record of the meeting.[13]

"A Frank Statement" to Smokers

It was John Hill of the public relations agency who told group members that they needed to sponsor research—it was not enough just to provide "information." Thus was born the Tobacco Industry Research Committee (TIRC), which in January 1954 published an advertisement that ran in 448 newspapers in 258 cities. Drafted by Hill and Knowlton, it was titled "A Frank Statement to Cigarette Smokers." Without attacking directly the scientific results pointing to tobacco's causation of cancer, the ad nonetheless said that, according to "distinguished authorities," lung cancer had many possible causes, that authorities did not agree about the cause, that there was no proof that cigarette smoking was a cause, and that statistics purporting to show such a cause were "questioned by numerous scientists." In the name of the TIRC, all of the major companies except Liggett & Myers signed the ad.[14]

From the standpoint of later litigation, the key sentence of this advertisement was: "We accept an interest in people's health as a basic responsibility, paramount to every other consideration in our business." This statement was disingenuous. Neither then nor at any time since has there been any evidence that cigarette executives regarded the public's health as paramount to preserving the lives and profits of their companies. But Hill and Knowlton solicited such an assurance from them, and, having received it, proceeded to incorporate it into the ad. If the statement seems duplicitous and ill-considered in retrospect, at least it was less explicit than two other sentences that the industry presidents did delete from Hill and Knowlton's draft: "We will never produce and market a product shown to be the cause of any serious human ailment. . . . [We] will undertake to keep the public informed of such facts as may be developed relating to cigarette smoking and health and other pertinent matters."[15]

Although it is possible to overstate the importance of the ad per se, its publication was surely a critical moment in defining the industry's posture. Instead of worrying about the quality and effects of its product, the industry began by worrying about its public relations. Fixed on the selling of cigarettes, industry executives were unable to transcend their roles so as to attach greater importance to their public responsibility. Edward DeHart, an account executive at Hill and Knowlton, offered this revealing account of their mental state:

> At the moment, these men feel thrown for a loop. They've competed for years—not in price, not in any real difference of quality—but just in ability to conjure up more hypnotic claims and brighter assurances for what their own brand might do for a smoker, compared to another brand. And now, suddenly, they feel all out of bounds because the old claims became unimportant overnight; they are suddenly challenged to produce just one, simple fact.

DeHart did not shrink from articulating the stakes:

> For the public, an issue touching on the deepest of human fears and instincts is involved—the issue of uncontrollable disease and death. Hence, cigarette companies might not readily be forgiven if their approach to this problem stemmed only from eagerness to protect their earnings and if they twisted the research of medical science . . . into a device to save stockholders.

For years, DeHart said, the industry had twisted research into "sales propaganda with few repercussions. Doing so now would be a grave mistake. The stakes are too large; the penalties for losing could be too great."[16]

Still, for all his appreciation of the stakes and the gravity of the situation, DeHart had a job to do, and he instructed others in the agency as follows:

> We have one essential job—which can be simply said: Stop public panic. There is only one problem—confidence, and how to establish it; public assurance, and how to create it. . . . And, most important, how to free millions of Americans from the guilty fear that is going to arise deep in their biological depths— regardless of any pooh-poohing logic—every time they light a cigarette.[17]

Privately, industry executives always saw the TIRC for what it was—a public relations device—and they did not necessarily deny as much in public. Quoted in the same edition of the *Winston-Salem Journal* as that in which the "Frank Statement" appeared, R. J. Reynolds's Edward Darr said—admittedly to a friendly readership, made up in no small part of his employees—that the companies had formed the TIRC as "a concerted effort . . . to combat a bit of propaganda, which we believe to be erroneous, unfair, and unjust."[18]

Fighting Mounting Evidence

For at least two years, until it could form an organization of its own, the TIRC was staffed by Hill and Knowlton, its near neighbor in the Empire State Building. Hill and Knowlton submitted budgets to the TIRC, which showed a staff of more than thirty. Progress reports documented a high level of public relations activity, including pamphlets for distribution to doctors' offices, reprints of favorable articles, press releases and press conferences, visits to major newspaper and magazine publishers and TV producers, coverage of scientific and medical conventions, and systematic counterattacks against adverse scientific findings.[19]

Eventually, the TIRC acquired a permanent chair from the industry, a staff of its own, a scientific advisory board, and a scientific director. The first occupant of this office, appointed in mid-1954, was Dr. Clarence Cook Little, a former president of the University of Michigan, former executive director of the American Cancer Society, and founder of the Roscoe B. Jackson Memorial Laboratory in Maine—on the face of it superbly qualified, except that the decision by such a man to accept such an office instantly reduced his stature. Little had a history as a bona fide cancer fighter, but, true to his role and the expectation of his new

employer, he began issuing statements that cast doubt on scientific findings that implicated cigarette smoking as a cause of cancer.[20]

Still later, the industry tried to protect the TIRC's appearance of
scientific integrity by forming the Tobacco Institute to take charge of
its public relations and political activities, removing from the TIRC
the burden of being the industry's mouthpiece. After 1958 it was
the Tobacco Institute that published *Tobacco and Health Research,* a
monthly distributed free to the medical community and designed to
broadcast whatever research findings cast doubt on the link between
smoking and disease. The TIRC was renamed the Council for Tobacco
Research (CTR). In time, its leaders would take refuge in giving grants
for basic science, which at once preserved their professional integrity
and kept them at a safe remove from any results that could be manifestly damaging to their employer, the tobacco industry.

The ascent of the lawyers within the industry dates from the mid-
1960s and the publication of the report to the surgeon general. However
disingenuous and delusionary the industry's initial stance, it had not
been wholly implausible in the early 1950s to treat the scientific case as
unproven. There were unanswered questions—about, for example, the
effects of industrial pollution on the incidence of lung cancer—but as
the decade progressed, evidence mounted.

In 1959 a team of scientists from BAT (the British-American
Tobacco Company in London) visited major U.S. universities and
research centers and found the medical opinion on smoking nearly
unanimous. They wrote, "Although there remains some doubt as to the
proportion of the total lung cancer mortality which can fairly be attributed to smoking, scientific opinion in the U.S.A. does not now seriously
doubt that the statistical correlation is real and reflects a cause-and-
effect relationship."[21]

In 1962 the Royal College of Physicians in Great Britain, a nation
that smoked even more than the United States, issued a report stating
that the weight of the evidence in approximately two hundred studies
was that smoking was a major cause of lung cancer, also caused bronchitis, and probably contributed to coronary heart disease. It said that
air pollution intensified the health problems induced by smoking but
found that the level of disease and premature death depended on cigarette use, independent of the smoker's place of residence.[22]

The publication of the U.S. report two years later by the Surgeon
General's Advisory Committee on Smoking and Health powerfully
strengthened the case against cigarettes both by amassing the scientific
evidence and by giving it government endorsement. Against its will, the
industry was now entering the realm of public policy and public law,
where the use of government power was at stake. To mount a defense

against this graver threat, the company presidents turned to their lawyers, whom they supposed were skilled in the use of public power. Hill and Knowlton receded and in 1968 resigned the tobacco account.[23]

The presidents set up the Committee of Counsel, consisting of the general counsels of the leading companies. Lawyers from BAT, visiting the United States in the fall of 1964 as the government was gearing up for warning labels, concluded that "the lawyers . . . are the most powerful group in the smoking and health situation."[24] They attributed particular power to Reynolds's Henry Ramm, committee chair and representative of what was then the biggest manufacturer (Reynolds had passed American Tobacco's sales in 1958). A different account attributes more influence to Philip Morris's Paul Smith, even before his company's spectacular rise in market share (Philip Morris would surpass Reynolds in 1983). Richard Kluger writes,

> Probably the ablest and most enlightened of the legal representatives was the team assembled by Philip Morris, which as a result wielded [disproportionate] power within the industry's councils. . . . Their passionately protective general counsel, Paul Smith, moved regularly and with the full joy of combat between New York, Washington, foreign parts, and even Winston-Salem [Reynolds's headquarters]."[25]

Still another account attributes leadership to David R. Hardy of the Kansas City law firm of Shook, Hardy and Bacon, which developed a specialty in defending tobacco companies after Hardy won a critical case in 1962 for Philip Morris. His performance in that case, which the jury took only an hour to decide, made him a hero within the industry. Hardy died in 1976, but not before turning his firm from a "small mid-western practice into a national power" by defending cigarette companies.[26]

Whatever the distribution of power within the Committee of Counsel, henceforth the committee itself—and individual members within their respective companies—would dominate the companies' policymaking in regard to smoking and health. The companies' deepening engagement with government—with the government's legislatures, regulatory agencies, and courtrooms—made lawyers the most powerful force within the industry.

On the relation between smoking and health, the lawyers would admit nothing. The visiting BAT lawyers wrote in 1964 that "their policy, very understandably, in effect is, 'Don't take any chances.' It is a situation that does not encourage constructive or bold approaches to smoking and health problems, and it also means that the Policy Committee of lawyers exercises close control over all aspects of the problems."[27]

Hill and Knowlton, in contrast, had shown ambivalence. On one hand, they had served to their client for public consumption the kind of language needed to keep alive the idea that the causes of lung cancer were unknown and still in dispute—which, at the utmost depths of the science, may have been technically true but was certainly misleading.[28] At the same time, they sometimes cautioned against too uncompromising and callous a stance. As the threat of government regulation began to develop, Hill and Knowlton suggested voluntarily adopting an advertising code, putting warnings on packages, and urging customers to use moderation in smoking. Company lawyers, however, resisted acknowledging any hazard and refrained from implying that there was any known standard of safety.[29]

A letter written by Hardy in August 1970 and addressed confidentially to "legal counsels only" illustrates the lawyers' mentality. He was alarmed because the industry had recently come close to losing a case, and he wanted to make sure that remarks made by company officials, the scientists especially, would not be revealed. He cited a recent conference, the record of which contained a "number of statements or expressions which could be most damaging. . . . a real threat to the continued success in the defense of smoking and health litigation." Among the potentially damaging phrases were:

1. research "will continue in the search for a safer product";
2. an "attractive" product is one that is less "biologically active"; and
3. the industry seeks a "healthy cigarette."

If such language were introduced in court, "the average juror" might not be able to "follow or accept the subtle distinctions and explanations we would be forced to urge." Such language would tend to establish

> actual knowledge on the part of the defendant that smoking is generally dangerous to health and should be removed, or that smoking causes a particular disease. This would not only be evidence that would substantially prove a case against the defendant company for compensatory damages, but could be considered as evidence of willfulness or recklessness sufficient to support a claim for punitive damages.

Hardy and the company lawyers devised record-keeping procedures designed to bring as many documents as possible under the cloak of the lawyer-client privilege and the lawyer's "work product," thereby helping to shield them from discovery.[30]

There was an Alice-in-Wonderland quality in the companies' willfully ignorant stance. Not only did they profess not to know what everyone else knew. Absurdly, they also were in the position of covering up the earnest efforts of their own scientists to make cigarettes as safe as they could. Nevertheless, this surreal stance, and the evasive corporate language it inspired, made perfect sense to lawyers, designed as it was by specialists in legal contestation to serve legalistic ends.[31] The company lawyers aimed to win in court, the arena they knew. Their policy of admitting nothing was buttressed by their litigating tactics, which from the start of tort litigation in the 1950s called for fighting every case to the very end. Settling rather than going to trial could have conceded some responsibility for smokers' illness. Without either denying or conceding that smoking posed a risk, the companies built their cases on the premise that smokers assumed the risk.

The ignorance prescribed by lawyers on strategic grounds had effects outside the companies' legal departments and the governments' courtrooms. In particular, it had chilling effects on in-house research. Company scientists who came too close to learning what the companies did not want to know—because it could weaken their position in court if they were shown to know it—found that their laboratory operations could be shut down, their jobs jeopardized, and their scientific papers denied company approval for publication.[32] One infamous event was the closing in 1970 of Reynolds's "mouse house," which resulted in the sudden and unexplained firing of twenty-six scientists, an event unparalleled in the history of a company known for its job security. Uncertain at the time why they were fired, the scientists later concluded that the company's lawyers and top executives feared that they were "getting uncomfortably close to uncovering a link between smoking and emphysema." The lawsuits that such a finding might spawn could be avoided only by ending the experiments.[33]

The lawyers' influence spread also to the CTR, which had a category of "special projects" that did not go through the usual scientific review process. They were given preferential treatment because the lawyers anticipated that the results might be useful in buttressing the companies' position in court. In particular, the lawyers sought research results that demonstrated environmental or genetic origins of cancer. After all, it was obviously the case that not everyone who smokes dies of lung cancer—about one in ten do. Some smokers live to advanced ages and die of illnesses unrelated to smoking. Those who develop lung cancer conceivably have a trait that predisposes them to the illness, or have been exposed to hazardous substances other than cigarette smoke. Company lawyers liked to finance scientists who would go looking for these other causes, and, except for the fact that the tobacco companies were surreptitiously supporting it, this work would not have been a reprehensible scientific enterprise. It is not clear whether the scientists who did such work—for example, Theodor Sterling of Simon Fraser University in British Columbia—did not perform it honestly, but accepting CTR grants certainly compromised them. Of course, the lawyers' role in allocating the CTR's grants compromised the council.[34]

The companies' obdurate stance, grounded though it may have been in a rational calculation of efficacy in the courtroom, put them in an anomalous position. Long before science had much to say about the subject, cigarettes were known colloquially as "coffin nails." In 1949, even before the publicized cancer scare developed, more than half of smokers (52 percent) told the Gallup poll that they believed smoking to be harmful. In 1954, soon after the cancer threat made news, 70 percent of respondents said smoking was harmful, and 42 percent believed that it caused lung cancer.[35] Moreover, if the companies were at odds with the general public, they were the devil incarnate to their active enemies. Rather than view them as a well-established and legal industry mounting a morally dubious defense of a popular product with the aid of the country's most famous law firms, the antismoking movement saw them as a bunch of murderous, lying outlaws. "Pond scum," one California activist was fond of calling them.[36]

After the cigarette companies were humbled, there was recrimination against the lawyers. Edward Horrigan, who had been an executive of both Reynolds and Liggett, said that "[lawyers] were like ostriches. They stuck their heads in the sand and hoped it would go away. . . . Lawyers thought they were protecting the industry, but in my opinion the lawyers were the downfall of the industry."[37]

In defense of the lawyers, it may be said that they had been guided by one of the central tenets of their profession, which prescribes partisanship on behalf of clients. From the start, they presumed adversarial relations with both regulatory agencies and cigarette users. Anticipating a fight, they were not naïve or stupid in supposing that it would be a fight for the lives of their corporate clients.[38] In summer 2000 a state-court jury in a Florida class-action suit imposed $144.9 billion in punitive damages on the industry—far and away the biggest such penalty in U.S. history—for its deceit about the health risks of tobacco. The amount could have threatened the industry with bankruptcy if it had not been overturned or reduced on appeal (as, in fact, it was in 2003).[39] This suit was precisely the sort of event that the lawyers feared.

Also in defense of the lawyers, it may be said that for three decades their approach had succeeded at least in protecting the narrow self-interest of the companies. The case against them was, in large part, that they succeeded too well—that their rigid denials, heavy-handed litigating tactics, and long string of victories against weak opponents heightened the fury and fired the ambition of their opponents, who hungered for revenge against a seemingly invincible foe.

· The Search for a Safer Cigarette ·

Despite the moral obtuseness and irresponsibility with which they would later be charged, the cigarette executives of the 1950s and 1960s certainly did not wish to kill anyone. While turning to practitioners of public relations and law to protect their companies, they simultaneously hoped that their scientists would be able to remove from cigarettes whatever harmful substances were present. For a time, scientists in the federal government also pursued the goal of a safer cigarette. The failure to produce and successfully market one, along with the failure of the companies and the government to sustain a cooperative search, is important background to the official assault against the companies that began in the mid-1990s.

The big companies had research and development departments of four hundred to five hundred employees, and they had well-qualified research directors who were much more willing than were other executives to admit the possibility that the indictment of cigarettes had merit. When the results of the Graham-Wynder mouse-painting experiments were published in the early 1950s, Claude Teague, a scientist at Reynolds, searched the literature and concluded that it tended "to confirm the relationship between heavy and prolonged tobacco smoking and the incidence of cancer of the lung." He "recommended that management take cognizance of the problem and its implications to our industry, and that positive research action be planned and initiated without delay." A few years later another Reynolds scientist, Alan Rodgman, summarized in an internal document the conclusions of the English scientist Richard Doll, and concurred with him that "it is a reasonable presumption that the changes which have taken place in tobacco consumption (in amount and method) are responsible for the major part of the increase in mortality."[40]

In 1961 Helmut Wakeham, Philip Morris's research director, outlined a three-part "Research and Development Program Leading to a Medically Acceptable Cigarette," one part of which was "Reduction of the General Level of Carcinogens in Smoke."[41] Murray Senkus, who was Reynolds's director of chemical research throughout most of the 1950s and became research director in 1961, told reporters years later that ". . . we explored all the avenues that were floating at the time." He added, "They [company executives] didn't know a damn thing about science but they assumed we are going to get the answers with proper research. A very profound scientist knew at the beginning that you had a helluva problem. . . . I had that feeling but that doesn't mean that you shouldn't keep on trying."[42] Senkus's colleague Rodgman echoed the thought: "One by one, we did things—all of which lowered and lowered and lowered different things in proportion. What else could you do? There was only one alternative: Close the place down."[43]

Research and development departments worked hard at three different approaches. One strategy that seems to have led nowhere was to add metal nitrates, such as palladium, platinum, or magnesium, to achieve a cleaner burn and cut down on the proliferation of free radicals, which produced carcinogenic compounds.[44] A second approach, technically more feasible and universally adopted, was to reduce the tar (the residual solids that remain after burning) and nicotine content of cigarettes. The most radical strategy, which Reynolds in particular experimented with, was to change the design of cigarettes so that they heated tobacco rather than burned it.

In addition to scientific intractability, rooted in the chemical complexity of tobacco, the effort to make cigarettes safe encountered three main obstacles: company lawyers, ever fearful of the danger of liability in acknowledging, even obliquely, a hazard in the original product; customers' preferences; and opponents of smoking, who preferred eradication to amelioration.

In 1966 the Public Health Service found that "the preponderance of scientific evidence strongly suggests that the lower the tar and nicotine content of a cigarette, the less harmful will be the effect."[45] The average tar yield per cigarette was down from thirty-seven milligrams in 1955 to seventeen milligrams in 1977, and some brands had fewer than ten or five milligrams, or even one. Manufacturers typically reduced nicotine and tar yields by using more of both reconstituted tobacco and puffed tobacco. They made reconstituted leaf by mixing scraps of tobacco with water in a slurry and then drying and pressing them with flavorants and preservatives; the result looks much like the paper in a grocery bag. Puffed tobacco, inflated with carbon dioxide, is like popcorn. With equivalent volume in the cigarette rod, puffed tobacco contains less nicotine than does the untreated leaf. Both processes made cigarettes cheaper to produce as well as safer. Filters reduced tar and nicotine and became more efficient over time. Porous paper and paper additives increased the burn rate, which reduced the number of puffs required to finish the cigarette. How much safer such changes made cigarettes was debatable. Behavioral research showed that smokers sometimes compensated for the changes by smoking more cigarettes or inhaling more deeply.

Reynolds was the principal developer of the radically revised cigarette, to which it turned, with some desperation, in the 1980s. The company was shocked between 1982 and 1983 by a 10 percent decline in sales, the result partly of a general drop in cigarette sales and partly of a loss of market share. A company known for paternalism, in which everyone who did not steal cigarettes could count on a lifetime job, Reynolds paid more than one thousand employees to leave. Soon thereafter the company was further traumatized by a radical change in leadership styles. Historically, Reynolds executives had been rooted both in their place, Winston-Salem, and in their industry, tobacco manufacturing. This situation began to change, however, in the early 1970s with the arrival of Paul Sticht, formerly of Federated Department Stores of Cincinnati, who headed the company in fact if not always in name from 1972 to 1983, and it changed with a vengeance in 1986. Reynolds had acquired Nabisco Brands in 1985, and along with the Oreos and Ritz crackers came Nabisco's erratic, ingratiating, and wildly ambitious chief executive officer, Ross Johnson. It took him only a year to induce Reynolds's board to install him in place of Tylee Wilson, who had made that deal. "Ross was a citizen of the world," according to David Fishel, a veteran public relations executive at the company. "He was not a guy who was tied to anything. He was a guy who thought nothing about getting on an airplane, flying all night, meeting all day, going out to dinner, sitting in a bar until 2 o'clock in the morning and starting all over again." A company whose executives had once prided themselves on driving to work in their own cars—nothing more extravagant than a Buick—now owned fleets of airplanes and limousines and had a headquarters in Atlanta. "Wrenched . . . from its century-old North Carolina home," Reynolds was "transformed . . . into a monument to nouveau-riche excess."[46]

Obsessed with the stagnation of Reynolds's stock, Johnson decided that the way to beat Philip Morris and get Reynolds moving again was to bring out the cleanest cigarette the world had ever seen, although his subordinates warned him that the product was not ready. The new brand, named Premier, was unveiled with much fanfare at a press conference in New York City in 1987. It looked like a normal cigarette but did not perform like one. Smokers lit a carbon element at the tip. Heated air inhaled through the tip passed over a small aluminum capsule that contained tobacco extracts, including nicotine, flavorings, and glycerin. Because nothing burned, there was virtually no tar and only a fraction of the chemical compounds normally found in cigarette smoke.

Premier was a fiasco and was pulled from test markets in February 1989. It tasted and smelled terrible, was hard to draw, and was assaulted by antismoking groups, who bragged about helping to kill it. "We ambushed them in the test markets," the leader of one antismoking group claimed in 1989. "I think we created a lot of doubt in consumers' minds." Fishel called the reaction of the health groups to Premier "the major disappointment" of his twenty-six years in public relations at Reynolds. "My basic feeling is within the public health community . . . 'The only good tobacco company is one that's out of business.' "[47]

In addition to the companies' search for a safer cigarette, the U.S. government's National Cancer Institute (NCI) pursued such a project for approximately a decade. Begun in March 1968 as the Less Hazardous Cigarette Working Group, it was soon renamed the Tobacco Working Group (TWG), in deference to the companies' reluctance to speak of hazard. Among others, the group included Ernst Wynder, who by then had published several hundred articles on the health effects of tobacco. A veteran crusader against smoking, Wynder was also a pragmatist who believed that it would be impossible to eradicate smoking and that it was therefore incumbent upon public health officials to seek a safer cigarette.

The industry research directors, who participated in the TWG as consultants or observers rather than as full-fledged members, seemed reluctant to talk about anything except the chemistry of smoke, about which they knew a great deal. "The industry crowd wasn't telling us much," one government participant recounted. "I knew damned well we were talking about problems they had worked on two years earlier. . . . It took quite a while for our people to interface with them and understand that these guys wanted to prevent deaths, too, but couldn't afford to say so." The effort died in 1978 after the TWG's director, Gio Batta Gori, angered the secretary of Health, Education, and Welfare, Joseph Califano, then in the middle of a crusade against tobacco. Gori's offense was co-authoring an article in the *Journal of the American Medical Association* claiming that cigarettes with a tolerable level of risk were at hand. Gori was removed from the project and before long left the government. NCI shifted from an effort at modifying cigarettes to an emphasis on preventing smoking.[48]

The "safe" cigarette encountered so many obstacles that it is hard to tell which was the most formidable. There were always the lawyers. Soon after Reynolds announced Premier, William S. Ohlemeyer of Shook, Hardy and Bacon, the Kansas City firm specializing in tobacco litigation, lamented that the new cigarette could undermine "the tobacco industry's joint defense efforts." He wrote, "The industry position has always been that there is no alternative design for a cigarette as we know them. Unfortunately, the Reynolds announcement . . .

seriously undercuts this component of the industry's defense."[49] A twenty-seven-year veteran of Philip Morris who had worked closely with research director Helmut Wakeham told Richard Kluger:

> There was a conflict in the company between science and the law that's never been resolved. . . . [Wakeham] was addressing the issue purely as a scientist—lawyers look at the problem in a different way, and so we go through this ritual dance—what's "proven" and what isn't, what's causal and what's just an association—and the lawyers' answer is, "Let's stonewall." . . . If Helmut Wakeham had run things, I think there would have been some admissions. But he was outflanked by the lawyers, led by Paul Smith, who some people felt walked on water. The lawyers were saying, in effect, "My God, you can't make that admission" without risking liability actions against the company. So there was no cohesive plan—when critics of the industry speak of a "conspiracy," they give the companies far too much credit. . . . None of us at that time was sure what we could do, what we should or shouldn't do—or say.[50]

Then there were the antismoking forces, which, apart from occasional exceptions such as Wynder, refused compromise. "I was a little bit naïve," Wakeham said many years later, "in thinking that our critics would really like us to find a more acceptable product. I was forced to come to the conclusion after many years that they weren't really interested in such a thing."[51]

"We really thought that the world would welcome us with open arms," said J. Donald deBethizy, a Reynolds toxicologist who worked on Premier. "We went out to the best scientists with this message and we were hugely disappointed at the reaction."[52] Among antismoking activists, Donald Shopland, who had helped prepare the report of 1964 and for years thereafter worked on the annual reports of the surgeon general, conceded that it might have been a mistake to assault Premier. "I was one of them. I slammed them like everybody else did. It may not have been the smartest thing to do."[53]

Without a genuinely cooperative effort between government and industry, accompanied by some willingness to accept the fact that complete safety would probably never be attained and certainly not proven, the search for a safer cigarette was doomed. To this day, scientists remain the most honest and skeptical industry commentators on the search. Murray Senkus, retired as Reynolds's director of research, told reporters: "Looking at it in retrospect, we tried everything possible, but I'd have to say, now talking as a scientist, that tobacco is tobacco. Whatever changes you made are not likely to change the risk at all. . . . People who smoke should know the risk, and that's all there is to it."[54]

· Notes ·

1. Peter Pringle, *Cornered: Big Tobacco at the Bar of Justice* (New York: Holt, 1998), 7.
2. This account of the litigating history relies almost exclusively on the work of Robert Rabin, which can be found in two places: "A Sociolegal History of the Tobacco Tort Litigation," *Stanford Law Review* 44 (April 1992): 853–878; and "Institutional and Historical Perspectives on Tobacco Tort Liability," in *Smoking Policy: Law, Politics, and Culture,* ed. Robert L. Rabin and Stephen D. Sugarman (New York: Oxford University Press, 1993), 110–130. My citations are to the law journal article. Rabin's work is updated in "The Third Wave of Tobacco Tort Litigation," in *Regulating Tobacco,* ed. Rabin and Sugarman (New York: Oxford University Press, 2001), 176–206.

    The industry's opponents shared this view of the likely consequences of defeating it in court. Professor Richard A. Daynard, head of the Tobacco Products Liability Project in Boston, told a worldwide conference on tobacco and health in 1990:

    > I would like to focus here on what I see as the tobacco cartel's Achilles' heel. Its victims have begun to seek justice. Lawsuits are now being actively pursued in 10 American states. . . . Though each suit involves only one afflicted smoker, the fate of the entire cartel hangs on each one. If any single smoker finally receives justice from a tobacco company, every other victim becomes a potential claimant. If a single plaintiff's attorney proves he can make money suing tobacco companies, all plaintiff's attorneys are thereby encouraged to try. The wound, once opened, cannot be closed. (See 5.2 *Tobacco Products Litigation Reporter* 4.1.)

    The *Tobacco Products Litigation Reporter* (hereafter *TPLR*) is a serial that was published between 1985 and 2006 at the Northeastern University Law School in Boston under the direction of Professor Daynard, a leading antitobacco activist. Designed mainly as a service to attorneys, it contained a variety of materials pertinent to litigation against the industry, including judicial opinions, litigation documents, trial testimony, news reports, and journal articles. In citing it I have followed a form recommended by its editors. The first number in the citation is the volume; the number following the first period is the issue. Thus, the quotation in this note may be found in volume 5, issue 2. The third number is the section of the *Reporter*, and the fourth number is a page number. Thus, the quotation starts on page 1 of section 4. I have sometimes added as well other identifying information—for example, the year of publication (in parentheses), a case number, or the title of an article—when it was available and seemed likely to be helpful to the reader.

3. Frank Tursi, Susan E. White, and Steven McQuilkin, "Lost Empire: The Fall of R. J. Reynolds Tobacco Co.," a Web-only account of the recent history of R. J. Reynolds. See chap. 28, part 2, "A Privilege Denied," at www.journalnow.com, the Web site of the *Winston-Salem Journal.*

4. Cited in Rabin and Sugarman, "Institutional and Historical Perspectives," 867. The original source is William E. Townsley and Dale K. Hanks, "The Trial Court's Responsibility to Make Cigarette Disease Litigation Affordable and Fair," *California Western Law Review* 25 (1989): 277. This article is reprinted in 4.5 *TPLR* 4.11.

5. Rabin and Sugarman, "Institutional and Historical Perspectives," 861.

6. Ibid., 863.

7. The industry's counterargument was that millions of users found satisfaction in the product, governments enjoyed a large return in excise taxes, and various sectors of the economy, including tobacco growers, retailers, and advertising agencies, as well as the manufacturers, profited.

8. For a full account of the *Galbraith* case, see John A. Jenkins, *The Litigators* (New York: Doubleday, 1989), 142–148 and 159–184. The quotation is on page 121.

9. A detailed account of the Horton trial may be found in Michael Orey, *Assuming the Risk* (Boston: Little, Brown, 1999), 9–143, and a briefer one in Jenkins, *The Litigators,* 185–189.

10. Orey, *Assuming the Risk,* 142–143.

11. Richard Kluger, *Ashes to Ashes: America's Hundred-Year Cigarette War, the Public Health, and the Unabashed Triumph of Philip Morris* (New York: Knopf, 1996), 674.

12. Ibid., 654.

13. House Energy and Commerce Committee, *Regulation of Tobacco Products: Hearings before the Subcommittee on Health and the Environment,* part 1, 103d Cong., 2d sess., 1994, 546, 558.

14. The ad is reproduced in Stanton A. Glantz et al., *The Cigarette Papers* (Berkeley: University of California Press, 1996), 34.

15. Tursi, White, and McQuilkin, "Lost Empire," chap. 4, "Manning the Ramparts."

16. Ibid.

17. Ibid.

18. Ibid.

19. *Regulation of Tobacco Products,* part 2, 446–502.

20. Kluger, *Ashes to Ashes,* 166–167.

21. Tursi, White, and McQuilkin, "Lost Empire," chap. 7.

22. Kluger, *Ashes to Ashes,* 224.

23. Ibid., 324.

24. Tursi, White, and McQuilkin, "Lost Empire," chap. 8, part 1, "The Minister of Defense."

25. Kluger, *Ashes to Ashes,* 228.

26. Dan Zegart, *Civil Warriors* (New York: Delacorte, 2000), 41–42, 44–48, 82–84, 205, and passim. The quotation is on page 83. See also Milo Geyelin, "Smoking Guns: A Missouri Law Firm Finds Tobacco To Be a Lucrative Cash Crop," *Wall Street Journal,* March 28, 1996, A1.

27. Tursi, White, and McQuilkin, "Lost Empire," chap. 8, part 1.

28. Kluger, *Ashes to Ashes*, 324.

29. Ibid., 229.

30. Philip J. Hilts, *Smokescreen: The Truth Behind the Tobacco Industry Cover-up* (Reading, Mass.: Addison-Wesley, 1996), 198–199.

31. The deformation of industrial speech through fear of litigation is not peculiar to the cigarette industry. In his autobiography, IBM's Thomas J. Watson Jr. says this of the effects of an antitrust suit on his company: ". . . it depressed me to see IBM back in the lawyers' hands. The antitrust case began to color everything we did. For years every executive decision, even ones that were fairly routine, had to be made with one eye on how it might affect the lawsuit. To keep damning evidence to a minimum, the lawyers even dictated what we could and couldn't say at meetings. There were all sorts of code words and strange uses of language. . . ." See Watson's *Father, Son & Co.* (New York: Bantam, 1990), 386.

32. On censorship at Reynolds, see Tursi, White, and McQuilkin, "Lost Empire," chap. 11, part 1, "The Mouse House," and part 2, "Protecting the Kingdom."

33. Ibid., part 1.

34. Kluger, *Ashes to Ashes*, 479–483; and Glantz et al., *Cigarette Papers*, chap. 8.

35. Lydia Saad, "A Half-Century of Polling on Tobacco: Most Don't Like Smoking But Tolerate It," *Public Perspective* (August/September 1998): 1–19.

36. Kluger, *Ashes to Ashes*, 556.

37. Tursi, White, and McQuilkin, "Lost Empire," chap. 11, part 2.

38. Don Barrett, the tort lawyer from Lexington, Mississippi, who litigated the *Horton* case, did judge them stupid. When Marc Kasowitz, a lawyer for financier Bennett LeBow of Liggett & Myers, asked Barrett if there was a way out of the impasse between the industry and its opponents, Barrett "said no, because the tobacco company executives are too stupid to understand that we are not trying to put them out of business. If they would be socially responsible and pay some measure of damages and quit marketing to children, then we could make a deal." See Pringle, *Cornered*, 227. By Pringle's account, that was the beginning of an independent deal by LeBow. See chap. 5.

39. Rick Bragg, "Jurors in Florida Give Record Award in Tobacco Case," *New York Times*, July 15, 2000, A1. The largest previous such award was $5 billion in 1994 in the case of the *Exxon Valdez* oil spill. Although an appeals court threw the jury verdict out in 2003, the Florida Supreme Court reinstated the case in May 2004. In 2006 the Supreme Court likewise invalidated the $145 billion award, calling it "excessive as a matter of law," but it allowed many of the findings from trial to stand with the result that individual suits could go forward. Vanessa O'Connell, "Tobacco Industry Wins Big at Florida High Court," *Wall Street Journal*, July 7, 2006, A3.

40. Tursi, White, and McQuilkin, "Lost Empire," chap. 5, part 3.

41. Kluger, *Ashes to Ashes*, 231–232.

42. Tursi, White, and McQuilkin, "Lost Empire," chap. 20, part 1, "A Safer Cigarette."

43. Ibid., chap. 20, part 2, "One-Fanged Rattler."

44. See Kluger, *Ashes to Ashes,* for an account of Liggett & Myers's effort to develop a cigarette that incorporated palladium. See also Tursi, White, and McQuilkin, "Lost Empire," chap. 20, part 1.

45. U.S. Department of Health and Human Services, Office of Smoking and Health, *Smoking, Tobacco & Health: A Fact Book,* pub. no. 80-50150 (PHS) (Washington, D.C.: 1980), 18.

46. Bryan Burrough and John Helyar, *Barbarians at the Gate: The Fall of RJR Nabisco* (New York: Harper and Row, 1990), 5. This source quotes a Reynolds employee as follows (page 40): "Imagine you lived in this great old house. You grew up in it, and all your happy memories are in it, and you take special care of it for the next generation. Then one day, you come home to discover it's been turned into a brothel. That's how I feel about RJR." Chapter 2 of this book contains a vivid historical portrait of Reynolds.

47. Reynolds's experience with Premier is recounted in Tursi, White, and McQuilkin, "Lost Empire," chap. 26, part 1, "In Pursuit of the Holy Grail"; part 2, "A New Weapon"; and part 3, "Firing Blanks."

48. There is a full account of the NCI effort in Kluger, *Ashes to Ashes,* 421–434, 448–452; the quotation is on page 428. See also Glantz et al., *Cigarette Papers,* chap. 4.

49. Tursi, White, and McQuilkin, "Lost Empire," chap. 26, part 3.

50. Kluger, *Ashes to Ashes,* 277.

51. Ibid., 231.

52. Tursi, White, and McQuilkin, "Lost Empire," chap. 26, part 1.

53. Ibid., chap. 26, part 3.

54. Ibid., chap. 20, part 2.

S641

CHAPTER FOUR

The Drive for FDA Regulation

PUBLIC HEALTH AGENCIES WERE LEADERS of the campaign against tobacco, and the leader among all agencies for several decades was the Office of the Surgeon General in the federal government. Even before President John F. Kennedy's surgeon general, Luther Terry, appointed his famed advisory committee in 1962, his predecessor in the Eisenhower administration, Leroy E. Burney, had gone on record against smoking. In 1957 he stated that "the weight of the evidence is increasingly pointing in one direction . . . that excessive smoking is one of the causative factors in lung cancer." [1]

The report of 1964, followed by the legislation of 1965, laid the foundation for a series of annual reports that were prepared by the Office on Smoking and Health—a small agency in the Department of Health, Education, and Welfare (HEW)—with dozens of collaborating authors from the public health and medical research professions. These reports regularly compiled, reiterated, and extended the scientific case against smoking. Although some were no more than rehashes of what had gone before, others were milestones and agenda setters. The volume, freshness, and power of these reports gave witness to the commitment of public health professionals to the cause of tobacco control. Along with scientific periodicals such as the *Journal of the National Cancer Institute* and the quarterly journal *Tobacco Control,* which began publication in London in the early 1990s, they were the principal publication outlets for the scientific and medical opponents of tobacco.

Among the readers whom these reports could influence were the surgeons general in whose name they were issued. Of particular consequence was the case of C. Everett Koop, who was appointed by President Ronald Reagan in 1981. Koop's confirmation was delayed for a long time by Senate liberals who feared his evangelical Christianity, believing that it could affect government policy toward abortion rights. They failed to anticipate that his evangelical approach to public policy would advance a cause of which they approved—opposition to smoking. It was not a cause with which he had previously been identified, but once installed in office, exposed to the facts and the arguments, and presented with the opportunity, he seized it with prophetic zeal and continued the pursuit even after leaving office. Koop's goal, enunciated in a speech to the American Lung Association in May 1984, was a "smoke-free society" by the year 2000.[2]

Another agency of the Department of Health and Human Services (HHS, formerly HEW) that has played an important part in the campaign against tobacco use is the Centers for Disease Control and Prevention (CDC), based in Atlanta, whose mission is to combat preventable diseases and respond to public health emergencies, such as outbreaks of disease. Since the mid-1980s, the CDC has published figures for smoking-attributable mortality. The CDC has estimated that for the years 1990–1994, an average of 430,700 deaths per year were attributable to smoking, or one of every five deaths in the United States. The agency arrived at the figure by attaching "smoking attributable fractions" to twenty-four different categories of fatal diseases. The fractions range from a low of 0.138 for sudden infant death syndrome to highs of 0.85 for chronic bronchitis, emphysema, and chronic airways obstruction.[3]

The figure of 430,000 deaths per year, though obviously subject to challenge as an estimate, became the antismoking movement's mantra, endlessly repeated in editorials and public documents.[4] Since the early 1980s, Public Health Service publications have regularly characterized smoking as the leading preventable cause of death and disability in the United States—a succinct and arresting statement that is echoed in other media outlets. This statement is often coupled with the additionally dramatizing assertion that cigarettes kill more Americans than do AIDS, alcohol, car accidents, murders, suicides, drugs, and fires combined.

Secretaries of HEW and HHS have also taken up the cause, some with more fervor than others. Secretary Joseph A. Califano Jr. embraced it vigorously in the late 1970s. On January 11, 1978, the fourteenth anniversary of the advisory committee's report, he labeled cigarettes "Public Health Enemy No. 1" and said their users, of whom he had been one, were committing "slow-motion suicide."[5] In 1989 HHS Secretary Louis Sullivan contributed to a growing campaign to combat youth smoking by instructing his department's Office of the Inspector General to investigate how well state governments were enforcing laws prohibiting the sale of cigarettes to minors. The resulting report, *Youth Access to Cigarettes,* documented a lack of enforcement.[6]

In addition to acting through the agencies for which safeguarding public health is a mission, the federal executive branch, as a major employer and office manager, can influence society with its personnel policies. In 1972, during the Nixon administration, the secretary of HEW prohibited smoking in departmental conference rooms, auditoriums, sections of cafeterias, and certain work areas. In 1976 the General Services Administration began issuing smoking guidelines for government buildings generally.[7] In 1990 the secretary of veterans affairs, Edward J. Derwinski, announced that Veterans Administration (VA) hospitals would not sell tobacco products after September 1991 and that VA health facilities were to be tobacco-free by the end of 1993. This declaration created such an outcry from veterans that Congress, after heated debate, reversed the ban and required the VA to designate smoking rooms. The U.S. government had, after all, distributed cigarettes to its armed forces or made them available at below-market (because tax-free) prices at post exchanges for much of the twentieth century. Cigarettes had been the serviceman's companions in combat, as General Pershing had said. Ex-servicemen felt entitled to them in civilian life as well.

Missing from this broad panoply of executive action prior to the mid-1990s were the Food and Drug Administration (FDA) and the president. When they joined each other and the rest of tobacco's opponents in 1995, the antitobacco coalition was very much strengthened, and tobacco politics was profoundly changed.

· Kessler Engages the Issue ·

An appointee of President George H.W. Bush in 1990, Commissioner David A. Kessler came to the FDA with excellent credentials. A Phi Beta Kappa graduate of Amherst, he had an M.D. degree from Harvard and a law degree from the University of Chicago, as well as experience as a staff member on Capitol Hill and as medical director of New York's Einstein-Montefiore Hospital. Ironically, a scion of the R. J. Reynolds tobacco fortune, C. Boyden Gray, who was White House counsel under George H. W. Bush, was instrumental in his selection. Gray's uncle, Bowman Gray Jr., was president of Reynolds in the late 1950s and early 1960s, when the company was at a peak of success, and he had testified on behalf of the industry before Congress during the first big fight over regulation in the mid-1960s.

Kessler's principal goal was to invigorate the agency's enforcement with expanded powers and staff. For example, he sought to build a one-hundred-person office of criminal investigation within the agency so that it would no longer have to rely on the FBI. Substantively, he began with food labeling and seized twenty-four thousand cartons of orange juice to demonstrate to Procter and Gamble's beverage division that the FDA would not tolerate the company's calling "fresh" what was actually reconstituted. He proceeded from that confrontation to a more sweeping one over nutritional labeling.

Congress had enacted the Nutrition Labeling and Education Act in 1990, and it was up to the FDA to design implementing regulations, though the Department of Agriculture also had some claim to jurisdiction. Kessler showed his mettle by doing battle against this rival agency and winning the fight at the level of the White House. The core issue was whether the standard for the average daily intake of calories should be set at 2,350, as Agriculture wanted, or at 2,000, as public health specialists preferred. Kessler, holding the view that "diet accounted for the second largest cause of preventable death in the United States [after tobacco]," was prepared to resign over this issue and managed to convey as much through a talk with the food reporter for the *New York Times*. He also found backing in the editorial pages of the *Times* and the *Washington Post*. Kessler reported that Ed Madigan, who was Bush's secretary of agriculture and who had helped pass the labeling act as a member of Congress from Illinois, "was furious at being portrayed as a tool of the meat industry," whose products would have benefited from a more lenient standard.[8]

Having thus honed his skills as an uncompromising regulator in a political environment, Kessler turned to tobacco. Within FDA he had early been prodded on this subject by the associate commissioner for public affairs, Jeffrey Nesbit. Like Kessler, Nesbit was a hard man to classify politically. He had worked for the muckraking journalist Jack Anderson, the public-interest organizer and lobbyist Ralph Nader, and the Indiana senator and Republican vice president Dan Quayle. An evangelical Christian, he was, like Kessler, principled and zealous in his approach to public issues. Moreover, like many antitobacco activists, he had a personal stake in the issue. His father, a smoker, was dying of lung cancer, and he had a younger brother who smoked. At FDA, which he joined before Kessler's appointment, he kept asking why the agency did not do something about cigarettes: "Here's this product that cuts short the lives of millions of Americans, and it's totally unregulated. And here's the premier consumer-protection agency in the world. Why isn't it doing its job?" Nesbit's attitude, Kessler says, "was that if something could be done, and should be done, there was no excuse for not trying to do it. . . . He did not ask me if I wanted to take on tobacco. He told me I should."[9]

The problem was how to regulate tobacco in the face of Congress's preference to the contrary. At least since the late 1970s, antitobacco organizations had been petitioning the agency to claim jurisdiction. FDA commissioners had consistently responded that they lacked it. "I'll be

glad to go to work on the cigarette ban as soon as you give me the legislative authority to do so," Commissioner Donald Kennedy had told a
senator who asked why he was trying to ban saccharin, an artificial
sweetener, but not cigarettes.[10] A federal appeals court had upheld the
FDA's position in *ASH v. Harris* in 1980. In the early 1990s the industry's
opponents in Congress had introduced bills that would have given the
FDA authority over tobacco, but these did not pass or even receive serious consideration.

This history might have seemed an insuperable obstacle to most
people, but not to an official convinced that protecting the public's
health required regulation. In the practice of politics and government,
laws are not necessarily treated as fixed things. Much of the activity of
American policymaking consists of attempts not to pass new laws but
to invest old ones with new meanings. In this case, two conceptual
breakthroughs were critical.

The first was supplied by Scott Ballin, chairman of the Coalition
on Smoking OR Health, the antitobacco consortium composed of the big
health voluntary organizations—the American Heart Association, the
American Lung Association, and the American Cancer Society. According to Kessler, "Ballin thought the appropriate federal laws to regulate
tobacco might already be somewhere on the books, and for months he
sat in his office studying them." Ballin noticed that all of the recently
passed consumer protection laws—those from the 1960s and 1970s—
contained provisions explicitly excluding tobacco from regulation. However, the FDA's statutory charter (the Federal Food, Drug, and Cosmetic
Act), much of it dating from 1938, contained no such provision. No
doubt, as a practical matter this was because it would not have occurred
to Congress or to the tobacco industry in 1938 that any such protection
was necessary. Now Ballin saw the omission as an opportunity: if the
FDA's law alone failed to prohibit tobacco regulation, then this absence
of prohibition could be taken as permission. Ballin kept taunting the
FDA with petitions.[11]

There needed to be a second step. It was not enough to find a
lacuna in the FDA's law. It was necessary also to identify language that
could be used affirmatively to cover the case. Here the key was supplied
by a lawyer in the agency's policy office, David Adams—"a freelance
artist of the law," as a colleague called him. Adams told Kessler in a
private meeting that instead of regulating tobacco, the agency should
regulate its active ingredient, nicotine. "Cigarette manufacturers can
take the nicotine out, but they leave it in," Adams said. "That goes to
the question of intent." Such intent could bring nicotine within reach of
the FDA statute, which authorized the agency to regulate products that

were intended by their manufacturer to affect the structure or function of the body. "The idea was powerful, as elegant as it was succinct, and I recognized it as a dramatic way to approach an old problem," Kessler writes. "From that moment on [it was the fall of 1992]. . ., I began to focus on tobacco." [12]

More than a year passed before Kessler made a public move. In the interim, Bill Clinton became president, and Kessler was retained as commissioner. On February 25, 1994, he sent a letter to Scott Ballin that in essence announced an intention to regulate the nicotine in cigarettes:

> Under the [Federal Food, Drug, and Cosmetic] Act, products are subject to regulation as drugs based on the intent of the product vendor. . . . Evidence brought to our attention is accumulating that suggests that cigarette manufacturers may intend that their products contain nicotine to satisfy an addiction on the part of some of their customers. . . . Should the agency make this finding based on an appropriate record or be able to prove these facts in court, it would have a legal basis on which to regulate these products under the drug provisions of the Act. [13]

There are at least two explanations for the timing of this letter. Kessler knew that ABC-TV was about to show an exposé of the tobacco industry's "last best secret . . . never before disclosed to consumers or the government"—that manufacturers were "spiking" or "fortifying" their cigarettes with extra nicotine to keep smokers addicted. [14] The sinister implication was that the nicotine in cigarettes exceeded that which occurred naturally in the tobacco plant. The program aired on February 28 and March 7. Kessler wanted both to precede it and to take maximum advantage of it.

Second, the Clinton plan for universal health insurance, a major domestic policy initiative announced in fall 1993, was not going anywhere. Containing a large increase in the tax on cigarettes, it indicated the administration's willingness to oppose the industry. At the same time, its faltering prospects suggested that a vacuum might be impending in the health policy agenda.

By Kessler's account, he hoped to goad Congress into action. Democrats on the Subcommittee on Health and the Environment of the House Commerce Committee did not need much goading. Rep. Henry Waxman, the chairman and a longtime foe of the industry, had been kept informed of what Kessler was planning to do, and another leading opponent of the industry, Rep. Mike Synar of Oklahoma, was urging him on. As soon as Kessler's letter was released, the subcommittee scheduled hearings on the regulation of tobacco products. These hearings were held on seven days between March 25 and June 23, 1994, and were a leading event in the gathering assault on the industry. According to Waxman, they marked "the beginning of a new relationship between Congress and the tobacco companies. The old rules are out. . . ." [15] Tobacco executives had thought that the old rules went out in 1979, when Waxman became the subcommittee chairman.

The hearings gave Kessler an opportunity to attack the defense of smoking that both smokers and the industry had traditionally employed— that Americans had a right to smoke if they wanted to. Kessler now replied that it was a right not freely exercised because smokers were addicts who did not control their own actions. His presentation to Waxman's subcommittee opened as follows:

> Mr. Chairman, the cigarette industry has attempted to frame the debate on smoking as the right of each American to choose. The question we must ask is whether smokers really have that choice. Consider these facts:
>
> - Two-thirds of adults who smoke say they wish they could quit.
> - Seventeen million try to quit each year, but fewer than one out of ten succeeds. For every smoker who quits, nine try and fail.
> - Three out of four adult smokers say that they are addicted. By some estimates, as many as 74 to 90 percent are addicted.
> - Eight out of ten smokers say they wish they had never started smoking.[16]

Of greater public effect than Kessler's testimony was the appearance in April of the executives of the major cigarette companies, who were captured on TV testifying that they did not believe nicotine was addictive. This exposed them to public ridicule as liars and constituted a propaganda coup for their opponents; more will be said of this moment in chapter 6.

In the year following the hearings, Kessler pursued twin objectives. One was to catch his quarry, the cigarette industry, in the act of purposely manipulating the nicotine content of cigarettes to addict smokers. A second was to win support for his campaign from the Clinton White House. Whatever chance there had been of securing support from Congress vanished with the congressional elections of 1994, in which the Republican Party, on the whole more sympathetic to industry interests than were the Democrats, captured the House of Representatives. Waxman was out as chairman of the Subcommittee on Health and the

Environment, which was abolished. Rep. Tom Bliley of Richmond, whose district included a big Philip Morris manufacturing plant, became chairman of the full committee, now called Energy and Commerce. Officials at the top of the Department of Health and Human Services, who were Kessler's nominal superiors, hesitated in the face of the changed political environment and the growing backlash against big government that had developed in response to the Clinton health care plan, but Kessler, far from finding the election results a reason to desist, was more than ever determined to press on and correctly perceived that he would need the president's support to do so.

· Getting the Goods on the Industry ·

If Kessler had felt constrained by organizational channels, it is possible that he would have been inhibited by opposition within the FDA. In 1991, when he took his first steps in response to Jeff Nesbit's plea to do something about tobacco, he assembled a meeting of a dozen or more of the agency's scientists, lawyers, and administrators. Nesbit made his argument for tobacco control, stressing that the industry was no longer the power in Congress that it was thought to be. There was opposition from two agency veterans, Gerry Meyer, deputy director of the Center for Drug Evaluation and Research, and Dan Michels, head of drug compliance, both of whom feared reprisals from Congress and a compromise of the agency's core mission, the regulation of pharmaceuticals. On the other hand, there was support from within the counsel's office.[17] This support was not surprising—in government agencies today, lawyers often are activists.[18]

In 1991 Kessler was still noncommittal. After he embraced the cause late in 1992, he assembled a tobacco task force that reported directly to him, either recruiting members from outside the agency or handpicking them from among its eight thousand employees. His principal deputy, Mitch Zeller, came from outside, with a record that made him less than fully welcome in the FDA. As counsel for the oversight committee of Rep. Ted Weiss of New York, Zeller had "turned the FDA upside down in his pursuit of documents," subpoenaed Kessler, and threatened to hold him in contempt. Earlier, he had angered the agency's Center for Veterinary Medicine and its food experts with confrontational tactics. Kessler admired his "tenacity."[19]

Two other key members of the task force were its criminal investigators, Gary Light and Tom Doyle. Light was a twenty-year veteran of the army's criminal investigation command, where he had been involved in undercover narcotics operations and investigations of larceny, robbery, rape, and murder. Doyle had been a transit police-man in New York City and an employee of the Secret Service and the CIA. They, too, were not entirely welcome among the FDA's employ-ees. "After twenty years of dealing with criminals, Gary and Tom were cynical as only cops could be," Kessler writes. "They never took any-body at face value and were predisposed to make an assumption of guilt." The typical members at FDA headquarters were "made of gen-tler stuff." [20] The typical employees of FDA also did not carry con-cealed guns, as did Light and Doyle.

Combining a prosecutor's zeal with a scientist's curiosity, Kessler directed his team of lawyers and detectives in a far-flung pursuit of tobacco's miscreants. They visited the major manufacturing plants, receiving a polite welcome at Philip Morris in Richmond and at R. J. Reynolds in Tobaccoville, North Carolina, but a hostile one at Brown & Williamson (B&W) in Macon, Georgia. To avoid arousing suspicion at the tobacco archives of North Carolina State University in Raleigh, they dispatched a student intern dressed in blue jeans and carrying a backpack. They went down back roads in Wilson, North Carolina, and Cynthiana, Kentucky, in search of farmers who had grown "Y-1," a nicotine-rich experimental tobacco. They interviewed employees of DNA Plant Technology in New Jersey, a genetic engineering firm that had been under contract to B&W to develop Y-1. They sought out James Chaplin, a plant scientist retired from the Department of Agri-culture, whose work in hybridizing new tobacco strains while a government employee formed the background of Y-1. They hunted through patents, foreign and domestic, and customs records in North and South Carolina, Virginia, and Georgia, to trace the movement of Y-1 seeds offshore to Brazil and back again—as tobacco leaf—through domestic ports. With an interest in the industry's early advertising practices, they hunted through the papers of John Hill, of Hill and Knowlton, in the Wisconsin Historical Society and through those of Clarence Cook Little, the first scientific director of the Council on Tobacco Research.

Besides the considerable digging they did on their own, the FDA investigators also benefited from a rising flood of inside information from whistleblowers, document thefts, and legal discovery.

The most renowned whistleblower of the time, who would become the hero of the movie *The Insider,* was first known to Kessler by the pseudonym "Research." He turned out to be Jeffrey Wigand, a biochem-ist who had become head of research and development at B&W in 1989, only to be fired four years later. He had been constantly at odds with Tommy Sandefur, B&W's president, whom he held in contempt as intel-lectually inferior, "just like a farm boy." [21] When Sandefur became CEO,

Wigand was sacked, but his four years in the industry had given him knowledge of the chemistry of cigarettes that made him valuable to tobacco's critics. Questioned for many hours at FDA headquarters, where he insisted on dealing with Kessler personally, Wigand tipped the FDA off to Y-1 and to the industry's use of ammonia additives to facilitate the release of nicotine. Very likely, he was the source of a bundle of B&W documents, including a manufacturer's handbook, that was mailed to the FDA anonymously.

Arguably even more helpful to the FDA was a still-employed B&W scientist whom Kessler calls "Macon" and whose identity remains a secret. Macon was more specific than Wigand—he named the brands in which Y-1 had been used and helped the FDA in locating patents. The actual use of Y-1 in commercial products was later confirmed by Drew McMurtrie, the company's director of product development, in a meeting with FDA officials at the agency's headquarters.[22]

The FDA benefited also from interviews with several former Philip Morris employees, especially William Farone, initially known to Kessler as "Philip." Farone had left the company in 1984 after eight years as its director of applied research. Articulate and cooperative, he developed rapport with Kessler as a fellow scientist in pursuit of knowledge. In numerous conversations and finally in a formal declaration to the FDA, Farone described attempts by the industry to maintain a satisfying level of nicotine—for whose stimulating yet relaxing effects smokers smoked—while reducing the tar, which contained carcinogens. Farone wrote,

> If we accept the premise—as the cigarette industry surely does—that cigarettes are a nicotine delivery system, and the current laws do not forbid the self-administration of nicotine via smoking by adults, then it becomes a desirable technical challenge to decrease the "tar" in a cigarette while maintaining the delivery of nicotine. This has been a key objective of the cigarette industry over the last 20–30 years. . . .

With a scientist's naïveté about the politics of tobacco, Farone closed his statement with an appeal for an "'open' environment, with cooperation on the nature of cigarette products between the industry and government regulators," such that new and safer products could be made and "agreement between regulators and industry would open up entirely new options for cigarette construction and progress in the industry."[23]

Then there was the melodramatic case of Merrell Williams, whom the FDA did not meet but from whose thefts it benefited. In mid-April 1994 Richard Scruggs, a Mississippi tort lawyer, took possession of approximately four thousand pages of B&W documents that Williams had stolen between 1988 and 1992 when he worked as a paralegal for the Kentucky law firm of Wyatt, Tarrant, and Combs, counsel to B&W. From Scruggs's hands and those of Mississippi attorney general Mike Moore, whom he consulted, the stolen documents quickly made their way to Waxman's subcommittee and staff; to Philip Hilts, a science reporter for the *New York Times;* and to the FDA investigators.[24] These documents contained a wealth of information on nicotine research in the 1960s and 1970s by B&W and its parent, the British-American Tobacco Company, which were engaged in the industry's longtime quest for a cigarette that would sustain nicotine delivery while reducing tar. They also contained a particularly useful one-line quotation from B&W's general counsel at that time, Addison Yeaman, who wrote, "We are, then, in the business of selling nicotine, an addictive drug. . . ."[25]

Williams's trove of stolen documents was indirectly a product of lawsuits, inasmuch as he would not have had access to them had the industry not been forced to search its files in response to the demands of legal discovery. Equally useful were numerous documents that had been produced more directly by discovery. There was, for example, a trove from the Philip Morris laboratory of William L. Dunn Jr., who had been known within the company in the 1970s as "the nicotine kid." Trained in psychology at Duke University, from which he held a PhD, Dunn had been hired by Philip Morris's director of research, Helmut Wakeham, because Wakeham thought the company ought to know why people smoked. Much in Dunn's work was now useful to the company's adversaries—probably more useful than it had ever been to Philip Morris, given the fact that it was often abstract or narrowly behavioral. Dunn was a clever and quotable speaker, who in 1972 had summarized a Caribbean island conference on "Motives and Incentives in Smoking" by telling co-workers back in Richmond that they should "think of the cigarette pack as a storage container for a day's supply of nicotine. . . . Think of the cigarette as a dispenser for a dose unit of nicotine. . . . Think of a puff of smoke as the vehicle for nicotine. . . . Smoke is beyond question the most optimized vehicle of nicotine. . . ."[26] These remarks may well have engaged his Richmond audience in the early 1970s. They were certainly helpful to Waxman's staff and the FDA investigators nearly a quarter century later.

Ann Ritter, a tort lawyer in pursuit of the industry, was puzzled by Philip Morris's inquisitiveness. "Tell me this," she asked a whistle-blower, Ian Uydess, who was describing the company's behavioral research for her in Charleston in the spring of 1996. "Why collect so much information? I mean, measuring brain-wave activity, hiring you and all these biologists. . . . It couldn't do anything except get them into trouble." Uydess replied, "You have to understand, Philip Morris loves to know. They want to know the truth. It's part of who they are. They don't like just *kind of* knowing. They want to *know.*" [27] Uydess was of course referring to the scientific side of Philip Morris. It did want to know, whereas the legal side did not want to tell. This inner conflict proved to have devastating consequences.

The FDA had gotten Dunn's laboratory documents from an archive maintained in Houston by an organization called DOC, for Doctors Ought to Care, founded in 1977 by a doctor named Alan Blum. An FDA staff member stayed there for five days, photocopying 2,867 documents. [28] A windfall of Reynolds documents came via yet another channel, a law firm in Charleston that was pursuing tobacco litigation and was more than willing to share its findings with the FDA. At Reynolds the key documents were written by the scientist Claude Teague in the 1970s. Teague wrote, for example, that

> nicotine is known to be a habit-forming alkaloid. . . . Thus, a tobacco product is, in essence, a vehicle for delivery of nicotine, designed to deliver the nicotine in a generally acceptable and attractive form. . . . If nicotine is the sine qua non of tobacco products, and tobacco products are recognized as being attractive dosage forms of nicotine, then it is logical to design our products . . . around nicotine delivery. . . . In a sense, the tobacco industry may be thought of as being a specialized, highly ritualized and stylized segment of the pharmaceutical industry. Tobacco products uniquely contain and deliver nicotine, a potent drug with a variety of physiological effects. [29]

If the FDA had set out to design its own findings, it could not have written anything better suited to its purposes, unless by substituting "addictive" for "habit-forming."

Throughout Kessler's investigation, which took his agents into homes, offices, tobacco fields, and factories, Kessler expected Congress to try to stop him by instructing the FDA not to spend funds for this purpose. [30] That did not happen, but Congress did refuse his funding request for a new building for the FDA, possibly a way of retaliating. Sen. Mitch McConnell of Kentucky secured signatures from 120 members of the House and 32 additional members of the Senate on a letter to the FDA protesting its reach into tobacco. [31] Also, members of Congress sympathetic to the industry asked Kessler to supply documents relating to the investigation. He refused. "Document requests are an appropriate part of oversight," Kessler writes, "but this request bothered me because I was sure the tobacco companies were behind it." Charlie Rose, a North Carolina Democrat who was chairman of the House Agriculture Committee, and then his Republican successor, Thomas Ewing of Illinois, turned to the General Accounting Office (GAO) when Kessler refused to provide documents. They asked the GAO to review the FDA's approach to tobacco rulemaking procedures and to consider possible criminal charges that the FDA had obstructed a congressional investigation. The general counsel at HHS backed Kessler, and Rose and Ewing backed down rather than try to get documents with a subpoena. The FDA agreed to allow the GAO to interview employees on the tobacco team.[32]

Fairly drowning in evidence obtained from the industry's files, Kessler had to decide how best to use it. This led him to the White House.

· Enlisting President Clinton ·

Historically, cigarette smoking had failed to engage the attention of presidents. In contrast to the surgeon general and the secretary of HHS, the president is elected rather than appointed and a generalist instead of a specialist. He is responsible for the full range of government activities, including foreign policy and national defense, and is attentive to the political implications of all. Opposition to the nation's habit of smoking cigarettes had not seemed sufficiently important or politically rewarding to reach the president's agenda.

Presidents did not send bills to Congress on the subject, and they signed Congress's several regulatory enactments without fanfare. President Jimmy Carter failed to support the antismoking campaign of his secretary of HEW, Joseph Califano Jr., whom he asked to resign in 1978.[33] On the campaign trail presidential candidates were, if anything, mildly derisive. In North Carolina in 1978, in a political appearance aimed at countering the appeal of Republican senator Jesse Helms, President Carter "lauded the beautiful quality of your tobacco" and pledged continued backing for the tobacco price support program and government research "to make the smoking of tobacco even more safe than it is today."[34] A farmer himself, Carter knew the satisfaction of growing a good crop. Presumably he also wanted to carry North Carolina in 1980, when he would run for reelection.

During his 1980 campaign, Ronald Reagan promised that his administration would "end what has become an increasingly antagonistic relationship between the federal government and the tobacco industry. . . . I can guarantee that my own cabinet members will be far too busy with substantive matters to waste their time proselytizing against the dangers of cigarette smoking."[35] In the administration of George

H.W. Bush, who had appointed Kessler, the assistant secretary of HHS for health, James Mason, had been receptive to Kessler's initiative, but Kessler doubted that the president would be equally so.[36]

Kessler's first stop in the higher levels of the federal executive branch was in HHS, of which FDA is a part. He found Clinton's department secretary, Donna Shalala, to be enthusiastic, except for some reservations about Kessler's desire to break the link between tobacco and sports sponsorships. As a former chancellor of the University of Wisconsin, Shalala had insight into the thrill of athletic competition. After Wisconsin's football team qualified for the Rose Bowl in 1994, she turned up in the gear of a "cheesehead," offering to share it with Kessler, who declined. Not a fun-loving person, Kessler recounts in his book how he took his young son to a minor league baseball game and plunged into the study of opinion poll data on tobacco as the first pitch passed over home plate.[37]

Shalala's subordinates in HHS, with whom FDA officials regularly met, were much less receptive than she was. They saw the FDA staff as "stubborn advocates," Kessler says, and thought him "mesmerized" by tobacco. It was not that they questioned the principle of the thing—that is, Kessler's claim to have authority even in the absence of an explicit grant from Congress and contrary to the interpretation of his predecessors. Rather, they questioned the substance of the proposed rules, which, for example, contained strict prohibitions on advertising and promotion and would have set the legal age limit for tobacco purchases at nineteen when almost every state legislature had set it at eighteen.[38] The department's assistant secretary for legislation, Jerry D. Klepner, who would have to bear the burden of defending the FDA before Congress, was enraged. "Are you people crazy?" he asked at one point. At another, he "pushed his chair away from the table, his breathing rapid and hard. He walked to the window, struggling to control his fury, and then walked back to the edge of the table. He looked directly at [Kessler] and said, 'I feel fucked.' " Unfazed, Kessler writes that "whether the Department was with me or not, I was going to move the issue forward. I decided we should quietly establish our own channels to the White House. It was a risk to circumvent the Department, and I did not want to offend my overseers, but I needed support from other quarters."[39]

Within the White House, Kessler found several allies, beginning with the president's wife, Hillary Rodham Clinton, who put Kessler's name on the guest list for the White House Christmas party in 1994. "I wanted you to come," she told him warmly. ". . . I really admire what you are doing. It's Orwellian to say that nicotine is not a drug."[40] Another ally was Vice President Al Gore, who had once helped grow tobacco on the family farm in Tennessee but had become the bereaved sibling of a lung cancer victim. His sister, Nancy Gore Hunger, had started smoking at the age of thirteen and died in 1984 at the age of forty-five, as he would tell the Democratic National Convention in 1996. Gore's moral fervor on the issue matched that of Kessler, while the range of his regulatory ambition reached even farther. At a State Department treaty-signing ceremony that they both attended, Gore whispered in Kessler's ear, "Can't we do something about smoking in Russia?" Kessler looked for the smile on his face and, failing to find one, concluded that Gore was serious.[41]

Other supporters were Abner Mikva, the White House counsel, and his associate Chris Cerf, particularly after they were assured that Kessler did not intend a ban on nicotine products but rather a set of regulations designed to restrict youth access. Kessler had dramatized this approach in February 1995 with a well-publicized speech at the Columbia Law School, in which he characterized smoking as "a pediatric disease" and emphasized the need to protect against nicotine addiction in children. "The speech had the intended effect," he says, "letting everyone know the direction in which the FDA was headed, regardless of who controlled Congress." [42] Mikva helpfully suggested that Kessler send the FDA's several hundred pages of jurisdictional claims and analysis to Walter Dellinger, head of the Office of Legal Counsel in the Department of Justice. By the middle of 1995, Dellinger had reviewed and approved this document, which very much strengthened Kessler's position.

It remained to secure the endorsement of the president. At the White House Christmas party, Clinton had remarked to Kessler that the Democrats had lost the congressional elections because of two issues— tobacco and gun control. Defeated southern Democrats had told the president that trying to increase the tobacco excise tax to fund health care reform had cost enough votes to be decisive in their races. Kessler's wife had reassured the president that he had done the right thing, and Kessler had quickly planted an idea: "We can do this, if we focus on kids." [43]

Most of the president's politically oriented advisers, such as Harold Ickes and Pat Griffin, who handled liaison with Congress, were leery of attacking tobacco, but one political operative argued for it. Dick Morris, the president's pollster, was trying to position him for victory in 1996 and insisted that tobacco would only be a help. Morris showed the president survey data from each tobacco state indicating that as long as he tied the issue to children's health he would do well. Morris was ardent on the subject, a self-proclaimed zealot. A professional tactician in politics, normally unburdened by conviction or principle, Morris nonetheless had convictions about tobacco use. He believed that cigarettes had killed his mother, who had started smoking at age four-teen and had died in 1993 of cancer, heart disease, and a bleeding ulcer after a lifetime of two to three packs of Pall Malls a day.[44] Kessler estab-lished a link directly with Morris, circumventing the White House chief of staff, Leon Panetta, who in Kessler's judgment had an aversion to Morris and not much interest in pursuing tobacco. Morris, however, credited Panetta with making the argument that the White House needed to identify opportunities to act unilaterally, independent of Con-gress, given the Republicans' capture of the House.[45] The FDA's pro-posed rules satisfied the president's interest in finding ways to act that did not depend on congressional cooperation.

The president decided to embrace youth smoking as an issue, per-suaded that it would not be fatal to him in the South and might even help him in such populous states as New York and California, which harbored strong antismoking movements. Also, by Kessler's account, Clinton was enraged by the industry documents dealing with nicotine. "I want to kill them," he said of industry officials, in a meeting in the private quarters of the White House. "I just read all those documents, and I want to kill them."[46]

In August 1995 the president held a televised press conference in the White House at which he endorsed the FDA's proposed regulations. Surrounded by children, he would turn opposition to youth smoking into a campaign theme:

> It is time . . . to free our teenagers from addiction and depen-dency. . . . When Joe Camel tells our children that smoking is cool, when billboards tell teens that smoking will lead to true romance, when Virginia Slims tells adolescents that cigarettes will make them thin and glamorous, then our children need our wisdom, our guidance, and our experience.[47]

The president stressed that he was acting "by executive authority" and taking "broad executive action." When a reporter chided him for being a cigar smoker, the president replied that it was well known that he was allergic to cigars and did not smoke them often.

The press conference took place on August 10. The FDA's proposed regulations appeared in the *Federal Register* on August 11. They were published in final form on August 28, 1996, and were scheduled to take effect for the most part one year later.

· The Regulations ·

At least in length, the FDA's rule was anticlimactic. It occupied a mere 3 pages at the end of 222 pages of text, which were followed by a

662-page annex of jurisdictional determination. (A circuit court would remark acidly that the basic premise of the more than 600 pages could be fairly summarized in a statement of one sentence that tobacco products fit within the literal definition of "drug" and "device" in the Food, Drug, and Cosmetic Act.[48]) This document was the most extensive administrative record in the history of the agency. The three pages did the following:

1. prohibited the sale of cigarettes and smokeless tobacco to individuals under the age of eighteen;

2. required sellers to verify a purchaser's age through photographic identification;

3. prohibited the distribution of free samples and the use of vending machines or self-service displays except in places where persons under eighteen were not permitted;

4. prohibited the sale of cigarettes in packs of fewer than twenty;

5. banned the use of advertising billboards and posters near schools and public playgrounds;

6. limited the advertising and labeling to which children and adolescents were exposed to a black-and-white, text-only format;

7. prohibited the sale and distribution of promotional items such as hats and T-shirts bearing cigarette brand names;

8. prohibited sponsorship of sporting and musical events and of sports teams using brand names; and

9. required each cigarette and smokeless tobacco package to bear the label "Nicotine-Delivery Device for Persons 18 or Older."

The last of these requirements in effect validated the FDA's regulatory regime by giving tobacco products a name that justified regulation.[49]

The rest of the 222 pages plus the annex, besides justifying the FDA's claim of authority to issue the regulations, responded in painstaking detail to the more than seven hundred thousand comments—a record number in the agency's experience—that had been received after the agency issued its notice of proposed rulemaking in 1995. For its claim of authority, which was set forth in seventeen pages at the outset, the agency relied heavily on a relatively recent statute—the Safe Medical Devices Act of 1990—even though Congress had not applied the law explicitly to tobacco products. That law had recognized the existence of products that, although neither drugs nor devices, were a combination of "a drug, device or biological product," and it allowed more products to be categorized as medical devices, a class of products that the FDA had had authority to regulate since 1938. The FDA had determined that cigarettes and smokeless tobacco were intended by their manufacturers to affect the structure or function of the body, thereby meeting one criterion for bringing them within the definitions of "drug" and "device" used in the Food, Drug, and Cosmetic Act, the agency's charter. It further determined that the nicotine in cigarettes and smokeless tobacco was a "drug" that "produces significant pharmacological effects in consumers, including satisfaction of addiction, stimulation, sedation, and weight control." Finally, cigarettes and smokeless tobacco were found to be "combination products consisting of the drug nicotine and device components intended to deliver nicotine to the body." The agency elected to regulate cigarettes under the scheme created by Congress for "devices"—typically including such items as cardiac pacemakers, lasers, and magnetic resonance imaging equipment—because this approach gave it a wider range of controls than it possessed for drugs.

The FDA's decision to assert authority even over the advertising and promotion of cigarettes was the boldest aspect of a generally very bold leap. No doubt the decision owed something to its disappointment in the Federal Trade Commission (FTC), which historically had regulated cigarette advertising. In 1991 the Coalition on Smoking OR Health had petitioned the FTC to act against the R. J. Reynolds Company's use of the cartoon character Joe Camel, on the ground that such use was an unfair appeal to minors. The FTC's Bureau of Consumer Protection conducted an investigation, which gained attention in spring 1993 after President Clinton took office, but the commission voted 3–2 not to prosecute the case. The majority argued that there was no evidence that Reynolds's advertising campaign had caused minors to begin smoking, as distinct from switching brands. This decision was controversial and apparently prompted the crusading Kessler to invade the jurisdiction of a "sister agency" to which the FDA had ordinarily deferred.[50]

* * *

Kessler did not act against cigarettes precipitously, without forethought. At the same time, there is no evidence in his account that he pondered how to weigh the public's health against the respect an agency head owes to law. Once he began his effort to reinterpret the law, he was utterly single-minded and uncompromising about it, trimming his goals only to the degree needed to take tactical advantage of the Clinton administration's and the larger society's concern for "kids," as children were empathetically called. Everyone knew that the issue would be carried to court. Within hours after the FDA formally announced its intention to regulate the nicotine in cigarettes, the five biggest manufacturers filed suit in a federal district court, contending that the agency had no statutory authority to do what it had done.

· Notes ·

1. Richard Kluger, *Ashes to Ashes: America's Hundred-Year Cigarette War, the Public Health, and the Unabashed Triumph of Philip Morris* (New York: Knopf, 1996), 201.

2. C. Everett Koop, *Koop: The Memoirs of America's Family Doctor* (New York: Random House, 1991), chap. 8. Koop recalls his initiation into the campaign against smoking as follows: "My first step in the anti-smoking crusade came with the 1982 *Surgeon General's Report on Smoking and Health,* then the most serious indictment of cigarette smoking the Public Health Service had ever made. During those long months of my confirmation struggle I had heard words here and there about this upcoming report, but no one had thought to include me in its preparation. It was not until the early weeks of 1982 that I began to realize that I would have to present the report at my first major press conference since assuming office" (page 165).

3. *Morbidity and Mortality Weekly Report* 46, no. 20 (23 May 1997): 444–451.

4. Critiques of the CDC's SAM reports are rare, but see Robert A. Levy and Rosalind B. Marimont, "Lies, Damned Lies and 400,000 Smoking-Related Deaths," *Regulation* 21 (Fall 1998): 24–29; Martha Perske, "Does Smoking Really Cause Over 400,000 Deaths Per Year in the U.S.?" http://www.forces.org/evidence/files/martha2.htm, accessed May 19, 2011; and Nickie McWhirter, "Computer Blows Out Smoking-related Death Figures with No Real Human Facts," *Detroit News,* October 18, 1992. Perske, who is one of the most able and persistent critics of the claims of tobacco's opponents, writes: "How does the CDC know that smoking caused 1,294 deaths from cervical cancer if other risk factors such as early and frequent sexual intercourse, multiple sexual partners, pregnancy at an early age, and the presence of sexually transmitted diseases (to name a few) were not considered?" For the McWhirter citation, I have relied on Don Oakley, *Slow Burn* (Roswell, Ga.: Eyrie, 1999), 239 ff. Oakley's book is a polemic against the antismoking movement by a retired journalist.

5. Jacob Sullum, *For Your Own Good* (New York: Free Press, 1998), 436.

6. Barbara S. Lynch and Richard J. Bonnie, eds., *Growing Up Tobacco Free: Preventing Nicotine Addiction in Children and Youths* (Washington, D.C.: National Academy Press, 1994), 203.

7. A. Lee Fritschler and James M. Hoefler, *Smoking and Politics: Policy Making and the Federal Bureaucracy,* 5th ed. (Upper Saddle River, N.J.: Prentice Hall, 1996), 161, 117.

8. The climax of the fight over nutritional labeling is described in David Kessler, *A Question of Intent: A Great American Battle with a Deadly Industry* (New York: Public Affairs, 2001), chap. 8. The quotations are on pages 55 and 59.

9. Ibid., 11–12, 26; and Alix M. Freedman and Suein L. Hwang, "How Seven Individuals with Diverse Motives Halted Tobacco's Wars," *Wall Street Journal*, July 11, 1997, A1.

10. Kessler, *Question of Intent*, 27.

11. Ibid., 50–51.

12. Ibid., 63.

13. House Energy and Commerce Committee, *Regulation of Tobacco Products: Hearings before the Subcommittee on Health and the Environment*, part 1, serial no. 103–149, 103d Cong., 2d sess., 1994, 25–27.

14. Kluger, *Ashes to Ashes*, 742.

15. *Regulation of Tobacco Products*, part 1, 528.

16. Ibid., 72.

17. Kessler, *Question of Intent*, 29–36. In 1997, three years after retiring from the FDA, Meyer told the *New York Times* that the agency's effort at tobacco regulation was "just off the wall. . . . far afield from the F.D.A.'s core responsibilities." See Sheryl Gay Stolberg, "Overloaded F.D.A. Is Facing Biggest Challenge, Tobacco," *New York Times*, August 3, 1997, A1.

18. See, for example, the description of the role of the Office of General Counsel of the Environmental Protection Agency in R. Shep Melnick, *Regulation and the Courts: The Case of the Clean Air Act* (Washington, D.C.: Brookings Institution, 1983), passim.

19. Kessler, *Question of Intent*, 78.

20. Ibid., 81.

21. Marie Brenner, "The Man Who Knew Too Much," *Vanity Fair*, May 1996, 170–181. The quotation is on page 178.

22. Kessler, *Question of Intent*, 241–244. For B&W's explanation of its use of Y-1, see *Regulation of Tobacco Products*, part 3, 138–145. B&W's president testified that the development of Y-1 was not secret and that adding it to the blend did not necessarily increase the nicotine content of the company's products.

23. "Declaration of William A. Farone to the Food and Drug Administration," 11.2 *Tobacco Products Litigation Reporter* 8.13.

24. On the transfer of the stolen documents from Williams to Scruggs and Moore, see Peter Pringle, *Cornered: Big Tobacco at the Bar of Justice* (New York: Holt, 1998), 67; and Carrick Mollenkamp et al., *The People vs. Big Tobacco* (Princeton, N.J.: Bloomberg, 1998), 46–48.

25. The Brown & Williamson papers were published in Stanton A. Glantz et al., *The Cigarette Papers* (Berkeley: University of California Press, 1996). For the quotation from Yeaman, see pages 15, 74, and 101.

26. *Regulation of Tobacco Products*, part 1, 154–159.

27. Dan Zegart, *Civil Warriors: The Legal Siege on the Tobacco Industry* (New York: Delacorte, 2000), 200.

28. Kessler, *Question of Intent*, 256–257.

29. Ibid., 257–260.

30. Ibid., 317.

31. Senate Appropriations Committee, *Agriculture, Rural Development, and Related Agencies Appropriations for Fiscal Year 1997: Hearings before a Subcommittee of the Appropriations Committee*, 104th Cong., 2d sess., 1996, 1165.

32. Kessler, *Question of Intent*, 288–290. The resulting report, which emphasizes the FDA's refusal to cooperate with the GAO, is *Food and Drug Administration: Regulation of Tobacco Products* (Letter Report, 09/29/97, GAO/HEHS-97-140). GAO reports issued since 1995 may be accessed on http://www.gpoaccess.gov/gaoreports/index.html.

33. Joseph A. Califano Jr., *Governing America: An Insider's Report from the White House and the Cabinet* (New York: Simon and Schuster, 1981), 182–197 and chap. X.

34. Kluger, *Ashes to Ashes*, 447.

35. Michael Pertschuk, *Giant Killers* (New York: Norton, 1986), 33.

36. Kessler, *Question of Intent*, 32, 64–65.

37. Ibid., 323.

38. Ibid., 294–298. Even before enactment of the Synar Amendment, which in effect set eighteen as the minimum age by making it a grant-in-aid condition, most states had chosen eighteen. After the Synar Amendment, all used eighteen except three (Alabama, Alaska, and Utah) that as of 1998 were using nineteen. See U.S. Department of Health and Human Services, Centers for Disease Control and Prevention, "State Tobacco Control Highlights—1999," CDC Publication No. 099-5621 (1999), 10–111.

39. Kessler, *Question of Intent*, 298–299.

40. Ibid., 299.

41. Ibid., 323.

42. Ibid., 319–320.

43. Ibid., 300.

44. Freedman and Hwang, "Seven Individuals"; and Dick Morris, *Behind the Oval Office* (Los Angeles: Renaissance, 1999), 215.

45. Morris, *Behind the Oval Office*, 217.

46. Kessler, *Question of Intent*, 331.

47. For the text of this press conference, see http://www.gpoaccess.gov/wcomp/index.html, choose "1995 Presidential Documents," and enter a search term.

48. *Brown & Williamson Tobacco Corp. v. Food and Drug Administration* (1998), http://scholar.google.com/scholar_case?case=3090108252127608858&hl=en&as_sdt=2,21&as_vis=1&scfhb=1, accessed May 19, 2011.

49. *Federal Register* 61, no. 168 (28 August 1996): 44615–44618. The full text begins on page 44396.

50. Richard A. Harris and Sidney M. Milkis, *The Politics of Regulatory Change: A Tale of Two Agencies* (New York: Oxford University Press, 1996), 325–327, 369. I am indebted to Professor Milkis for calling this event to my attention. In May 1997 the FTC reversed its position and brought a formal complaint against Reynolds for using Joe Camel to appeal to underage smokers. Within weeks Reynolds promised to replace Joe Camel. Early in 1999 the FTC formally dismissed the case, saying that the relief it sought had been largely accomplished by the multistate settlement between the industry and the state attorneys general in November 1998. See http://www.ftc.gov/os/1999/01/d09285.htm, accessed May 19, 2011.

CHAPTER FIVE

The New Wave of Litigation

FDA REGULATION WAS ONE OF two major fronts in the extralegislative assault on tobacco that took place in the mid-1990s. The other was litigation. In a law professor's eyes, the cigarette industry had become "low-hanging fruit"—fruit because it enticed by its wealth, arrogance, and power, and low hanging because of the nature of its product, the growing volume of internal documents becoming available, and the rising volume of antitobacco public propaganda, as illustrated by ABC's *Day One* exposé and the Waxman hearings.[1] Two new kinds of lawsuits appeared, in contrast to the lawsuits brought previously on behalf of individual plaintiffs.[2]

One type of new suit was the class action, which amassed the claims of individuals. On March 29, 1994, Wendell Gauthier, a New Orleans tort lawyer, in cooperation with twenty-five plaintiffs' law firms, filed *Castano v. American Tobacco Company* in the U.S. district court in downtown New Orleans. The lawyers called themselves the Castano Group after Peter Castano, a friend of Gauthier and fellow lawyer who had died from lung cancer at the age of forty-seven after smoking heavily since his teens. Several other individual plaintiffs were named, and the lawyers hoped to sue on behalf of all smokers who had tried to quit and failed to do so—"addicts," therefore. Addiction would be the central issue in the case, which would qualify as the biggest class action the nation had ever seen if the courts agreed to certify it as one. Seven other companies were named along with American Tobacco. The amount to be sought in compensatory and punitive damages, plus funds to treat smoking-related diseases, could be as high as $100 billion, or more than twice the combined annual revenues of the companies.

Little more will be said of this suit. Although it was certified as a class action in February 1995 by Okla Jones, a district judge, Jones was overruled by three judges of the Fifth Circuit Court of Appeals in May 1996. Thereafter, members of the Castano Group decided to file "sons of Castano" in state courts, seeking statewide certification, but most of these cases also failed to be certified as class actions.[3]

The other new category of suits, much more important than the first kind as things turned out, included those brought by the attorneys general of the state governments. The first of these, *Moore v. American Tobacco Co. et al.*, was filed by the attorney general of Mississippi, Mike Moore, in the chancery court of Jackson County, Mississippi, on May 23, 1994. Moore was assisted by ten Mississippi law firms located in six different cities, one South Carolina law firm, and Prof. Laurence Tribe of the Harvard Law School, who worked pro bono. Mississippi sought recovery of Medicaid expenses for smokers. The claim was that the tobacco companies had been "unjustly enriched" because the state had paid medical costs that were the consequence of the companies' having sold cigarettes to Mississippi citizens. Other state attorneys general followed Moore's example, with the result that they and the plaintiffs' lawyers combined to spearhead the shift at the level of state government from ordinary politics to adversarial legalism, as I call the method of policymaking by litigation. Eventually, by example, they changed the conduct of the national government as well. When the Clinton administration's Department of Justice filed suit against the cigarette industry in fall 1999, it was following a policymaking trail blazed by the attorneys general of the states. The task remaining for the rest of this chapter is to explain what brought the tort lawyers and attorneys general into the contest against Big Tobacco, and what then brought the industry to agree to a settlement with them in June 1997.

· The Lawyers ·

The tort lawyers were of course no strangers to legal contests with tobacco companies, but always before they had been on the losing side. The combination of industry money, legal talent, and legal tactics, along with supportive juries when the cases got that far, had been overpowering. This history could have discouraged the tort lawyers but for the fact that their assets had increased and the additional fact that the history per se gave them a powerful motive to try again. They loathed their opponent. At worst, in their eyes, the tobacco industry was not just one more courtroom adversary, it was an evil monster, comparable to the great killers of the twentieth century—Hitler, Stalin, the Khmer Rouge.[4] At the least, it was the ultimate prize in professional lives that were dedicated to winning prizes. As Richard Scruggs, a lawyer from Pascagoula, Mississippi, who was Moore's principal collaborator, coolly explained to an interviewer,

> Guys like [Ron] Motley [a renowned tort lawyer in Charleston]—and perhaps me, although it's hard to analyze yourself—get involved in cases like [tobacco] because they have a need

to be approved, they have a need for professional fulfillment and achievement, they need to be recognized by their peers as having done something that nobody else can do. It's a constant, insatiable desire of most successful men. . . . The prospect of making huge sums of money was always there. But the challenge was the professional and intellectual challenge of doing this for the first time. . . . We knew [the tobacco companies are] diabolical, they're guileful, they're savvy, they'd spent years preparing their defense."[5]

A tort lawyer could hardly imagine anything more rewarding than to defeat them.

Along with powerful motivation, the tort lawyers had the asset of money, which was new to them. For the lack of it in the past, they had been unable to endure in tobacco litigation, but they were newly enriched by fees from cases involving contraceptive devices, silicone breast implants, and, above all, asbestos. It was asbestos that had made Scruggs rich, and, as he told an interviewer, he felt a duty to reinvest his winnings from the asbestos cases in a public cause—had he retained all that wealth for purely personal use, he would have been subject to criticism.[6] Nor was money the only benefit from the asbestos cases. Another was knowledge. Experience with asbestos litigation introduced many of the plaintiffs' lawyers to the etiology of lung disease. As counsel to the industry in those cases, some of them had mounted the argument that tobacco, not asbestos, was responsible for the plaintiffs' illnesses.

One other critical asset was new to tort lawyers at this time: their clients. Until 1994 the lawyers had gone to court on behalf of ailing individuals or their families. This practice conformed to traditional tort law. The typical plaintiff was a lung cancer victim, an invalid who was on his or her deathbed—if not beyond it—by the time the case reached trial, if it ever did. It was a fundamental principle of tort law that parties harmed only indirectly by a tortfeasor's acts had weaker legal claims than did victims directly and physically injured. One tactic of the tort lawyers in 1994 was to aggregate individual clients in an attempt to create class-action suits, but the more important development for politics and policymaking was their union with a wholly new class of clients— the state attorneys general, who were elected officials of considerable vigor, dynamism, and political ambition. In news photographs they clustered in front of the camera, hair well groomed, jaws thrust forward, eyes intense, as if to pose for their next campaign poster.

But what gave anyone the idea that these particular clients had a cause of action against the tobacco companies? Personally, of course, they did not. They were acting on behalf of the state governments. The principal argument—by no means the only argument, but the one most persistently advanced—was that their governments were entitled to restitution for the costs of public health care for persons made ill by smoking. The public program involved was Medicaid, a joint federal-state program that originated with a congressional enactment in 1965. It is a means-tested program: to qualify for it, a recipient must demonstrate poverty. Nationwide the Medicaid program cost $124.8 billion in 1993. In Mississippi it cost approximately $1 billion.

Origins of new ideas in public policymaking are often hard to locate. The idea that governments could sue to reclaim health care costs from cigarette manufacturers might be traced to "Cigarettes and Welfare Reform," an article published in the *Emory Law Journal* in 1977 by Donald Garner, a law professor at the University of Southern Illinois. Garner suggested that state governments could get a cigarette manufacturer to pay the direct medical cost "of looking after patients with smoking diseases." He drew an analogy to the Coal Mine Health and Safety Act of 1969, under which coal mine operators are required to pay certain disability benefits to coal miners suffering from pneumoconiosis, or black lung disease.[7]

A memorandum from the files of the Philip Morris Company late in 1978 shows that someone in the cigarette industry anticipated the possibility of suits from governments:

> More industry antagonists are using an economic argument against cigarettes—i.e., cigarettes cause disease; disease requires treatment; major health costs are borne by the government; the taxpayers pay in the end.
>
> Thus, as health costs rise astronomically, the opposition becomes armed with more potent weapons. We must be prepared to counter this line of argument.[8]

Whatever the antecedents, journalistic accounts unanimously attributed the idea for Mississippi's pathbreaking lawsuit of 1994 to Michael Lewis, a plaintiff's lawyer from Clarksdale, Mississippi, who had been deeply affected by the sight of the dying mother of his legal secretary. A chain smoker, this forty-nine-year-old woman had had several heart attacks, angioplasty, and a triple bypass operation. When Lewis visited her in Baptist Memorial Hospital in Memphis, she was emaciated, bald, sallow, penetrated with tubes, and awaiting a combined heart-lung transplant operation. Her family was emotionally drained, although the costs of her care were now borne by the federal and state governments under Medicaid. Eventually these costs would pass $1 million.

Lewis emerged from the hospital room enraged. "The emotion that I was really feeling was a desire for revenge, for vindication," he recalled several years later. "I wanted to destroy the tobacco industry, to put them out of business." Rage turned to exhilaration as on the way home it occurred to him that it might be possible for Mississippi to sue the cigarette companies. He had to pull his car over to the side of the road to collect his thoughts. Once home, he talked the idea over with his wife, who was also his law partner, and after a couple of weeks he called Mike Moore, then in his second term as the state's attorney general, with whom Lewis had attended law school at Ole Miss. "Get down here," Moore said, summoning him to Jackson, the state capital.[9]

· Planning the Strategy ·

That was in the spring of 1993. In the ensuing year, Moore with associated tort lawyers would develop plans for the case. Moore began by referring Lewis to Scruggs, who then drew in other tort lawyers from around the state, including Don Barrett from Lexington, who had tried the Horton case against the American Tobacco Company. Scruggs reached also into South Carolina to include Ron Motley, a histrionic and celebrated figure in the world of tort litigation, the South's answer to San Francisco's aging Melvin Belli. The group had brainstorming sessions in Mississippi, South Carolina, and—for the purpose of consulting Professor Tribe of Harvard—Cambridge, Massachusetts.

They quickly ruled out using a theory of subrogation, whereby the state would become the surrogate for the thousands of individual smokers whose medical bills it had paid. This approach could lead to the filing of thousands of individual lawsuits, which would not be feasible for the attorney general or the courts to manage. Rather than depending on tort law, the suit would rely on equitable theories of recovery. Mississippi would claim that the tobacco companies had been "unjustly enriched" because they had not borne the costs of the by-products of their enterprise. The state would ask to be indemnified, as an innocent third party, for its medical expenditures on behalf of smokers.[10]

When litigators file lawsuits, they try to pick venues that will maximize their chances of winning. In this particular case, Moore and Scruggs had decided that they were more likely to win if they could avoid going before a jury. Scruggs knew the pollster Dick Morris—also the pollster of President Clinton, no less—who had previously done jury polling for him in an asbestos case. Scruggs wanted to assess the public's attitude toward a suit by a state government, as distinct from one by an individual, against the tobacco industry. On his instructions, Morris polled in four Mississippi counties: Hinds, Jackson, Smith, and

Jones. To Scruggs's surprise, the results were not encouraging: 55 percent of the eight hundred respondents opposed a lawsuit by the state, and the results were consistent across all four counties. Scruggs then asked Morris to do another poll in which he would weed out people who hated all lawsuits. This did not change the result. Morris reported that "there is no co-relation between dislike of lawsuits in general and a decision to oppose plaintiff's position in the contemplated tobacco lawsuit."[11]

Fortunately for Moore and Scruggs, there was a way to avoid a jury trial. Every county in Mississippi has two trial courts—a circuit court, which is considered a court of "law," and a chancery court, which is considered a court of "equity." The difference between the courts is traceable to medieval England and is rooted in the ancient power of the king to administer justice independently of the courts of common law, when a remedy in those courts was not available. Chancery courts became known as courts of "conscience" or "equity" because the chancellor (the king's agent) could seek to render true justice in individual cases. For present purposes, the main point is that judges in equity—or "chancellors," as they are still known in Mississippi—have more discretion than do judges in common-law courts. They have more freedom to fashion justice by considering fairness rather than formality.[12] Moore and his team of lawyers very much liked the idea of going into chancery court. In their view, the history of cigarette litigation exposed a defect of the common law of torts: the cigarette companies had perpetrated a wrong and had yet to be punished for it.

The tobacco companies would later complain that Moore had handpicked his judge, but it would be fairer to say that he had handpicked his court. The chancery court of Jackson County, in which Moore filed, has three chancellors. When a case is filed, a computer randomly assigns it to one of the three. The first two to be picked recused themselves, one because he had served on Moore's campaign committee, the other because he had publicly opposed Moore in an issue over judicial redistricting in Mississippi. The case then went by default to Chancellor William Myers, who was relatively new to the bench and not well known. Because he was an appointee of the outspokenly probusiness incumbent Republican governor, Kirk Fordice, there was no prima facie reason to expect him to be hostile to the tobacco companies.

In venue-shopping of their own, the tobacco companies tried to take the case to a federal court. Anticipating that state courts would be biased against out-of-state defendants, federal law permits such defendants to "remove" a state civil action over which federal courts would have original jurisdiction. In Mississippi and later in other states, the tobacco industry tried to remove the cases filed by the attorneys general by arguing that they were founded on claims arising under the federal law that authorizes the Medicaid program. The attorneys general in turn sought to protect against removal by naming as defendants in-state retailers and distributors of tobacco products. In Mississippi and elsewhere, the industry's attempts to get into federal court failed. Federal courts ruled that they did not have original jurisdiction over the subject matter of the suits.[13]

Even if Myers had been handpicked by Moore, he could hardly have been more supportive of the state's case. In a series of pretrial rulings he came down repeatedly on the side of the plaintiffs. The first ruling, in February 1995, was to keep jurisdiction over the case. The industry's lawyers argued that the state's claim was really a claim in products liability and therefore belonged in a court of common law, the circuit court. They also argued that the issues in the case were political and therefore fell within the jurisdiction of the state's legislature. Without explanation, Chancellor Myers rejected these claims, and the plaintiffs began to celebrate. Scruggs thought, as he later explained, that Myers must be keeping the case for a reason. "He's not keeping it . . . to be the eight hundredth judge in America to rule for the tobacco industry."[14]

Thereafter, Governor Fordice filed a petition with the Mississippi Supreme Court arguing that Attorney General Moore lacked authority to bring the suit. Fordice maintained that the state's Medicaid Division was part of the governor's office and the attorney general was the governor's lawyer—he could not bring a suit for recovery of Medicaid expenses without the governor's permission. The industry also petitioned the state supreme court to block the suit on other grounds, drawn from federal regulations on suits for recovery of Medicaid expenses.[15] The companies then petitioned Chancellor Myers to delay the case until the supreme court, which was notoriously slow, responded to the petitions of the governor and the industry. In July 1996 Myers made only a minor concession to the defendants, moving the trial date from March to July 1997. (In March 1997 the Mississippi Supreme Court rejected the Fordice and industry petitions, declining to rule on their merits. As a lawyer for Philip Morris acidly put it, the supreme court by a vote of 6 to 1 "denied extraordinary relief and said it would determine, after the trial was over, whether or not it should ever have begun."[16])

In April 1997, with the trial only three months away, Myers issued a ruling that deprived the industry of a potentially effective defense. If its opponents were going to argue economic harm to the state government from smoking, the industry wanted to argue economic benefit. For years state governments had realized sizeable revenues from excise taxes on tobacco, which they had begun to impose in the 1920s, both to take advantage of the rising popularity of cigarettes and to compensate for the loss of revenue from alcohol taxes as a result of Prohibition.[17] Far from discouraging use of cigarettes, governments had reaped the benefits of their popularity. Then there was the newly developed and tendentious argument, coming from academic economists, that calculations of health care costs generated by tobacco use should be set against the savings to government from smokers' premature deaths—there would be no need to pay health care costs or pensions for the prematurely deceased. Plaintiffs called this argument uncivilized and offensive to human decency. In any event, it would not be heard in the chancery court of Chancellor Myers. Already deprived of standard tort defenses such as "assumption of risk," which they had used for decades in individual cases, the cigarette companies were now additionally deprived of an economic defense, which Myers rejected with a ruling of eight lines. He did not agree with the defendants' plea that an equity court's "duty to look at the 'whole situation' requires the Court to look at the full economic impact of the sale of cigarettes on the State." The companies were heading for trial "with both hands tied behind their back."[18]

They made one desperate, last-ditch plea for a change of venue. They accepted the trial date and the judge but asked for a jury: "Defendants propose a procedure under Mississippi law that would permit transfer while preserving the trial date and retaining Chancellor Myers to preside over the trial. The transfer would result in only one change: the placement of twelve Mississippi citizens in the jury box to ultimately decide this case." Myers denied the motion.[19]

· Entry of Other States ·

This pretrial history of the Mississippi case begins to explain why the industry accepted the settlement of June 1997. That case had been lost in its pretrial phase, but to understand more fully the industry's position, it is necessary to look at events in other states, for Mississippi did not stand alone as a plaintiff. By the end of May 1997, thirty-one other states had filed.

Merely in monetary terms, the Mississippi suit alone was not very threatening to the industry. Mississippi was seeking just under $1 billion in damages. Tobacco stock analysts on Wall Street calculated that to raise this sum the industry had only to raise cigarette prices five cents a pack for one year.[20] However, if Mississippi were joined by other states, the stakes would multiply. Others did follow, though slowly at first. Minnesota, where Attorney General Hubert H. Humphrey III was an impassioned foe of the industry, filed suit in August 1994, followed by West Virginia in September. Two more states—Florida and Massachusetts—filed in 1995, and four more—Connecticut, Maryland, Texas, and Washington—in the first half of 1996. All had Democratic attorneys general.

In one of these early filers, Florida, the industry appeared to face certain defeat because the state legislature had passed a law depriving it of a defense. The law provided that "principles of common law and equity as to assignment, lien subrogation, comparative negligence, assumption of risk, and all other affirmative defenses normally available to a liable third party, are to be abrogated to the extent necessary to ensure full recovery by Medicaid from third-party resources."[21] The industry mounted an appeal to the Florida Supreme Court, which would eventually reject it on a split decision. Elsewhere, however, outcomes initially seemed uncertain, given the novelty of the states' claims, and some attorneys general were deterred by the uncertainty. In West Virginia a judge early on ruled that the attorney general lacked authority to sue except on behalf of state-agency clients.

It was not until the summer of 1996 that the effort of the attorneys general became bipartisan and snowballed. The first Republicans to file—Carla Stovall of Kansas and Grant Woods of Arizona—did so in August. In all, nine more states filed in the second half of 1996, and twenty-one more did so before the conclusion of the industry-state agreement on June 20, 1997.

There are several explanations for this gathering of momentum. One is that Moore and Scruggs together worked very hard to achieve it, flying around the country in Scruggs's Lear jet and touching down in state capitals to plead their cause. For Moore, at least, defeating the industry truly was a cause. A man on a mission, obsessed with Big Tobacco, he combined a politician's hunger for public recognition with a social activist's desire to do good. Scruggs, a cooler sort with a background as a military pilot, shared his determination, if for a different set of reasons, which in his case included financial reward. The two men had been friends since starting their careers simultaneously in Pascagoula, and Scruggs had helped Moore's campaigns with cash contributions and the use of his plane. As attorney general Moore had hired Scruggs as counsel to the state in cases brought to compel the removal of asbestos from public buildings.[22] When it came time to fight tobacco, their personal bond both linked and gave leadership to two different political forces—the attorneys general and the tort lawyers.

The ready availability of private counsel encouraged the attorneys general as a group to proceed. Because the plaintiffs' bar saw a potential for immense profits in these cases, lawyers were ready and eager to help the state governments prepare them. For their part, the attorneys general, who as elected politicians were disposed to build followings and cement friendships, engaged many lawyers. For example, twelve firms participated in the Florida case—ten from Florida and one each from South Carolina and Mississippi (Scruggs's firm)—and they were joined by Professor Tribe, who again participated pro bono. The Massachusetts case employed five firms, three from that state and one each from South Carolina and California. Virtually all of the early cases—those filed up to the spring of 1997—employed abundant outside counsel.

The provisions for fees were imprecise, at least in the flagship case of Mississippi. Moore and Scruggs had been criticized for their collaboration in the asbestos cases, in which Scruggs received a contingency fee. This arrangement was patterned after that in the typical private case, where the lawyer's fee was a stipulated percentage of the award to the plaintiff. Anticipating the tobacco case, Scruggs had managed quietly to get a provision inserted in state law that authorized the attorney general to hire counsel for a contingency fee, but Moore still thought this approach too risky politically. Instead he promised that in case of victory he would join the lawyers in asking the court to order the cigarette makers to pay their fees. Among themselves, the Mississippi lawyers fashioned a joint venture that stipulated the contribution each would make to preparing the case and, correspondingly, the share of fees each would receive.[23]

· Division within the Industry ·

A final source of momentum as time passed was a growing belief that the cases could be won. In part this conviction arose from a breakthrough in a lawsuit brought on behalf of an individual plaintiff, which was historically the typical case. Early in August 1996 a Florida jury awarded an ailing smoker, Grady Carter, $750,000 in damages in a suit brought against Brown & Williamson. The lawyer in this case, Woody Wilner, was the first to make use of the documents that Merrell Williams had stolen in Louisville. With them he bolstered a case that the industry had acted negligently by failing to reveal what it knew about the health effects of smoking.

Even more important was an unprecedented division within the industry. Bennett LeBow, a financier who held a controlling interest in the Liggett Corporation, smallest of the major cigarette manufacturers, offered to settle independently with the Castano lawyers and the attorneys general early in 1996. From the standpoint of the industry, which had always fought its legal battles to the bitter end, this offer was an act of utter treachery. For LeBow, it served several ends.

Most obviously, a deal could save LeBow's company from insolvency. A specialist in generic, discounted cigarettes as well as a manufacturer of the fading Chesterfield and L&M brands, Liggett made only $11 million in pretax profit in 1996 while spending $10 million on legal services.[24] But LeBow had more complex and devious objectives than merely keeping Liggett afloat. Since the early 1960s he had made a practice of buying distressed companies cheaply and then attempting to rebuild them in order to sell at a profit. He had done this with products as varied as jewelry, microfilm, computers, airplanes, and trading cards. In combination with financier Carl Icahn, a takeover specialist, he now cast a covetous eye on RJR Nabisco (Reynolds, that is, in its post-1985 incarnation), whose value he judged to have been reduced by the liability of its tobacco products. He hoped to win a hostile takeover, after which he planned to merge RJR Tobacco with Liggett, thereby rescuing Liggett, and to split off the food division to protect it from tobacco lawsuits. LeBow designed his settlement to make this scheme attractive to RJR Nabisco stockholders. The terms, which would apply to any tobacco company that merged with Liggett, promised to give RJR an advantage vis-à-vis rival Philip Morris. Also, his deal provided that the tobacco plaintiffs would not fight an RJR effort to spin off (and thus protect) its food unit.[25]

The deal was concluded in March 1996 but did not last long or have the effects LeBow had primarily intended. In April he lost his fight for control of RJR Nabisco, and in May the Fifth Circuit Court of Appeals decertified the Castano class-action suit, which in effect canceled his settlement. Yet LeBow's separate deal had consequences for the larger contest between the industry and its opponents. The willingness of one company to settle, however small the company and however devious the motives of its leadership, undermined the industry's position. It lent credibility to the suits of the state governments, the novelty of which had cast doubt on their outcomes, and it compelled other companies to begin asking whether they, too, should settle. Talks opened behind-the-scenes in New York and Washington, informally involving the White House and Senate majority leader Trent Lott as well as the industry and its opponents. However, these talks were inconclusive and failed to engage the main adversaries face-to-face until LeBow again entered into a separate deal.[26] In March 1997 he signed an agreement with twenty-two states, in contrast to the mere five with which he had signed a year earlier.

When LeBow's first deal was concluded in 1996, Mississippi's Mike Moore termed it "a crack in the wall." When the second was concluded, he said that the wall had been knocked down.[27] The states agreed to drop their suits, and there was a companion agreement with the plaintiffs' lawyers, who abandoned hundreds of private pending suits, including several class actions. In return, Liggett agreed to contribute 25 percent of its pretax income for twenty-five years to a fund from which the states and other plaintiffs would be compensated. In Liggett's case, this amount was only about $575,000 a year. The company made various admissions of wrongdoing, even though doing so galled LeBow, who had not been around when the companies were plotting their strategies in the 1950s and 1960s and who had not to his knowledge ever sold cigarettes to children. "For Christ's sake," he would say, "children don't buy *Chesterfields*. No one under the age of fifty has bought a Chesterfield since the Korean War."[28] In the end the company acknowledged that cigarette smoking "causes health problems, including lung cancer, heart and vascular disease, and emphysema," and that nicotine is addictive. It also promised

1. to attach the warning "Smoking is addictive" to its cigarette packages and ads;
2. to cease using cartoon characters in advertising and promotion;
3. to refrain from challenging the FDA's tobacco regulations and to observe some of those rules immediately; and
4. to assist the attorneys general and plaintiffs' lawyers with suits against the other companies by providing documents and witnesses.

In particular, LeBow agreed to turn over notes taken by Liggett lawyers in meetings with the other company lawyers in the industry's Committee of Counsel, its policymaker on smoking and health. The industry had maintained that such documents were protected by the lawyer-client privilege.[29]

· The Settlement ·

Even if LeBow had not done his separate deal and turned state's evidence, the bigger companies would have come under intense pressure to settle, given the course of the litigation in Mississippi and the rising costs of litigation generally. The legal expenses of the six biggest companies were around $600 million a year.[30] More than three hundred lawsuits were pending against them, with potential damages of hundreds of billions of dollars. Shareholders were nervous, and share prices were becoming volatile. Reynolds was $9.5 billion in debt as a result of the leveraged buyout and had less than $400 million in cash on hand.[31]

Although diversification had provided financial protection for the cigarette manufacturers, it had the correlative effect of exposing their other businesses to the liabilities of tobacco. Finally, it was one thing to fight lawsuits to the bitter end when facing individual victims of lung cancer. It was another to do so when facing half or more of the state governments and dozens of the richest, most aggressive members of the plaintiffs' bar. Under these conditions, settlement was at least thinkable—and arguably imperative. It was difficult to run a business while under a mass assault.[32]

It was also difficult to defend against governments in the governments' courts. In spring 1997, as the likelihood of a comprehensive settlement became evident, states rushed to file and claim their share of the anticipated proceeds. By June 20, the date of the agreement, only eleven states had failed to bring suit. Facing this much governmental force, not to mention private class-action suits, private individual suits, and an active investigation by the Department of Justice, the industry was overwhelmed. Vis-à-vis the amassed power of its foes, its bargaining power was at a low ebb. Perhaps with some bravado, Russ Herman, a tort lawyer from New Orleans, put it to the tobacco attorneys: "This isn't about how much you're willing to give in order to settle this, it's about how much we will accept for not destroying you in court."[33]

Negotiations proceeded over a period of more than two months, from a meeting on March 30 at the Washington office of the National Center for Tobacco-Free Kids through sessions at hotel conference rooms and law offices in Crystal City (Virginia), Chicago, Dallas, New York City, and downtown Washington. In the end, not surprisingly, the key issue was how much money the companies would pay and how much protection from legal damages they would get in return. The theory on which the individual lawsuits mainly rested was that states were being compensated for health care expenses, but this fiction was not maintained during the negotiations. When the companies' opponents assembled to consider how much to ask for, they examined instead how much the companies could pay without going bankrupt.

The industry had offered $230 billion over twenty-five years. Its opponents arrived at a figure of $300 billion, using as one guide a three-page financial analysis of the industry prepared by a private attorney from Washington State. He judged that R. J. Reynolds, with a large debt but also a large obligation because of its 28 percent market share, would be in trouble. Loews Corporation, the parent of Lorillard, should by comparison have an easy time, since its brands had less than 10 percent of the cigarette market, and the parent company had ample income from its holdings of life insurance, hotels, oil-drilling operations, and Bulova watches. Philip Morris, the industry leader, would be able to borrow or sell stock if need be.[34]

For its part, the industry was determined in the future to avoid punitive damages for past misconduct. For this assurance, it offered an additional $15 billion. The attorneys general asked for $50 billion, which happened to equal the industry's entire annual sales. However, the Clinton White House, participating behind-the-scenes, rejected that as insufficient. Bruce Lindsey, in the office of Counsel to the President, insisted on $368.5 billion, of which $60 billion was understood to cover punitive damages for past misconduct. The industry would also get a promise that class-action lawsuits would be banned, and there would be an annual combined $5 billion cap on judgments or settlements in future lawsuits by individual smokers.[35]

The added industry payments, combined with caps on liability, removed the last big obstacle to a settlement and enabled its drafters to propose it to Congress. This settlement was in effect a draft piece of legislation, but it would not be binding until approved by Congress, where it would have to be recast as a bill and formally introduced for the members' consideration.

The agreement incorporated the FDA's restrictions on advertising and marketing and went beyond them in some respects. Carefully crafting its rules to apply to adolescents, for example, the FDA had not banned all cigarette vending machines and self-service displays but only those to which the retailer could not ensure that persons under eighteen years of age would be denied access. Similarly, the FDA had not banned all color and pictures in print advertising but had confined their use to "adult" publications—that is, those "whose readers younger than eighteen years of age constitute 15 percent or less of the total readership" and those that are "read by fewer than 2 million persons younger than 18 years of age. . . ." The agreement, in contrast, would have banned all vending machines as well as the use of human images and cartoon characters in all tobacco advertising and on tobacco product packages. Whereas the FDA rules would have banned billboards only near schools and public parks and playgrounds, the agreement banned all outdoor advertising, as well as advertising on the Internet unless the ad were designed to be inaccessible in the United States.

The agreement provided for a new series of nine rotating warnings on cigarette packs—including "Smoking can kill you," "Cigarettes cause cancer," and "Tobacco smoke causes fatal lung disease in non-smokers"—and specified that the warnings occupy 25 percent of the front panel of the package. An appendix specified type sizes. The FDA would be required to promulgate a rule governing the testing, reporting, and disclosure of tobacco smoke constituents. Authority over such rules had previously rested in the FTC, but critics of the industry felt that it had not been exercised with sufficient vigilance, and they expected the FDA to do better.

The agreement broke new regulatory ground in requiring the industry to pay the costs of enforcing the rules against itself. Normally, the activities of federal regulatory agencies are financed through appropriations by Congress, which in turn depend on raising tax revenues. Indeed, the Constitution provides that "no Money shall be drawn from the Treasury, but in Consequence of Appropriations made by Law. . . ." The agreement instead contemplated that the industry would finance government activity through "industry payments," a sizeable fraction of which would go into a public health trust fund that would be administered by a presidential commission consisting of the industry's opponents— presumably the state attorneys general, the trial lawyers attacking the industry with class-action suits, and representatives of organizations devoted to public health, such as the American Cancer Society. In addition to paying for the FDA's oversight (including grants to the states for help with enforcement), the purposes named for the trust fund included enforcing restrictions on smoking in public places, financing a national advertising campaign against smoking, supporting various health programs and product liability judgments at the state level, and encouraging the efforts of individuals to quit smoking.

There were also audacious provisions on the internal organization of the industry, whose "corporate culture" the agreement was dedicated to changing. Title I, dedicated to "reformation of the tobacco industry," included a section on compliance and corporate culture. This section required the creation of internal organization, rules, and oversight and reporting requirements designed to ensure less hazardous products and reduced sales to minors. There would be compliance standards, compliance officers, training programs, internal audits, hotlines, protections for whistleblowers, compliance reports to shareholders, and the like.

To bend the industry further to the regulators' purpose, there were "lookback" provisions that imposed fines if teenage smoking rates did not fall. The agreement specified that underage use of cigarettes must fall by at least 30 percent by the fifth year after the legislation took effect, at least 50 percent by the seventh year, and 60 percent by the tenth year. If these targets were not met, the FDA would impose a fine on the industry—a "mandatory surcharge"—of up to $2 billion a year. This provision rested, obviously, on the unrealistic and unreasonable assumption that the industry fully controlled consumers' decisions to buy its products. It did provide, however, for partial abatement of the fines if manufacturers could demonstrate to the FDA that they had fully complied with the agreement, "had taken all reasonably available measures to reduce youth tobacco use and had not taken any action to undermine the achievement of the required reductions."

The agreement disbanded the Tobacco Institute and the Council for Tobacco Research, the industry's lobbying and research arms, respectively. Although to a political scientist it seems extraordinary that government should compel abolition of a lobby, inasmuch as lobbying is basic to the letter and spirit of the Constitution and Washington is full of industry lobbies, this provision seems not to have been controversial. To be sure, abolition of the Tobacco Institute was not tantamount to denying the industry a right to engage in political activity. The institute might be reconstituted in another form, or the industry might hire lobbyists. The agreement stated that "tobacco product manufacturers may form or participate in any new tobacco industry trade association," but the very fact that this provision was framed as a grant of permission implied that such permission might have been denied. Moreover, the agreement specified how a new trade association should be organized: "Any such new trade association shall have an independent board of directors, in accordance with the following requirements." The requirements were designed to make the trade association independent of its members, the manufacturing companies—an arrangement that would seem to defeat the purpose of forming a trade association. They were also designed to guarantee that the records of the trade association be open for inspection by an oversight committee consisting of the state attorneys general.

This account of the agreement's provisions is far from exhaustive, but it is sufficient to convey a sense of the deal's radical nature. The regulatory regime was unprecedented in its severity; the monetary settlement—the several hundred billion dollars to be paid in twenty-five years by the industry—was unprecedented in size; and the legislative grant of protections from civil liability would be unprecedented, too.

The agreement acknowledged that some of its provisions might be unconstitutional. The restrictions on advertising and marketing seem to have been regarded as particularly subject to legal challenge, though restrictions on industry political activity might have been vulnerable as well. However, by signing the agreement, the industry promised to refrain from mounting constitutional challenges:

> ... The parties recognize that certain provisions of the consent decrees and the agreement may require them to act (or refrain from acting) in a manner that they might otherwise claim would violate the federal or state constitutions. They will therefore in the consent decrees expressly waive any claim [of a constitutional violation]. The consent decrees will also state

that if a provision of the Act covered by the decrees is subsequently declared unconstitutional, the provision remains an enforceable term of the consent decrees.[36]

Note that the agreement did not depend exclusively on congressional enactment for its effects. Because the lawyers who drafted it understood that Congress presumably would not pass acts known to be unconstitutional and that legislators could be reversed by courts if they did pass such laws, it relied on consent decrees—agreements between the negotiating parties in lawsuits, and enforceable through courts—as substitutes for legislation. These decrees were superior to legislation precisely because they could be used to circumvent both constitutional law and the political constraints assumed to operate in legislatures. The tort lawyer Stanley Chesley later explained the logic to a skeptical Congress:

> Now, why should Congress accept the basic terms of this deal when it can instead simply penalize tobacco by imposing taxes and fees and still leave the industry to face civil liability for its past misdeeds?
> While taxes alone could raise the price of cigarettes, they would not accomplish the advertising restrictions, the unquestioned acceptance of regulatory authority, or the wholesale changes in corporate culture.[37]

Why would the industry agree to such radical terms? Not to buy peace, insisted the attorney general of Arizona, Grant Woods, in reply to David Kessler. This was hardly peace, Woods said:

> This is not peace when they pay record amounts, when they have more regulation than any industry ever has, when they restrict their advertising as no one else has, when the money is used—their money is used, to counter-market against their product—when billions of dollars are used to persuade people [to] no longer use their product, and at the same time every individual in the United States is still free to sue them. This is not peace. They did not get peace.[38]

What they got, Woods said—and tobacco executives undoubtedly would have agreed—was "certainty," which is to say, a predictable environment. They were relieved of the state governments' suits and of class-action suits, and they were assured that they would not have to pay more than a stipulated amount ($5 billion per year) in judgments or settlements in individual suits.

· Closing Ceremonies ·

On June 20 Moore, six other attorneys general, and Scruggs announced the outcome in a hotel ballroom in Washington before a horde of print journalists and TV camera crews. ABC television broke away from the Oprah Winfrey show to do a live broadcast. For an hour the attorneys general denounced the industry. Moore opened with the following statement:

> Today is V-day for the American people in the war on tobacco. . . . We wanted this industry to have to change the way it did business, and we have done that. . . . If enacted by Congress, [this agreement] will save more lives than any public agreement in [history].
>
> The attorneys general of America, the trial lawyers of America, the public health community has [sic] fought a war. A very long war. We had to punish this industry in such a way that everybody in this country, and everybody in this world, would recognize that they had paid a higher price than any other corporation in history. Because, frankly, this corporation has done more harm than any other corporation in history.

Connecticut's attorney general, Richard Blumenthal, was particularly scathing, declaring that the attorneys general had been "dealing with the devil," an industry responsible for millions of deaths.[39] The *New York Times* gave the story a full-page double-banner headline, the kind normally reserved for such momentous events as presidential elections or assassinations.

The settlement did not bring to a halt those state lawsuits that were already heading for trial, of which Mississippi's was the first. On July 3, 1997, thirteen days after he had held his press conference in Washington and three days before his case was to go to trial, Moore stepped up to another bank of microphones, this time in the rotunda of the Mississippi state capitol, to boast:

> A little over three and a half years ago, now, way down south in Mississippi, not many people gave us much of a chance for this little ol' lawsuit. Matter of fact, some people here in this state said it probably wasn't worth a nickel. Well, we have a settlement today that's worth 3.6 billion dollars.

The first installment on that amount, $170 million, would reach Mississippi on July 15.[40]

The actual amount of the Mississippi settlement was $3.366 billion. Determined by extrapolating Mississippi's share from the comprehensive settlement just concluded, that was more than three times what the state had initially asked for. Florida's suit was settled the following month for $11.3 billion, a figure again arrived at by calculating the state's share of the national settlement. In Florida the companies also agreed to pull down billboards and ads on mass transit and in stadiums.

* * *

Tobacco politics had come a long way from the congressional committee hearing rooms of 1964 to the hotel ballroom of 1997. Along with the change in venue had come a change in technique and tone. Once compelled by legislative enactment to put health warnings on cigarette packs and to give up radio and TV advertising, the industry was now compelled by the threat of devastating lawsuits to send multimillion- and even billion-dollar checks to state governments. Government policy had shifted from an emphasis on public persuasion to an emphasis on punishing manufacturers, reordering their businesses, and extracting revenues from them, while their executives were pilloried on television as satans and mass murderers.

An early manifesto of the campaign against cigarettes was *Smoke Screen: Tobacco and the Public Welfare,* ostensibly authored by Sen. Maurine B. Neuberger of Oregon but largely ghostwritten by her aide Michael Pertschuk. The introduction to that book reflects philosophically on who would be blamed for the failure to bring smoking to an end as soon as its health dangers were revealed:

> . . . *Which* segments of our society and *which* institutions will [historians] indict? The tobacco industry, for its callous and myopic pursuit of its own self-interest? The government, for its timidity and inertia in failing to formulate a positive program of prophylaxis? The medical profession, for abdicating its role of leader in this crucial area of public health? Or is the individual—smoker and nonsmoker alike—incriminated by his failure to accept responsibility for his own and his society's well-being? I am convinced that no indictment would be sufficient if it failed to name each of these parties jointly responsible for the "cigarette epidemic."[41]

By 1997 the epidemic had been much reduced, while the blame for what remained had been fixed squarely by tobacco's enemies on the industry, which they portrayed as worse than callously self-interested, the very epitome of evil.

• Notes •

1. *Regulation by Litigation: The New Wave of Government-Sponsored Litigation* (New York: Manhattan Institute for Policy Research, 1999), 63. The law professor was Richard Epstein of the University of Chicago, and what he actually said was: ". . . lawyers and prosecutors always go after the low hanging fruit first. Tobacco was on the ground, waiting to be picked up."

2. To understand the legal case that could be mounted against the industry, there is, ironically, no better source than a memorandum of more than four hundred pages prepared in the mid-1980s by Jones, Day, Reavis and Pogue of Cleveland, a large law firm that RJR employed in the hope of improving its representation. Not imagining, of course, that this document, which was labeled "confidential, attorney work product, attorney-client privileged," would become public fifteen years later in lawsuits against the industry, Jones, Day lawyers constructed a "worst-case analysis" of industry misconduct, writing hypothetically from the plaintiffs' point of view. (As of May 19, 2011, this document could be found at http://www.tobacco.org/resources/documents/jonesday1.html.) On Reynolds's decision to replace Jacob Medinger of New York with Jones, Day as its national trial counsel, see Frank Tursi, Susan E. White, and Steven McQuilkin, "Lost Empire: The Fall of R. J. Reynolds Tobacco Co.," chap. 21, part 1, "Tortes and Torts." This Web-only account of the recent history of R. J. Reynolds may be found at www.journalnow.com, the Web site of the *Winston-Salem Journal.* In the early 1980s, Reynolds was spending about $1 million a year on outside legal costs; by 1985, it was spending that much each month.

3. The *Federal Rules of Civil Procedure* contain standards for certifying class actions. These guidelines say that (1) a class action must have too many plaintiffs to conduct individual trials, (2) the claim must be typical of the class as a whole, (3) the representatives of the class must be able to safeguard adequately the interests of the class, (4) questions of law common to members of the class must predominate over questions affecting individual members, and (5) the class approach must be superior to other methods available for the fair and efficient adjudication of the claims. See Peter Pringle, *Cornered: Big Tobacco at the Bar of Justice* (New York: Holt, 1998), 258–263.

4. Michael Orey, *Assuming the Risk: The Mavericks, the Lawyers, and the Whistle-Blowers Who Beat Big Tobacco* (Boston: Little, Brown, 1999), 222.

5. Ibid., 264–265.

6. Pringle, *Cornered,* 26.

7. Ibid., 28–29.

8. Orey, *Assuming the Risk,* 225.

9. Ibid., 223–224. Though details sometimes differ, there are parallel accounts in Pringle, *Cornered,* 29–30, and in Carrick Mollenkamp, Adam Levy, Joseph Menn, and Jeffrey Rothfeder, *The People vs. Big Tobacco: How the States Took on the Cigarette Giants* (Princeton, N.J.: Bloomberg, 1998), 23–26. In Orey's account, for example, Lewis drives a Cadillac, while in the Mollenkamp book, it is a Chevy Blazer.

10. For a fuller statement, see Pringle, *Cornered,* 31–32.

11. Orey, *Assuming the Risk,* 268–269.

12. Ibid., 270–271. I draw heavily on Orey's work, paraphrasing him here and elsewhere in my account of what happened in Mississippi.

13. 11.1 *Tobacco Products Litigation Reporter* 1.6 and 3.42. I am indebted to Richard Drew for urging me to address the issue of removal. Inasmuch as federal law permits removal of lawsuits to a federal court when a citizen of one state sues a citizen of another, why, he asked, did the tobacco companies, which were not headquartered in Mississippi, not remove Moore's lawsuit to a federal court on grounds of "diversity"? An attorney familiar with tobacco litigation explained to me that that particular option was not open to the companies: ". . . In general, a state as a state does not satisfy the statutory definition of being a 'citizen' of a state. Therefore, under most circumstances, a state filing a lawsuit in its own name, in its own behalf, and in its own state courts will generally not find its lawsuit subject to removal on diversity grounds. Other grounds for removal may, however, exist under other federal statutes." The industry hoped to find another ground, but failed, with its claim that under the federal law on Medicaid, federal courts had original jurisdiction over the lawsuits. Despite the fact that removal on grounds of diversity was not legally available to the tobacco companies in the states' cases, the lawyers for the attorneys general sometimes took the step, which is routine in cases of tort litigation by private individuals, of adding minor in-state defendants, such as retailers, wholesalers, and distributors, to protect against removal. Assuming that my source, who asked for anonymity, is correct on the law, this precaution was superfluous. The quotation is from an e-mail message to me dated June 19, 2001.

14. Orey, *Assuming the Risk*, 281–282. Myers and Scruggs appear eventually to have developed a cordial relationship. A picture of them taking a walk together in Pascagoula appears in John Mintz and Ceci Connolly, "Small-Town Blow Exposed Cigarette Industry's Soft Spot," *Washington Post*, March 30, 1998, A1.

15. Pringle, *Cornered*, 217–218.

16. Remarks of Michael Wallace in *Regulation by Litigation*, 8.

17. Cassandra Tate, *Cigarette Wars: The Triumph of "The Little White Slaver"* (New York: Oxford University Press, 1999), 150–151.

18. The phrase is Orey's. See *Assuming the Risk*, 347.

19. Ibid., 347–348.

20. Ibid., 299.

21. Jonathan Rauch, "Bob Dole, Tobacco Racketeer," *National Journal*, October 2, 1999, 2787.

22. Mollenkamp et al., *The People vs. Big Tobacco*, 44; and Pringle, *Cornered*, 25.

23. Orey, *Assuming the Risk*, 265–266.

24. Mollenkamp et al., *The People vs. Big Tobacco*, 58.

25. The fullest accounts of LeBow's dealings are in Pringle, *Cornered*, chap. 12, and in Alix M. Freedman, Suein L. Hwang, Steven Lipin, and Milo Geyelin, "Breaking Away: Liggett Group Offers First-Ever Settlement of Cigarette Lawsuits," *Wall Street Journal*, March 13, 1996, A1.

26. Mollenkamp et al., *The People vs. Big Tobacco*, chaps. 4 and 5.

27. Pringle, *Cornered*, 242.

28. Dan Zegart, *Civil Warriors: The Legal Siege on the Tobacco Industry* (New York: Delacorte, 2000), 215.

29. Jacob Sullum, *For Your Own Good: The Anti-Smoking Crusade and the Tyranny of Public Health* (New York: Free Press, 1998), 181–182; and Pringle, *Cornered*, 242.
30. Pringle, *Cornered*, 230.
31. *Hoover's Handbook of American Business 1999* (Austin, Texas: Reference Press, 1999), 1213.
32. On this point, see the testimony of Steven F. Goldstone in Senate Committee on Commerce, Science, and Transportation, *Tobacco (CEOs): Hearing before the Committee on Commerce, Science, and Transportation,* 105th Cong., 2d sess., February 24, 1998 (Washington, D.C.: GPO, 2000), 39–42.
33. Mollenkamp et al., *The People vs. Big Tobacco,* 181. This excellent book is the source for my account of the negotiations.
34. Ibid., 210, 173–174.
35. Ibid., 220.
36. The text of the settlement is an appendix in ibid., 265–317. The quotation is on page 288.
37. Senate Committee on Commerce, Science, and Transportation, *Liability Issues Regarding the Global Settlement of Tobacco Litigation: Hearing before the Committee on Commerce, Science, and Transportation,* 105th Cong., 2d sess., February 26, 1998 (Washington, D.C.: GPO, 1999), 63. On the use of consent decrees more generally in American government, see Ross Sandler and David Schoenbrod, *Democracy by Decree: What Happens When Courts Run Government* (New Haven: Yale University Press, 2003).
38. Senate Committee on Commerce, Science, and Transportation, *Global Settlement of Tobacco Litigation: Hearing before the Committee on Commerce, Science, and Transportation,* 105th Cong., 1st sess., July 29, 1997 (Washington, D.C.: GPO, 1999), 52.
39. Mollenkamp et al., *The People vs. Big Tobacco,* 33, 231–232.
40. Orey, *Assuming the Risk,* 355–356.
41. Maurine B. Neuberger, *Smoke Screen: Tobacco and the Public Welfare* (Englewood Cliffs, N.J.: Prentice Hall, 1963), xii–xiii.

CHAPTER SIX

The Changed Context of Policymaking

ALTHOUGH NO ONE COULD HAVE predicted the widened scope and heightened intensity of opposition to cigarettes in the late 1990s—and anyone who is old enough to remember the smoke-filled, butt-strewn America of the 1930s and 1940s is bound to be astonished—in retrospect the change in tobacco politics does not appear so puzzling when set against changes in American politics and culture generally. Rather, it is a dramatic example of changes that have ramified through the political system. The purpose of this chapter is to deepen the explanation of the new politics of smoking by exploring some of these changes.

The modern (post-1964) assault on tobacco is by no means the first such assault in American history. Today's opponents of smoking had predecessors in the early part of this century. Opposition to smoking can plausibly be interpreted as falling well within a long American political tradition of moralism that produced such phenomena as a constitutional prohibition on the manufacture, sale, and transportation of intoxicating liquor and state laws against gambling, birth control, abortion, and sexual relations outside of marriage. The early twentieth century crusaders against tobacco associated it with other vices.

That the earlier crusade had so little lasting effect may have led cigarette manufacturers into the error of complacency. One of their reactions as the modern campaign got under way was that this was an old story and should be discounted as such—tobacco had always had critics. This time, however, besides being grounded in scientific evidence about smoking as a cause of disease, the story unfolded in an altered setting of politics and government. Several factors were critical specifically to the mid-1990s escalation of the campaign: the rise of the "culture wars"; the institutionalization of cause advocacy; the growth of government; and the nationalization and media-ization, through technological change, of politics.

• New Issues and the Culture Wars •

Through much of the twentieth century, American politics was dominated by economic issues such as how to control business cycles, set tariffs, manage currency, regulate monopolies, secure the right of workers to organize and strike, and protect individuals against the economic hazards of old age, ill health, unemployment, industrial injury, and exploitative working conditions. In the latter part of the century, with many institutions in place to regulate an industrial economy, other kinds of issues gained prominence. These included racial equality, gender relations, abortion rights, prayer in the schools, the quality of the environment, and the moral content of public life. At issue were "lifestyles," "culture," and claims to "rights."

Tobacco consumption has become one battle in the culture wars. To be sure, opponents of tobacco use bring to the fight a variety of motives. At the core of the antitobacco coalition, providing its scientific base and much of its moral fervor, are specialists in public health, such as the FDA's David Kessler, various surgeons general, and contributors to the annual reports of the surgeon general. Some of the opponents are members of evangelical or fundamentalist religious sects—for example, Mormon holders of congressional seats and executive offices in the federal government—who bring to the coalition a traditional morality. Others have become active out of rage at victimization, either their own (as angry ex-smokers) or that of near-relatives, heavy smokers whom they have watched die prematurely. Some of the most committed activists of the 1990s were children of the heavy smokers of the 1940s and 1950s, and this generational sequence may account for the intensity of the recent movement. The middle-aged adults who have watched smoking parents die of pulmonary diseases, besides being enraged, are fearful that children or grandchildren will take up the habit.

Finally, the issue has had a powerful and somewhat paradoxical appeal to the left wing of modern American politics—paradoxical because the left generally supports a libertarian lifestyle. If premarital sex and pot-smoking are approved, why not cigarettes? The answer seems to be both that cigarettes kill (as opponents of tobacco are wont to say, with eyes blazing) and that they are commercial products, manufactured for profit. Tobacco enrages the left wing just as abortion enrages the right wing, and for a parallel reason: it is perceived as murder. Additionally, these "murderous" products have historically yielded immense profits and have been heavily advertised, with seductive, alluring images evoking glamour and sexual gratification. Thus, in the eyes of the left, they epitomize American capitalism at its greedy, vulgar, deceptive worst. What is more, they pollute the atmosphere, offending protectors of the environment. Given R. J. Reynolds's three hugely successful decades of NASCAR sponsorship, they have also been associated with overpowered, gas-guzzling, ear-splitting, bone-crushing, and life-extinguishing automobiles, yet another symbol of American vulgarity. And, to top it all off, they originate in a region of the country that the left continues to associate with racism and reactionary politics. Virtually all tobacco growers and many tobacco manufacturers speak with southern accents.[1]

Not surprisingly, given the political high ground represented today by rights claims, both sides in the tobacco wars have sought to occupy that ground. When smokers claim a right to smoke, with prompting and financial help from the companies, opponents counter with claims of a right to a smoke-free environment and charge that smokers, rather than freely exercising a right, are victims of addiction.

The cultural foundations of the clash over tobacco use have emerged as smoking has become differentiated by social class. When cigarette consumption increased in the mid-twentieth century, it spread through all strata of the population, but following the post-1964 drop in smoking, it has become heavily concentrated among the poor and less well educated. An English author speculates that "smoking may even have become a defiant badge of lower class status." In the United Kingdom smoking rates exceed 50 percent among families in public housing or receiving welfare. "Only among the poorest communities is smoking still a normative behaviour."[2] In the United States 5.6 percent of persons who have graduate degrees smoke, whereas 28.5 percent of those who lack a high school diploma do so.[3] Increasingly, the war against tobacco is waged by a well-educated elite on behalf of the working class and the poor, with the proximate targets being the manufacturers, who are excoriated for making victims of the users.

· The Institutionalization of Cause Advocacy ·

Politics does not arise solely out of political actors' pursuit of self-interest, narrowly conceived. Some political actors pursue causes or principles with little or no expectation of material benefit. Historically, however, most of the durable organizations in American politics that have sought to influence government policy have had a grounding in material self-interest. Typically, they have been marketplace or occupational entities such as business corporations, trade associations, professional associations, labor unions, and organizations of farmers. Or they have been organizations of veterans—who have a stake in government benefits such as pensions, job preferences, and medical care—and, more recently, retirees, who benefit from Social Security and Medicare. Government programs tend to elicit the formation of organized interest groups that are composed of the programs' beneficiaries.

In the past several decades political analysts have noted the increasing importance of groups or movements that espouse causes, the interests of consumers (as distinct from those of producers), or the interests of "the public" (as distinct from narrower, more specialized interests). The terminology varies, but there is considerable agreement among students of American politics, not that the pursuit of material interest is in decline, but that rival forces have been on the rise. Such forces have been central to the assault on tobacco, and the case therefore illustrates their contemporary importance.

Foundation Funding

Founded in the early 1980s, the Coalition on Smoking OR Health was for approximately a decade the principal organized, nongovernmental opponent of tobacco use at the level of national politics. It was formed by the big three voluntary associations in the field—the American Cancer Society, the American Lung Association, and the American Heart Association—all of which had their own lobbyists but recognized the need for a coordinated effort targeted at tobacco use. Matthew Myers became their paid coordinator, the executive director of the coalition, and a leading player in the tobacco politics of the national capital.

The scale of Myers's activity was initially modest. Supported only by the sponsoring organizations, the coalition had an annual budget of around $150,000.[4] Still practicing law, Myers did the coalition's business out of his office. In the mid-1990s, however, coinciding with the general escalation of antismoking activity, the coalition underwent a metamorphosis. It acquired a president, William Novelli, who was a professional public relations man. His firm, Porter/Novelli, "was founded to apply marketing to social and health issues, and grew into an international marketing/public relations agency with corporate, not-for-profit, and government clients."[5] Under Novelli's leadership, the coalition changed its name to the National Center for Tobacco-Free Kids; added many more organizational constituents, such as the Parent Teacher Association and an array of youth and religious organizations; and secured large grants.

Some of these grants came from foundations, such as the Annie E. Casey Foundation, that have a particular interest in children's welfare, but the bulk of them came from the Robert Wood Johnson (RWJ) Foundation, specializing in health. RWJ announced in 1992 that it would seek in the coming decade to establish substance abuse as the nation's leading health problem and to reduce the harm caused by tobacco as well as alcohol and illegal drugs. A wealthy foundation, with many millions of dollars to give away from an endowment of stock in the pharmaceutical manufacturer Johnson & Johnson, it would become by far the most important source of private funding for the antitobacco movement, giving hundreds of grants for a wide range of purposes, including prevention, research, advocacy, training of antitobacco activists, and support of their quarterly journal, *Tobacco Control.*

The center, like any organization of its kind, also benefits indirectly from government support in that contributions to it are tax deductible under section 501(c)(3) of the tax code. In contrast, a nominally independent organization, the Campaign for Tobacco-Free Kids, which engages in lobbying and advocacy, does not so qualify.

The budget of Myers's expanded operation was a hefty $10 million a year, and as of the end of 1999 its Web site carried short biographies of twenty-eight staff members in addition to those of Novelli as president and Myers as executive vice president and general counsel. (Shortly thereafter, Myers succeeded Novelli, who moved to the American Association of Retired Persons.) The organization produced a large volume of antitobacco propaganda, sponsored events such as an annual "Kick Butts Day" to encourage youth activism, and engaged in grassroots organizing, taking it for the first time far outside of Washington.[6] Meanwhile, Myers was very much a player in the new politics of tobacco. When negotiations between the industry and its opponents in litigation, the state attorneys general and the Castano lawyers, got under way, he was at the table, a place he secured partly because the Clinton White House wanted him there. He acted virtually as the White House's representative in the negotiations.[7]

Faculty Activists

Besides benefiting from the organized cause advocacy represented by the Coalition on Smoking OR Health and its successor, the National Center for Tobacco-Free Kids, the antitobacco movement has been aided by the political activity of members of university faculties. Three stand out: John Banzhaf III of the George Washington University Law School, Stanton A. Glantz of the medical school of the University of California at San Francisco, and Richard Daynard of the Northeastern University Law School.

Banzhaf got involved early, when both he and the antitobacco movement were young. In 1966 he was twenty-five years old and about to join a New York law firm, having gotten a law degree at Columbia and clerked for a federal appellate judge in the D.C. circuit. Watching televised football interspersed with cigarette commercials on Thanksgiving

Day, Banzhaf was struck with the idea that the fairness doctrine of the Federal Communications Commission (FCC), which prescribed balanced treatment of controversial public issues, ought to apply to commercials as well as programming. He fired off a letter saying so to WCBS-TV in New York, and then, unsatisfied with the station's reply, he carried his case to the FCC, which was more receptive. The FCC had an activist general counsel in Henry Geller, who had been convinced by the surgeon general's report that the broadcasting industry was "hawking a product causing an enormous health risk." It also had a chairman, Rosel Hyde, who as a Mormon was no friend of the cigarette industry. Using Banzhaf's letter as a starting point, the FCC proceeded to apply the fairness doctrine to cigarette commercials.[8]

Banzhaf boldly expanded upon this initial move. He filed a petition in the D.C. circuit challenging the FCC's ruling, mainly as a way of pre-empting an appeal by the industry and ensuring that the FCC's action would be reviewed by a sympathetic court rather than one chosen by the industry—a ploy that succeeded. Later, he personally monitored the broadcasts of WNBC-TV in New York for compliance with the FCC's new rules and petitioned the commission to strip the station of its broadcast license when he found compliance wanting—a move that improved compliance generally.[9]

Later, as a member of the law faculty of George Washington University, specializing in tort law and consumer advocacy, Banzhaf was a frequent public speaker on tobacco issues and a witness before Congress. Along with Ralph Nader, a consumer advocate on behalf of many causes, he took the initiative in asking the Federal Aviation Administration to regulate smoking on passenger flights, prompting the creation of separate sections for smokers and nonsmokers.[10] Though he attempted to create an organization to pursue his cause, his creation, called ASH (Action on Smoking and Health), remained very much a personal vehicle. Brash, egotistical, and prone to alienating potential allies, Banzhaf was essentially an individual operator and was not a major figure in the events of the 1990s.[11]

Stanton Glantz, at the other end of the continent from Banzhaf, was one of a cluster of California antismoking activists who had helped put that state, often a bellwether in American politics and policymaking, into the forefront of regulation. Their strategy was to stigmatize smoking by prohibiting it in public places. Twice defeated in statewide referenda, they responded by concentrating instead on passage of local ordinances, which, starting with a Berkeley law in 1977, mounted by the dozen as the 1980s advanced. Ironically, they did not lead the fight for Proposition 99, "the largest tobacco control program in the world," as Glantz called it, which California voters approved in 1988. That advocacy was guided instead by a coalition of public health and environmental activists who saw an opportunity to raise funds for a range of causes by increasing California's cigarette sales tax to thirty-five cents from ten cents a pack, where it had stood since 1967. This approach had considerable appeal in a state then in revolt against the property tax.[12]

Glantz brought a potent combination of professional skills and personality traits to the California—and then the national—effort. Trained in applied mechanics and economics, he combined scientific expertise in cardiovascular physiology with technical skill in biostatistics, and proficiency in research and writing with a passion for political agitation. Though active in Californians for Nonsmokers' Rights (CNR), which evolved into Americans for Nonsmokers' Rights (ANR), he was too obsessive and confrontational to be well suited to organizational activity.[13] A photograph of him in a book that he co-authored on California tobacco politics shows him in a T-shirt that says, "Here Comes Trouble." And trouble he was—for the industry above all, for politicians who took contributions from the industry, for California officials who did not spend the proceeds of Proposition 99 as he thought they should be spent, and for other antitobacco activists whose strategies he disagreed with. Glantz was a guerrilla warrior, a movement leader at the grassroots who distrusted anything done in a state or national capital, by its legislature especially, the members of which he believed to have been bought. And he was a modern guerrilla, with, after 1996, an e-mail network of more than a thousand of the most aggressive opponents of tobacco, whom he daily bombarded with exhortations and guides to strategy.[14]

Glantz had a niche also in analyzing antitobacco advocacy at the state level, mainly in California but also in other states, and in documenting and disseminating exposures of the industry, an activity in which he was aided by his employer, the University of California, and by collaborators among its research institutes, library, academic press, and graduate programs. His initial venture involved circulating in the United States a pirated tape of *Death in the West,* an antitobacco documentary made for Thames Television by a British investigative journalist, Peter Taylor. A British judge in 1977 had granted Philip Morris an injunction to prevent further showing of the film on the grounds that the company had been fraudulently induced into cooperating and that its Marlboro commercials, which the program juxtaposed with images of cowboys dying of lung cancer, had been deceitfully obtained. The documentary was a powerful piece of antitobacco propaganda.

The British judge commented that this program "gave me all the indications of intending as its purpose the complete discrediting of the defendants." Saying that he did not doubt the value and importance of its message, he asked nonetheless, "Can a civilized legal system survive side by side with the proposition that the end can always justify the means?" Glantz received a pirated copy of the tape, which by order of the British judge was supposed to be confined to the Thames Television archives, and, with some help from Michael Pertschuk and the general counsel of the University of California, succeeded in having it shown on San Francisco's NBC affiliate, KRON-TV, and Boston's public TV station, WGBH. It was thereafter offered for sale by a private distributor, with royalties payable to the California Board of Regents, which administers the state university system, and to antismoking groups.[15]

In view of this history, it is not surprising that the documents stolen by Merrell Williams from Brown & Williamson via its law firm also became public through the efforts of Glantz and the University of California. For a long time, Williams had been unsure what to do with these papers. He had approached Richard Daynard, an antitobacco activist at Northeastern University in Boston. After warning of the legal risks of peddling these products of theft, Daynard had suggested that he meet with Morton Mintz, retired as an investigative reporter for the *Washington Post* but still fighting industry malfeasance as a freelancer. Mintz, too, was wary of the legal risks.[16]

Eventually, a tort lawyer in Mississippi, Don Barrett, using the name "Mr. Butts," mailed the documents to Glantz. Barrett had acquired them from Richard Scruggs, who had gotten them from Williams (who then received from Scruggs, presumably in appreciation, the gift of a house). Glantz gave them to the University of California library, where they would be open to users generally. After receiving a favorable ruling from the California Supreme Court, which rejected Brown & Williamson's plea that they were private property, the library posted them on a Web site, which within a year had been hit a half-million times.[17] Beyond that, Glantz and several collaborators proceeded to publish the documents, with analysis and interpretation, in the *Journal of the American Medical Association* and in a book, *The Cigarette Papers,* which the University of California Press brought out in 1996. Thus, a sizeable portion of Brown & Williamson's papers, with a blurb calling them "a shocking collection of secret industry documents," came into the public domain. Scruggs had also given them to Representative Waxman's staff, which passed them on to a science reporter for the *New York Times,* Philip J. Hilts, who functioned virtually as a member of the antitobacco coalition, so they were certain to become public. Glantz's distinctive contribution was to maximize the impact with collection, interpretation, and publication under eminent academic auspices.

Glantz's research and publication activities, which also included a series of cowritten articles that detailed the tobacco industry's expenditures in California state politics, were financed initially out of funds from Proposition 99, via a research account managed by the University of California. Later, he was supported by a grant from the National Cancer Institute.[18]

From his base in Boston, Richard Daynard campaigned for a strategy of litigation. Ranking tobacco below only nuclear weapons as a threat to the human race, he was dissatisfied with the strategy of local ordinances, which he had pursued as president of the Massachusetts GASP (Groups Against Smoking Pollution). Inspired by the example of asbestos litigation, in which the Johns Manville Corporation had been sued by twenty-five thousand claimants and forced into bankruptcy, he organized the Tobacco Products Liability Project in the mid-1980s to proselytize for a similar attack on the cigarette manufacturers. With the aid of a $30,000 annual grant from the Rockefeller Foundation, he began in 1985 to hold annual conferences at Northeastern on how to sue the tobacco industry, and he started to publish the *Tobacco Products Litigation Reporter*, a compendium of legal opinions, briefs, laws, and other material useful to plaintiffs' lawyers.[19]

Although Daynard litigated no cases himself, he helped fashion arguments for those who did, and he promised that there would be important policy and political payoffs from victory. Cigarette manufacturers, if forced to bear the costs of the harm from their products, would have to raise prices, which would discourage cigarette consumption. Litigation would also generate publicity, which would focus "media and public attention on the plaintiffs' cigarette-induced suffering, as well as exciting widespread discussion and debate on the larger issues of personal and corporate responsibility." Finally, the discovery process of litigation could be made to yield material that would embarrass the industry and "outrage jurors and judges." Even one favorable verdict, Daynard promised, could have dramatic results:

> Until a case is won, most lawyers, public health advocates and journalists will likely stay on the sidelines. . . . Once a case is won, the general perception of the value of the strategy should change rapidly. The useful economic, educational, and political effects described at the beginning of this commentary would follow.[20]

Just as Myers's activity expanded in the late 1990s with more liberal funding, so did Daynard's. Through Northeastern University and the

Tobacco Control Resource Center, created as a nonprofit organization under section 501 (c)(3) of the Internal Revenue Code, he received a grant of more than $1 million from the National Cancer Institute to do "the legal research and analysis needed to support states, municipalities, health insurers and public interest groups as they pursue innovative legal interventions to reduce tobacco use." The center's Web site in early 2000 described an organization with Daynard as president, seven attorneys of various ranks, a special projects coordinator, an administrative assistant, a financial administrator, and a publications manager.[21]

The cases of Myers, Banzhaf, Glantz, and Daynard illustrate how cause advocacy becomes institutionalized, counteracting the power of profit-making corporations. Each of these men brought a fierce commitment to the cause, but in the real world political action becomes feasible and effective only when fierce commitment is combined with discretionary time, money, and stable organizational support. Individuals can matter in politics, but individuals generally have to work for a living. For the most part (with the partial exception of Banzhaf, who seems to have started out as a genuine freelancer), these men were enabled to pursue the antitobacco cause by a combination of foundation grants, government grants and tax exemptions, and subsidies and other support from university employers.

Government agencies, foundations, and large, research-oriented universities are not new in American society, but they are a more muscular part of the organizational universe—better financed, better staffed, and more active politically—than they were several decades ago. The Robert Wood Johnson Foundation gave grants of nearly $267 million in 1996, of which more than $103 million went to fighting substance abuse. Universities help not only by channeling grants and offering legal counsel and office space, as just described, but also by being secure and accommodating employers. Tenured faculty members, who enjoy a great deal of discretion over the use of their time once their classroom obligations have been met, have greater freedom to undertake cause advocacy than do most private-sector employees. Also, graduate students are readily available as capable assistants employable at modest wages.

Cause advocacy engaged in by private parties, even if with much government support, only begins to explain what brought the tobacco companies to heel in the 1990s. The key actors in the antitobacco drama of the 1990s were the state attorneys general, whose principal asset was the power that comes with public office.

· The Growth of Government ·

In the three decades between the start of the public antitobacco campaign in 1964 and its transformation in 1994–1997, the role of government in the domestic affairs of the American people expanded enormously, rendering individuals, the society, and the economy ever more dependent on public policy. Any harm, hazard, risk, injustice, or inequality now became potentially fair game for government regulation or redress. Whereas arguments for government intervention once bore a very heavy burden of proof in the United States, that burden had rapidly shifted since the New Deal to the opposite, noninterventionist side.

Simple statistics hint—but no more than hint—at the change. Federal government outlays rose from $176.2 billion in 1965, amounting to 17.2 percent of gross domestic product (GDP), to $1.46 trillion in 1994, or 21.4 percent of GDP. State and local government spending, at $1.26 trillion in 1994, consumed another 18.4 percent of GDP, bringing the share for all governments to nearly 40 percent. Measured simply in number of pages of statutes enacted by Congress, the output of laws rose from 1,500–2,300 pages per Congress in the 1940s and 1950s to as high as 7,000 pages per Congress in the 1980s. The effects are cumulative, of course, inasmuch as the new pages do not simply substitute for the old. Pages in the *Federal Register*, in which new regulations implementing the laws are published, rose from 10,528 in 1956, to 16,850 in 1966, to 87,012 in 1980.

Perhaps the growth is captured more vividly by increases in the numbers of key participants. In describing how government in Washington had changed since the early 1960s, the journalist Hedrick Smith recounts that

- whereas 365 lobbyists were registered with Congress in 1961, 23,011 were registered in mid-1987;
- whereas the District of Columbia Bar Association had 12,500 members in 1961, it had 46,000 in 1987;
- whereas 1,522 journalists were accredited to congressional press galleries in 1961, 5,250 were accredited in 1987, and the 1980 census showed 12,612 journalists citywide;
- Washington in 1986 contained the headquarters of 3,500 trade associations, more than triple the number of 1960, and they employed a workforce of roughly 80,000; and
- Congress in 1985 employed more than 24,000 staff members, compared with 11,500 in 1973.[22]

Dollars spent, pages published, and lobbyists registered are the crudest measures of what was going on, giving no indication of scope, depth, and detail, nor do they capture even superficially the impact of judicial activity. However, such facts suffice to make the general point that government was growing. This growth contributed to the change in tobacco politics in ways both direct and indirect, manifest and subtle.

Most obviously, as the welfare state grew, governments undertook to finance health care. Governments spent roughly $386.5 billion for health care programs in 1993, of which $151 billion went for Medicare, a federal government program of insurance for persons sixty-five and over and for those with disabilities, and $125 billion for Medicaid, a joint federal-state program for persons who cannot afford to pay for health care. Authorized by amendments to the Social Security Act in 1965, these two big programs have given all of the major governments in the United States a direct stake in the control of health care costs—a stake that, in turn, has caused them to claim a large regulatory role. In 1964 no one could have conceived of lawsuits brought by governments to recover health care costs as a strategy of tobacco control because few such costs existed outside of veterans' programs. The indispensable precondition having been met, such a strategy could be conceived of in the 1990s, novel though it was.

As governments' role grew, government officials' conceptions of what is appropriate for governments to do expanded correspondingly. It would be inconceivable for a Democratic secretary of health and human services to say today what Joseph Califano Jr., a Democrat who was secretary of health, education, and welfare, said in 1979—that "in a free society, research and education must be the major tools of any public-health program to deal with smoking."[23] Today's Democratic advocates of tobacco control seek heavy regulation and taxation—even, at the extreme, public ownership—which aim at suppression or near-elimination of the product.

Similarly, the huge expansion in the government's role helped elevate the expectations of political activists outside of the government. That cigarette manufacture, as distinct from advertising and place of use, was unregulated by government struck antitobacco activists in the 1990s as worse than an anomaly—it was an outrage. When products less harmful than tobacco were heavily regulated by the Food and Drug Administration (FDA) and the Consumer Product Safety Commission, activists found it absolutely intolerable that tobacco, of all things, escaped. Their outrage was understandable in the contemporary United States, in which government regulation of commercial products had become the norm; decades earlier, when regulation had been exceptional, the outrage would have been anomalous.

As the role of governments changed, so did that of officeholders in government. From city councillor to U.S. president, they all have more to do than they did three decades ago. "More to do" does not, however, simply translate into "more power," because officials often are constrained by law, limited resources, conflicts with other officials, and competing pressures from interest groups. Most officials today probably find it harder to get anything done than did their predecessors of three decades ago, who led less harried lives. However, some officials clearly do have more power—that is, more ability to use discretion to influence public policy and to allocate penalties and rewards—than they formerly did. The attorneys general of the state governments are a striking instance.

All fifty states have attorneys general, and in nearly all, the office is defined in the state constitution and located in the executive branch. In forty-three states the attorney general is elected. In five states (Alaska, Hawaii, New Hampshire, New Jersey, and Wyoming) the attorneys general are appointed by the governor; in Maine the holder is elected by the legislature; and in Tennessee he or she is appointed by the supreme court. Because the elected ones are chosen independently of the governor, they may be of a different party. As of 1998 there were only seventeen Democratic governors, whereas there were thirty Democratic attorneys general—a fact that is pertinent to tobacco politics and specifically to the events of the 1990s. Although tobacco control sometimes elicits bipartisan alliances, as a general rule Democrats have been far more committed to it than Republicans, and the partisan difference sharpened in 1994.

The powers and functions of the office of attorney general typically include (1) rendering advisory opinions on questions of law to government officials; (2) representing the state's legal interests, either directly or as amicus curiae, in judicial proceedings; (3) drafting and promoting legislative proposals; (4) administering state expenditures in areas such as contracting and bonding; and (5) disseminating information regarding legal issues confronting the state.[24] On their face these duties may seem modest, but attorneys general also typically have common law authority allowing them to represent "the public interest"—which amounts to a very broad charter indeed. The U.S. Fifth Circuit Court of Appeals explained this authority as follows in 1976:

> The attorneys general of our states have enjoyed a significant degree of autonomy. Their duties and powers typically are not exhaustively defined by either constitution or statute but include all those exercised at common law. There is and has been no doubt that the legislature may deprive the attorney general of specific powers; but in the absence of such authority he typically may exercise all such authority as the public interest requires.[25]

The activities of the attorneys general expanded rapidly in the 1970s and 1980s, along with the size of their staffs. They tried many more cases and filed many more amicus briefs in the Supreme Court. In most states the attorney general became the official principally responsible for enforcing environmental protection laws, for which states bear a heavy burden prescribed by federal statutes. They grew active as well in the fields of hazardous waste disposal, antitrust enforcement, consumer protection, and civil rights, covering both race and gender.

So powerful an office has attracted able and ambitious politicians. It is often said in jest that "A.G." stands for "aspiring governor," an aphorism that does not reach far enough. Many have gone beyond state politics to offices in the federal government, typically the Senate but including also the cabinet, the Supreme Court, and even the presidency. Among former attorneys general who have made their mark in Washington are John Ashcroft, Bruce Babbitt, Jeff Bingaman, Bill Clinton, John Danforth, Dennis DeConcini, Thomas Eagleton, Slade Gorton, Jacob Javits, Jim Jeffords, Joseph Lieberman, Walter Mondale, Elliot Richardson, Warren Rudman, William Saxbe, David Souter, and Robert Stafford.

Against this background of the development of the attorney general's office, it is unsurprising—perhaps it was even predictable—that attorneys general would have become engaged in tobacco control, just as later nineteen of them would join with the Department of Justice in suing Microsoft. Their lawsuits were crucial to the change in tobacco policy that took place in the mid-1990s.

· The Nationalization and Media-ization of Politics ·

If initiatives by state attorneys general seem predictable as one examines recent history, one still must ask: Why the attorney general of Mississippi? The leader of the litigating campaign for tobacco control was from a Deep South state long known for its reactionary politics. The answer lies partly in the growing nationalization of American politics, by which I mean two things. First, interstate and interregional differences in politics and policy preferences have tended to erode as demographic, economic, and cultural changes make the country more homogeneous. Second, it becomes easier for interest groups, political movements, and political actors generally to mobilize on a national scale as technological change facilitates communication among them.

Once a radically deviant region, set apart by a large African American population, a high proportion of native-born white Protestants, a racial caste system, extreme poverty, an agricultural economy, defeat in a civil war, and the uniform loyalty of its voters and officeholders to the Democratic Party, the South today has become much more like the rest of the country. Its politics are less bound by a traditional culture and increasingly are characterized by two-party competition between conservative Republicans and progressive Democrats.[26]

As of the late 1980s, Mississippi in particular was in reaction against its own reactionary past. In the state elections of 1987, voters installed in office "a group of progressive, reform-minded politicians in their 30s who are pledged to help their new Governor to 'unravel the status quo,' as one of them put it."[27] The new governor, Ray Mabus, who was a Harvard-trained lawyer with experience in a liberal Democratic law firm in Washington, remained governor for only one term, but Mike Moore, who was elected attorney general along with him after making his mark fighting official corruption as district attorney in Jackson County, was repeatedly reelected.[28] The victorious progressives of 1987 came into office vowing that "Mississippi will never be last again." There would be an end to proud—or complacent—provincialism. Rather than last, Mississippi, with Moore in charge, was first in the campaign of official litigation against big tobacco.

As attorney general, Moore had demonstrated his belief in the cause of tobacco control. Between 1988 and 1997, he made more than two thousand appearances in schools to warn against smoking and drug abuse.[29] According to the journalist Peter Pringle, "When he talked about 'li'l ole Mississippa takin' on Big Tobacca,' it was said with deep feeling— from a Southerner who was determined to make his mark on the Northern Establishment and, if possible, on the rest of the world."[30] Moore lost a campaign for Congress in 1989. The antitobacco crusade promised to be a different route to participation in national policymaking.

Nothing in the social or economic structure of Mississippi stood in his way—although a Republican governor, Kirk Fordice, whose party affiliation was another indication of a changed Mississippi, tried to. Tobacco is often loosely associated with the South as a region, but it is unevenly distributed there. Tobacco is neither grown nor manufactured in Mississippi. In suing big corporations for payments to his state, Moore was unambiguously serving Mississippi's interests by seeking to redress the state's historic poverty. "It could mean hundreds of millions of dollars to the people of Mississippi," an assistant attorney general, Trey Bobinger, exulted. That would be "tremendous." It would mean "better schools, better roads, better hospitals, better health care."[31]

Cooperation among Attorneys General

Still, Moore did not stop with his own state. He intended to lead the rest in a national campaign. This strategy was plausible, given a developing pattern of interstate cooperation among attorneys general. Formally organized in a national association since 1907, the attorneys general in the 1970s and 1980s had become much more active collectively at the same time that they had become more powerful individually. The National Association of Attorneys General (NAAG) had formed numerous study committees to address policy issues of common state concern, such as environmental protection, public land management, antitrust law, consumer protection, charitable trusts and solicitations, securities regulation, insurance regulation, and utility ratemaking. The association's committees aimed to standardize state enforcement standards, prepare model statutes, and fend off federal government preemption. They aimed, in short, to collaborate in making national policy.

More telling than the existence of NAAG committees have been concrete instances of coordinated policymaking. For example, in 1988, following federal deregulation of the airline industry, all fifty states adopted a set of guidelines for using their laws to regulate airline fare advertising. Opposed by both the Federal Trade Commission and the Department of Transportation, these guidelines placed strict new controls on the advertising of fares and frequent flyer programs. The attorneys general also organized ad hoc task forces to prosecute nationwide corporations—Chrysler, for example, for disconnecting odometers of cars driven by company executives, and Minolta, for inflating camera prices.[32]

It was against this background that Moore set out to fight the cigarette companies. He was following a path tested earlier in pursuit of smaller prey, and he had the advantage of acquaintance with other attorneys general as a result of his activity in the NAAG. In addition to doing its committee work, the NAAG holds three national meetings a year, one of which is a retreat to which outsiders are not admitted. None of this would have guaranteed concerted action by the states in the tobacco wars in the absence of powerful economic and political incentives to collaborate, but what Moore did regarding tobacco would have been far harder without the prior creation of institutions for interstate collaboration among attorneys general.

"Ambulance Chasing" Grows in Scale

Similarly, development of tort lawyers into an influential force in policymaking was rooted in the increasing geographic scale of tort litigation. The activities of two leading and sometimes rival figures, Wendell Gauthier and Ron Motley, will illustrate the point.

Wendell ("the Goat") Gauthier, the New Orleans tort lawyer who headed the Castano Group, was to the lawyers what Mike Moore was to the attorneys general: the entrepreneur who undertook to assemble a nationwide antitobacco coalition. A multimillionaire, Gauthier had begun his career with local cases. His first break was a $1 million verdict against Louisiana Gas in a case involving explosion of a gas line. He moved on to an explosion at a grain elevator, an airplane crash, a hotel fire in Las Vegas that was settled for $208 million, the DuPont Plaza fire in San Juan, Puerto Rico (for $230 million), and a class action brought against Dow Corning on behalf of two hundred thousand women who had received silicone breast implants. In this suit he was one of seventeen liability lawyers who secured a settlement of $4.2 billion, which forced Dow Corning into bankruptcy in 1995. At the time it set a new record for a civil damage award.

The others whom Gauthier brought into his coalition—sixty lawyers from twenty-five firms who put up $100,000 each—came from California, Maryland, Mississippi, Ohio, South Carolina, Texas, and Washington, D.C., as well as Louisiana. They included flamboyant figures, many of them pioneers in class-action litigation. "Ambulance chasers," the colloquial term for their profession, implies limited geographic horizons, but these were ambulance chasers on a worldwide scale. Flying off to the Asian subcontinent, some had jockeyed with one another for action in the Bhopal disaster—the release of toxic gases from a Union Carbide plant in India that had killed 1,861 people and injured another 27,000 in 1984. Often in competition, disrespected by one another as well as their adversaries, they came together in the hope of profit from a *national* class-action suit against the tobacco companies, the largest class action ever filed.[33] This mobilization took extraordinary boldness even in the 1990s, but in an earlier time, before nationalization of the public sphere, it would have been inconceivable.

Ronald Lee (Ron) Motley, of the Charleston, South Carolina, firm of Ness, Motley, Loadholt, Richardson and Poole, joined the Castano Group but dropped out after a federal court declined in May 1996 to certify the national class-action suit. Thereafter the influence of the Castano Group per se waned, although its members had decided to file "sons of Castano" class actions in state courts. Motley thought the "sons" were losers and wanted to focus instead on the attorney general suits and several cases of private individuals that he had secured. Having been engaged by states as far-flung as Hawaii, Iowa, Kansas, and Utah, Motley, like Richard Scruggs, was a one-man embodiment of nationally coordinated tort actions. High-living, hard-drinking, passionate, profane, and very smart, Motley flew in his Cessna Citation III from one deposition to another, one document cache to another, one negotiation to another, all over the country.[34]

As they gained wealth and nationwide fame, these tort lawyers were redistributing power and status within the legal profession. Disproportionately from the South, they were reducing the distance between Washington and Pascagoula, Wall Street and Charleston, in the sociolegal hierarchy of the United States. They were also reducing the traditional imbalance of power between corporations and plaintiffs in tort cases. Speaking of Ron Motley's firm, Prof. Marc Galanter, a student of the legal profession, remarked: "This is the first time in history when a large plaintiffs' law firm has faced the financial ability to become a national megafirm."[35]

The Role of the Media

Historically, assembling a national coalition of any kind of political actor for any purpose has not been easy work. James Madison, who more than any other man shaped and then promoted the U.S. Constitution, thought that forming a national coalition would be extremely difficult in a large country. In a famous passage in *Federalist* No. 10, he wrote:

> Extend the sphere and you take in a greater variety of parties and interests; you make it less probable that a majority of the whole will have a common motive to invade the rights of other citizens; or if such a common motive exists, it will be more difficult for all who feel it to discover their own strength and to act in unison with each other. . . . The influence of factious leaders may kindle a flame within their particular States but will be unable to spread a general conflagration through the other States.[36]

Madison, however, knew no telephones, television, faxes, e-mail, Web sites, or Cessna Citations. As transportation and communications technologies have advanced at a revolutionary pace, beginning in the new American nation in the nineteenth century with the railroad and the telegraph, it has become steadily easier for like-minded actors to find one another and concert their activities. It is also easier for political actors who have access to mass media to influence opinions instantly and on a grand scale.

Propaganda—the manipulation of words and visual symbols to shape attitudes—is a political act as old as speech and drawing. In blunt form it is a crucial instrument of totalitarian regimes that monopolize its use, but a subtler form is pervasive in free, democratic regimes, where it is competitively employed by rival political parties, interest groups, and individuals. We are surrounded by "spin." However they start, political struggles in a democracy tend to become wars of propaganda sooner or later, escalating for some period of time as opposing sides compete to enlist the support of public opinion. In this struggle opponents of tobacco felt themselves to be at a severe disadvantage because the companies annually spent many millions and then billions of dollars to promote their products. As of 1983, for example, they spent $1.9 billion on advertising and promotion, including sampling and premiums, which was more than they spent in wages and salaries and nearly as much as they spent for tobacco.[37]

Yet the critics were not without rhetorical tools of their own, beginning with the nearly annual reports of the surgeon general. Starting in the early 1980s, the reports regularly pronounced cigarette smoking "the chief preventable cause of death" in the United States, a phrase that became a mantra for the antismoking movement. To a committed political activist, an evil that is "preventable" must therefore be prevented. By the 1990s the Centers for Disease Control and Prevention were attributing approximately 430,000 deaths per year to smoking—nearly 20 percent of all deaths.[38] Another statistic that was deployed as the focus shifted to youth smoking was that three thousand children started smoking every day. In the escalating conflict of the 1990s, the opponents of tobacco proved to have superior skills in political propaganda and in access to the most potent medium of the time—television. Moreover, they found an easy mark as they increasingly targeted cigarette companies and their executives, rather than cigarettes per se or the act of smoking. Quite deliberately, they demonized the makers of cigarettes.

Two events were of particular importance. One was an exposé of the industry that was broadcast by ABC's muckraking *Day One* program on February 28 and March 7, 1994. ABC's reporter, John Martin, announced, "Now, a lengthy *Day One* investigation has uncovered perhaps the tobacco industry's last, best secret—how it artificially adds nicotine to cigarettes to keep people smoking and boost profits." A voice-over continued, "The methods the cigarette companies use to precisely control the levels of nicotine is something that has never before been disclosed to consumers or the government. For years, growing and blending tobacco was an art, but about thirty years ago, it began evolving into something quite different." Clifford Douglas, a lawyer and lobbyist for the American Cancer Society who had urged ABC to do the program, said, "The public doesn't know that the industry manipulates nicotine, takes it out, puts it back in, uses it as if it were sugar being put in candy. They don't have a clue." An anonymous former employee of R. J. Reynolds, appearing only in a disguised silhouette, added, "They put nicotine in the form of a tobacco extract into a product to keep the consumer happy." In its promotion of the program, ABC had accused the manufacturers of "spiking" cigarettes, with the implication that there was more nicotine in the cigarette than occurred naturally in the tobacco leaf. Philip Morris responded with a $10 billion defamation suit.[39]

Rather than go to court, the TV network recanted more than a year later (in August 1995), broadcast two apologies, and agreed to pay $15 million in legal expenses to Philip Morris. But the program had spread the idea that the companies could manipulate nicotine levels to keep smokers hooked, a premise of the campaign to achieve FDA regulation. The program also influenced litigation. Wendell Gauthier in New Orleans ran and reran the thirteen-minute tape in his office, pondering how he could mount a class-action suit on the charge of nicotine addiction.[40]

An even greater propaganda coup occurred during hearings that Henry Waxman's subcommittee in the House held between March and June 1994. These hearings built on the work of ABC and the FDA, magnifying its public effects. The chief executive officers of the cigarette companies had resisted attending, but, berated by Waxman for not appearing and urged by a putative ally, Virginia's Rep. Tom Bliley, to do so, they came as a group on April 14 to an overflowing hearing room with full TV coverage. As a group they were filmed with hands raised, swearing to tell the truth. Rep. Ron Wyden of Oregon, one of their principal antagonists, then led them in mid-hearing into the following sequence of exchanges:

> Mr. WYDEN: . . . Let me ask you first, and I'd like to just go down the row, whether each of you believes that nicotine is not addictive. . . . Yes or no, do you believe nicotine is not addictive.
>
> Mr. [William I.] CAMPBELL [president of Philip Morris, U.S.A.]: I believe nicotine is not addictive, yes.
>
> Mr. WYDEN: Mr. Johnston?
>
> Mr. JAMES JOHNSTON [chairman, R. J. Reynolds]: Mr. Congressman, cigarettes and nicotine clearly do not meet the classic definition of addiction. There is no intoxication.
>
> Mr. WYDEN: We'll take that as a "no." Again, time is short. I think each of you believe nicotine is not addictive. We would just like to have this for the record. . . .
>
> Mr. [Andrew H.] TISCH [chairman, Lorillard Tobacco Co.]: I believe that nicotine is not addictive.
>
> Mr. [Edward A.] HORRIGAN [chairman, Liggett Group, Inc.]: I believe that nicotine is not addictive.

Mr. [Thomas E.] SANDEFUR [chairman, Brown & Williamson Tobacco Corp.]: I believe that nicotine is not addictive.

Mr. DONALD JOHNSTON [chairman, American Tobacco Co.]: And I, too, believe that nicotine is not addictive.[41]

This bit of theater, which admitted no discussion of what "addiction" might mean, was a trap. If the executives made any concessions to addiction, they invited regulation by the FDA, which the committee aimed to achieve and the executives were struggling to avoid. If they answered no, they were made to seem liars before a national audience. If they tried to get out of the trap by giving an even slightly reasoned and qualified answer, as James Johnston did, they were silenced. All of this cost antitobacco activists only the effort involved in arranging it. Whatever monetary costs there were to holding this hearing were paid by the public.

For the industry's opponents, this session was an emotional high point in the war against tobacco, an event that exhilarated them as it touched the consciousness of the public. They would all remember where they were on this day, just as ordinary citizens could remember where they were when the Japanese bombed Pearl Harbor or President Kennedy was assassinated.[42] At the request of a Democratic member of Congress from Massachusetts, Martin Meehan, the executive branch of the government opened a criminal investigation of the company executives to see whether it could indict them for perjury. To help the Department of Justice, which lacked enthusiasm, Meehan hired Cliff Douglas in August 1994 to write a "prosecution memorandum," which eventually grew to 111 pages and bore signatures of seven members of Congress.[43] More than a propaganda coup, the hearings appear in retrospect as a form of entrapment.[44]

The opponents of tobacco also scored a victory at the movies with the release in 1999 of The Insider, based on the saga of the whistleblower Jeffrey Wigand. After being fired from Brown & Williamson, where he had for several years been director of research and development, Wigand became a source of information for the antitobacco movement, including the FDA under David Kessler; Mike Moore, the Mississippi attorney general, for whose lawsuit he gave a deposition; the Department of Justice; a law firm of ABC, which was defending itself in the libel suit brought by Philip Morris; and Lowell Bergman, a producer of investigative reporting for the CBS show Sixty Minutes.[45] As a result of this media explosion, Wigand became, as Michael Orey observes, more than a witness: "He became a symbol for the antitobacco movement, a living embodiment of the righteousness of their cause."[46] He was helped in this by the industry's having hired private detectives in an attempt to discredit him. Besides portraying Wigand as heroic for revealing information about cigarette manufacture in violation of a legal agreement with his former employer, the media portrayed Brown & Williamson as having threatened murder in response.[47]

Not the least remarkable aspect of *The Insider* was that Mike Moore, a photogenic man, played himself as attorney general of Mississippi. (In 1994 he had been cited by *People* magazine as one of "the 25 most intriguing people of the year.") Campaigning against tobacco provided opportunities for uniting politics with celebrity. Moore and Scruggs attended the Beverly Hills premiere of the movie. Capture of the movie medium by tobacco's antagonists was the more notable given Hollywood's long love affair with cigarette smoke, which curled its way through many a black-and-white classic film. On and off the screen, movie stars in mid-century smoked, and manufacturers competed to place brands in their hands. *The Insider,* however, turned out to be a limited victory because it was a box office disappointment. The public was not gripped. Joe Roth, chairman of the Disney studio that produced it, told the *New York Times* a month after the movie opened that he was still hoping it "would find its audience." Box office returns at that point were less than a third of what would be needed to recover costs.[48]

Finally, there was the newest medium of all, the Worldwide Web, which utterly leveled the propaganda playing field. While Brown & Williamson went to court in a frantic attempt to protect stolen documents, the University of California library, a public agency, proceeded at little expense to make them available to anyone with a computer and a Web browser.

Money, which had been one source of Big Tobacco's comparative advantage in politics, could not prevent this media onslaught, which aided the industry's opponents in numerous ways. Individuals such as Gauthier and Wigand had their motives reinforced and their imaginations fired. Wigand claimed that it was watching B&W's Tommy Sandefur testify that nicotine was not addictive that pushed him over the edge into insurrection.[49] Mike Moore said that when he watched the tobacco executives "raise their right hands and swear that nicotine is not addictive . . . I said, 'We need to file and we need to file now.'" And file he did, within six weeks, although he also may have felt the need for speed because a tort reform act that would have made it harder to bring his case was due to take effect in Mississippi on July 1.[50] Cooperation among antitobacco activists became easier as prospects of success improved. Political movements are energized by the perception that they are making progress against powerful foes. Moreover, in the larger world, judges, juries, and the public generally were presumably affected—how much is impossible to say—by the damning media portrayals of the industry and recurring messages that shocking secrets were being revealed.

· Notes ·

1. See David Kessler's gratuitous reference to the use of the term "nigger farmhand" by the widow of Lloyd Vernon Jones, the farmer who had grown the experimental tobacco Y-1 for Brown & Williamson. Kessler, *A Question of Intent: A Great American Battle with a Deadly Industry* (New York: Public Affairs, 2001), 221.
2. Alan Marsh, "Tax and Spend: A Policy to Help Poor Smokers," *Tobacco Control* 6, no. 1 (spring 1997): 5. See also Alan J. Flint and Thomas E. Novotny, "Poverty Status and Cigarette Smoking Prevalence and Cessation in the United States, 1983–1993: The Independent Risk of Being Poor," *Tobacco Control* 6, no. 1 (spring 1997): 14–18.
3. "Vital Signs: Current Cigarette Smoking Among Adults Aged > 18 Years—United States, 2009," Morbidity and Mortality Weekly Report *(MMWR)*, http://www.cdc.gov/mmwr/preview, September 7, 2010, accessed September 9, 2010.
4. Richard Kluger, *Ashes to Ashes: America's Hundred-Year Cigarette War, the Public Health, and the Unabashed Triumph of Philip Morris* (New York: Knopf, 1996), 715.
5. The quotation is from the organization's Web site, http://www.tobaccofreekids.org/html/staff.html, accessed December 17, 1999. The Web address remains www.tobaccofreekids.org, accessed May 19, 2011.
6. The budget information is not from the Web site listed in note 5 but from Kluger, *Ashes to Ashes*, 765; and from Carrick Mollenkamp, Adam Levy, Joseph Menn, and Jeffrey Rothfeder, *The People vs. Big Tobacco: How the States Took on the Cigarette Giants* (Princeton, N.J.: Bloomberg, 1998), 185.
7. Mollenkamp et al., *The People vs. Big Tobacco*, 86.
8. Kluger, *Ashes to Ashes*, 303–306. The quote from Geller is on page 304.
9. Ibid., 307–310.
10. Ibid., 373.
11. In addition to Kluger, *Ashes to Ashes*, 308, see Michael Pertschuk, *Giant Killers* (New York: Norton, 1986), 50–52.
12. For a detailed account, see Stanton A. Glantz and Edith D. Balbach, *Tobacco War: Inside the California Battles* (Berkeley: University of California Press, 2000).
13. Stanton A. Glantz et al., *The Cigarette Papers* (Berkeley: University of California Press, 1996), 495–496; and Kluger, *Ashes to Ashes*, 475–478, 555–556.
14. Michael Pertschuk, *Smoke in Their Eyes: Lessons in Movement Leadership from the Tobacco Wars* (Nashville: Vanderbilt University Press, 2001), 40–42.
15. Kluger, *Ashes to Ashes*, 470–472, 477–478.

16. Peter Pringle, *Cornered: Big Tobacco at the Bar of Justice* (New York: Holt, 1998), 60–61.
17. Ibid., 74–75.
18. Glantz and Balbach, *Tobacco War*, xvi, 207–209.
19. Kluger, *Ashes to Ashes*, 559–561.
20. The original source is Richard Daynard, "Tobacco Liability Litigation as a Cancer Control Strategy," *Journal of the National Cancer Institute* 80 (March 1988): 9–13. I have relied on a summary in Lynn Mather, *Theorizing about Trial Courts: Lawyers, Policymaking, and Tobacco Litigation* 23 (fall 1998): 907–908.
21. The Web site remains active in 2011, and the staff is roughly the same size (Professor Daynard and twelve others). See http://www.tobacco.neu.edu, accessed May 19, 2011.
22. Hedrick Smith, *The Power Game: How Washington Works* (New York: Ballantine, 1988), 24, 29–30.
23. U.S. Department of Health, Education, and Welfare, U.S. Public Health Service, *Smoking and Health: A Report of the Surgeon General*, DHEW Publication No. (PHS) 79-50066 (Washington, D.C.: GPO, 1979), iii.
24. This list is drawn from Cornell W. Clayton, "Law, Politics, and the New Federalism: State Attorneys General as National Policymakers," *Review of Politics* 56 (summer 1994): 525–553, at 528. The Web site of the National Association of Attorneys General contains an overlapping yet somewhat different list of "typical powers": institute civil suits; represent state agencies and defend or challenge the constitutionality of legislative or administrative actions; enforce open meetings and records laws; revoke corporate charters; enforce antitrust prohibitions against monopolistic enterprises; enforce air, water pollution, and hazardous waste laws in a majority of states; handle criminal appeals and serious statewide criminal prosecutions; intervene in public utility rate cases; and enforce the provisions of charitable trusts. See http://www.naag.org.
25. *State of Florida v. Exxon Corporation*, 526 F.2d 266 (1976), 268–269, as cited in Clayton, "Law, Politics, and the New Federalism," 528. My discussion of state attorneys general is derived wholly from this article.
26. The changes are expertly summarized in Earl Black and Merle Black, *Politics and Society in the South* (Cambridge: Harvard University Press, 1987).
27. Peter J. Boyer, "The Yuppies: How They Took Over the Statehouse of Mississippi," *New York Times Magazine*, February 28, 1988, 24ff.
28. On Moore's political career before being elected attorney general, see Michael Orey, *Assuming the Risk: The Mavericks, the Lawyers, and the Whistle-Blowers Who Beat Big Tobacco* (Boston: Little, Brown, 1999), 240–243.
29. Mollenkamp et al., *The People vs. Big Tobacco*, 27.
30. Pringle, *Cornered*, 23.
31. Carolyn Lochhead, "The Growing Power of Trial Lawyers," *Weekly Standard*, September 23, 1996, 21ff.
32. Clayton, "Law, Politics, and the New Federalism," 540–543.
33. Pringle, *Cornered*, chap. 2.

34. Dan Zegart, *Civil Warriors: The Legal Siege on the Tobacco Industry* (New York: Delacorte, 2000), passim, but see especially 210–220.

35. Mark Curriden, "Tobacco Fees Give Plaintiffs' Lawyers New Muscle," *Dallas Morning News,* October 31, 1999, Business Section, 1. Motley's firm as of 1999 contained seventy-five members.

36. Alexander Hamilton, James Madison, and John Jay, *The Federalist Papers* (New York: New American Library, 1961), 83–84.

37. U.S. Department of Health and Human Services, Public Health Service, Office on Smoking and Health, *Smoking, Tobacco and Health: A Fact Book* (Washington, D.C.: GPO, n.d.), 23. This series of fact books was published periodically between 1969 and 1989. Data on cigarette advertising and promotion are compiled by the Federal Trade Commission.

38. U.S. Department of Health and Human Services, Centers for Disease Control and Prevention, *Morbidity and Mortality Weekly Report* (hereafter *MMWR*) 46, no. 20 (23 May 1997): 444–451. The 1987 report is reprinted in this publication with a current editorial note. See also *MMWR* 48, no. 3 (5 November 1999): 985–996.

39. A transcript of the program is in 9.1 *Tobacco Products Litigation Reporter* 4.1. There are secondary accounts of the *Day One* show in Zegart, *Civil Warriors,* passim; Kluger, *Ashes to Ashes,* 742–747; Philip J. Hilts, *Smoke Screen: The Truth behind the Tobacco Industry Cover-Up* (Reading, Mass.: Addison-Wesley, 1996), 113–120; and Pringle, *Cornered,* 33–34.

40. Pringle, *Cornered,* 39.

41. House Committee on Energy and Commerce, *Regulation of Tobacco Products: Hearings before the Subcommittee on Health and the Environment of the Committee on Energy and Commerce,* part 1, 103d Cong., 2d sess., serial no. 103-149 (Washington, D.C.: GPO, 1994), 628. The assertion that Bliley urged the executives to appear is from Kessler, *A Question of Intent,* 170.

42. Zegart, *Civil Warriors,* 127.

43. Ibid., 147, 154.

44. The government did not bring an indictment. In representations to the Department of Justice, the executives' lawyers argued that in stating that nicotine was not addictive, the witnesses were expressing an opinion, for which they could not be criminally prosecuted. See Ann Davis, "How a Lawyer Turned Tables in Tobacco Case," *Wall Street Journal,* October 4, 1999, B1. See also Marc Lacey, "Big Tobacco Grew Long Noses, but It's Not a Crime," *New York Times,* September 26, 1999, WK3.

45. The Bergman connection in particular brought fame to Wigand because CBS initially refused to broadcast Bergman's show about him. That refusal became a *cause célèbre* within the broadcasting industry, which became the subject of an article in *Vanity Fair,* which in turn became the film. See Marie Brenner, "The Man Who Knew Too Much," *Vanity Fair,* May 1996, 170–181.

46. Orey, *Assuming the Risk,* 309.

47. The FBI investigated this alleged threat, for which no substantiation was found. See the comment in Holman W. Jenkins Jr., "Forget the Movie and TV Show. I'll Wait for the Book," *Wall Street Journal,* November 3, 1999, A27.

48. Bernard Weinraub, "Outsider at Box Office," *New York Times,* December 3, 1999, B22.
49. Mollenkamp et al., *The People vs. Big Tobacco,* 111.
50. Michael Orey, "Fanning the Flames," *American Lawyer,* April 1996, 52ff. On the significance of the July 1, 1994, deadline, see the remarks of Michael Wallace in *Regulation by Litigation: The New Wave of Government-Sponsored Litigation* (New York: Manhattan Institute, 1999), 9.

CHAPTER SEVEN

The 1997 Settlement Dies in Congress

IN THIS AND THE NEXT two chapters, we return to the story of how a newly harsh regime of tobacco regulation was constructed in the 1990s. It did not come easily, and it did not come through legislation.

Congress did not agree to enact what the industry, state attorneys general, and tort lawyers had settled on in June 1997. This chapter will explain why not.

• The Tortuous Path to Defeat •

The 1997 settlement contained provisions that only the national legislature could enact—above all, extensive liability protections for the industry and authorization for the FDA to regulate tobacco. Congressional action was judged essential to a comprehensive resolution of the states' suits in combination with a new regime of regulation (although, as chapter 5 pointed out, the designers of the settlement expected to supplement the legislation with consent decrees).

One might have expected Congress to welcome this ready-made package. Here was a deal on which the participants had done much hard work, with behind-the-scenes help from the Clinton White House. They would continue to work hard. The industry began intensive lobbying in Washington immediately and planned a multimillion-dollar advertising campaign to promote the settlement.[1] Mike Moore and Richard Scruggs, its principal architects, would fly to Washington weekly from Mississippi to push for action. Scruggs's firm paid $2 million to three lobbying firms to promote the legislation.[2] However, other forces were also at work. The package was not complete politically.

The most zealous critics of Big Tobacco, activists on behalf of public health such as California's grassroots guerrilla Stanton Glantz, thought the deal was too soft on the industry. In their eyes, the tobacco companies were outlaws, with no right to sit at a bargaining table and no interests that were entitled to protection. They fought the deal from the moment it began to take shape. Mike Moore had met with one hundred such activists in a hotel ballroom in Chicago while the settlement was pending. Many wore stickers saying, "NO MOORE SELLOUT." Someone began by asking for a moment of silence to pay respect to victims of smoking. Then they assailed Moore with questions such as "Who gave you the right to make health policy for the country?" and "How could anyone give this bunch of killers amnesty in the courts?" After the meeting was over, Moore told Scruggs, who had known better than to attend, "I got no ass left at all, man."[3]

Once the deal was done, it was criticized by former FDA commissioner David Kessler, who had left the government to become dean of the Yale Medical School, for compromises it would make in his plan for regulating tobacco. Kessler's position was promptly endorsed by the White House and spelled out, in collaboration with C. Everett Koop and other public health advocates, in a formal set of recommendations to Congress. This advisory report, solicited by Rep. Henry Waxman and released on July 9, 1997, set the standard for the industry's critics in Congress, such as Waxman in the House and Edward M. Kennedy in the Senate.[4] The result was that the first congressional hearings on the settlement, rather than pitting the industry against its opponents, pitted one set of industry opponents—Koop, Kessler, and a dissident attorney general, Hubert Humphrey III of Minnesota—against another set, the attorneys general who had negotiated the settlement.

Tobacco farmers did not like the deal because it contained no protections for them. They had not been objects of the litigation and so had no claim to be represented in negotiations, but their interests were at stake. Moreover, members of Congress from tobacco-growing states were attentive to their interests. Often reluctant publicly to defend the manufacturers, members had no comparable reluctance in regard to growers, whom politicians and the press alike treated as innocent and deserving.

The Association of Trial Lawyers of America, the Washington lobby of the tort lawyers, did not like the deal because it would constrain future lawsuits against tobacco. Only those tort lawyers who had an immediate stake were in favor.[5]

Experts in antitrust law did not like the deal because it conferred on the tobacco companies broad immunity from antitrust laws. In a report solicited by Waxman and two colleagues in the House, the staff of the Federal Trade Commission warned that the cigarette manufacturers might profit from the settlement by increasing the price of cigarettes substantially above the amount of the annual payments to be made to governments.[6]

The public did not like the deal. An Associated Press poll taken in the summer of 1997 showed that two-thirds of the respondents thought that the companies would sell as many cigarettes as ever and that they should not be protected from liability.[7]

President Clinton welcomed the deal but declined to take the lead in pushing it through Congress, a role that a president might have been expected to play. In September 1997 he elected to outline broad principles for tobacco control, such as unfettered authority for the FDA, but not to propose a bill.[8] Further, his administration put the settlement at risk by asking for a share of the proceeds. In the fall of 1997 the Health Care Financing Administration notified state governments that the federal government would claim as much as 70 percent of their share of the industry payments intended as reimbursement for Medicaid expenses. This claim was solidly grounded, both legally and logically, in the fact that federal grants-in-aid to the states pay as much as 70 percent of the cost of the Medicaid program in any given state. (The federal share varies from state to state.)[9] Beyond that, as the president went to work on his budget for fiscal year 1999, he announced that he was planning to finance about 60 percent of $100 billion in new spending over five years from new tobacco revenues. Whether this financing would come from the federal government's anticipated share of settlement money or from new excise taxes or both was unclear. It was clear only that the administration expected to take maximum advantage of the industry's newly revealed vulnerability.[10]

Finally, congressional sponsors of the deal were lacking, and such sponsors usually are crucial to the formation of legislative coalitions, which they take the initiative in building. At one point Scruggs had alerted his brother-in-law, Trent Lott of Mississippi, the Republican majority leader in the Senate, that a deal was in the offing and had solicited help, but nothing came of that overture. Lott did not much like his brother-in-law's lawsuits. In general Congress had not been involved, and the chairman of the House Commerce Committee, Tom Bliley of Richmond, a longtime supporter of the industry, was bitter at not having been taken into its confidence.[11] Similarly, Henry Waxman, the leading congressional opponent of tobacco, was outraged at the effrontery of Matthew Myers of the National Center for Tobacco-Free Kids in undertaking to negotiate legislation directly with the industry, a role that he and his staff thought inappropriate for an advocate.[12] Waxman, like the grassroots activists in his home state of California, had been skeptical of the settlement from the outset, and he stood in the way of its swift endorsement by Congress.[13] Members generally were apprehensive about the scope and complexity of the proposed legislation, which fell within the jurisdiction of no fewer than seven Senate committees: Agriculture; Commerce, Science, and Transportation; Environment and Public Works; Finance; Indian Affairs; Judiciary; and Labor and Human Resources. Addressing Dr. Kessler, Sen. Olympia Snowe of Maine, a moderate Republican untainted by associations with the industry, expressed some of this apprehension:

> I think there is no question many of us share your concerns about the unprecedented nature of this settlement, not only in terms of impact, but in terms of scope. . . . I do not believe that the Congress should rush in blindly to codify this agreement without addressing a number of different issues raised by this settlement. . . . Many have said that this settlement would be a major step toward reducing smoking-related deaths, but that is only if this agreement is crafted properly.[14]

All of this apprehension introduced uncertainty into the prospects for action, yet tobacco had inescapably been placed on Congress's agenda, and the expectation among members and journalists early in 1998 was that something would happen. Democrats were "salivating" (the journalists' word) at the prospect of getting either strong antitobacco legislation for which they could claim credit or a fall campaign issue with which they could attack Republicans, who bore the political burden of having recently received large campaign contributions from the tobacco industry. The Republicans' leader in the House, Speaker Newt Gingrich, proclaimed that he would "not let Bill Clinton get to the left of me on this." "The Republican Party has been saddled with tobacco," Gingrich complained. "We're not going to support anything the industry is for."[15]

The McCain Bill

By the spring of 1998 tobacco legislation had acquired sponsors in the Senate—Kent Conrad of North Dakota for the Democrats and John McCain of Arizona for the Republicans. Because Republicans were the majority party and because he was chairman of the Commerce Committee—not to mention the fact that he turned out to have a zest for the task—McCain was the more important of the two. Two years later, as a candidate for the Republican nomination for the presidency, McCain would say that his mission as a politician was to combat evil, and nothing appeared more evil in the spring of 1998 than the tobacco companies, as their internal documents continued to be exposed to national view by state-level lawsuits. Major stories in January had focused on Reynolds's marketing to adolescents.[16] McCain had for several years declined to accept tobacco money, and now he refused to receive a visit from Geoffrey Bible, the CEO of Philip Morris, who was making the rounds of Capitol Hill in an effort to promote a bill endorsing the settlement.[17]

Moving to secure support from public health advocates and the Clinton White House, and confident of the industry's isolation, McCain put together a bill that was far harder on cigarette manufacturers than the 1997 settlement. It would have cost them more—$516 billion over twenty-five years instead of $368.5 billion—and given them less protection against lawsuits, such protection being the industry's overriding objective. The McCain bill offered no immunity from future class-action suits or punitive damage awards for past misconduct, and it raised the annual cap on liability payments from $5 billion to $6.5 billion, which was later raised further to $8 billion. It also increased from $2 billion to $3.5 billion the annual penalty the industry would have to pay if stipulated goals for reduction in youth smoking were not met. Whereas the cost of cigarettes per pack was expected to rise by $1.50 in ten years under the 1997 settlement, it was expected to rise by $2.55 under the McCain bill. Of that amount, an excise tax increase of $1.10 (above the existing tax of 24 cents) would go into a government trust fund, and the rest reflected retail price increases that would be needed to pay the costs imposed on the industry.[18] The McCain bill also expanded on the advertising restrictions in the 1997 settlement and on the proposed grant of regulatory authority to the Food and Drug Administration.

The Senate Commerce Committee approved the bill 19–1 on April 1, with only Missouri's John Ashcroft, a conservative Republican, in dissent. A week later, RJR president Steven Goldstone announced in a speech to the National Press Club that the industry would oppose it (see Box 7–1). Excluded from McCain's negotiations in any event, the industry was bailing out. "We are not," Goldstone said, "like a Brinks truck overturned on the highway," just lying there waiting to be robbed. A day after that, the industry began an advertising campaign that denounced the McCain bill as a government grab for money.[19] Yet in sacrificing the industry, McCain had not succeeded in securing support from the advocates for public health, who insisted that more changes must be made.[20] (For Koop's argument that the bill was too weak, see Box 7–2.)

It still seemed likely that something would pass. "We cannot be blackmailed or cajoled by the industry," McCain asserted.[21] But as April turned into May and May into June, the odds subtly shifted.

Box 7-1 RJR Chairman Claims McCain Bill Unfair

Remarks of Steven F. Goldstone, chairman and CEO, RJR Nabisco, to the National Press Club, Washington, D.C., April 8, 1998:

. . . Today, it is clear to me that we have failed in our effort to achieve a comprehensive resolution of the contentious issues surrounding tobacco in our country. The extraordinary settlement, reached on June 20th last year, that could have set the nation on a dramatically new and constructive direction regarding tobacco, is dead. And there is no process which is even remotely likely to lead to an acceptable comprehensive solution this year. By that I mean a comprehensive resolution that sets clear and fair rules for the future but acknowledges that tobacco companies have a legitimate right to exist in our country. . . .

I became chairman of RJR Nabisco two years ago. The company is the sixth largest consumer products company in the world. As chairman, I am accountable to thousands of shareholders and over eighty thousand employees all over the world. Our companies have developed some of the great brands of the world—such as Winston, Camel, Oreos, Ritz crackers, Planters nuts, and Lifesavers.

But I found it uniquely difficult to plan for the future when one of our companies is viewed as outside the mainstream of commerce—absorbed in massive litigation, under regulatory and political attack, with no normal working relationship with federal or state governments.

It was obvious to me that forty years of litigation—in which the industry never lost a case—was nonetheless not providing the best environment for my company and its employees. It was obvious to me that further escalation of the war . . . would not change anything for the better—for anybody—for my company, the public health community, or the country.

The result was a remarkable, comprehensive agreement—tougher and more wide-ranging than any of us had expected—that would have fundamentally changed the way tobacco products are regulated, marketed, and sold in this country. . . .

One attorney general, who had participated, said: "This is the biggest public health achievement and corporate settlement in the history of the country."

A leading public health advocate, Matt Myers, of the National Center for Tobacco-Free Kids, said: "This plan offers the best hope for protecting our children." He called it "the single most fundamental change in the history of tobacco control, *in the history of the world.*"

What has happened since June 20? Well, instead of any real consideration of the merits of the settlement, Washington has rushed to collect more tobacco revenues while playing the politics of punishment. . . .

The comprehensive resolution failed because some leading public health advocates who, seeing the realization of all the programs they had fought for years to obtain, and some others they never even dreamed of asking for, added a new cry: a demand for retribution. The comprehensive agreement, which should have been a public health advocate's dream come true, was left behind in favor of a surprising new public health agenda—the need to promote litigation and punitive damages against the industry.

The comprehensive resolution failed because the Congress, in the absence of leadership from the administration, dissolved into a taxing frenzy on a disfavored industry and the forty-five million customers it serves. . . .

. . . [T]he fair process of debate that we and the attorneys general had hoped for ended up instead [in] a process of discrimination and exclusion. The bill approved by the Senate Commerce Committee received significant input from interest groups of every shape and variety, *except* from the very industry sought to be regulated. We were expressly excluded. . . . It was a chilling reminder that many of our representatives in Washington believe that our industry simply has no right to be heard or to participate in the legislative process in the United States Congress. . . .

Why did this political process break down? My answer is one word—money.

[Three hundred sixty-eight billion dollars] is apparently not enough to satisfy all the wishes of the federal government. The amount has to be doubled or even tripled to pay for all sorts of new programs unrelated to kids' smoking. Just take a look at the president's budget submission this year and you get the idea. . . .

On top of Washington's urge to use the tobacco controversy as a unique opportunity to raise revenue, the debate has also taken on a truly coercive, big-brother tone. Not only do politicians not think twice about proposing huge tax burdens on adult smokers, but the adults of our country apparently cannot be trusted or allowed to exercise their own personal judgment freely.

I'll give you just one example. The Commerce Committee bill, in a stroke of a pen, would completely eliminate the camel image from my company's packaging. This is a trademark Reynolds has used for more than eighty years. It is known worldwide. Yet the committee determines, with no debate, that a picture of a camel on a pack of cigarettes is too dangerous, even for adults, to see.

So I come back to it. The legislative process that produced these proposals does not give me any hope that it can produce a reasonable or rational result. . . .

We're going to talk about protecting our constitutional right to advertise, market, and communicate with adults, and protecting the rights of adults in a free society to hear us and make their own personal judgments, free from government coercion. We're going to see if adults want their federal government to censor the images they are permitted to see, like that dangerous camel. . . .

This may all sound simply like political rhetoric to you, but I assure you that it is not. These are real issues facing real people involved in this business. They are issues that could not be more serious to them, and to me as a chief executive officer. I have a responsibility to them and a duty to my shareholders and employees to do what I can to advance their interests in this commercial enterprise. . . .

Source: 13.2 *Tobacco Products Litigation Reporter* 4.9.

Box 7-2 Koop Tells Senate to Get Tough on Tobacco

Remarks of C. Everett Koop, M.D., former surgeon general of the United States, to the Democratic caucus of the U.S. Senate, April 20, 1998:

. . . May I say in a preambulatory way that it is time we stood back and assessed the industry with which we are dealing. . . .

Abundant evidence has established the causal relationship between the use of tobacco and cancer, cardiovascular disease, chronic obstructive lung disease, peripheral vascular disease, stroke, and a variety of serious pediatric maladies in children exposed to environmental tobacco smoke.

These illnesses are so severe that nearly one of every five deaths in the U.S. are attributed to tobacco.

Now the world knows the amazing, consistent, antisocial behavior of the tobacco industry—that the industry has deceived the American people with bald-faced lies about the harmful effects of their products and the addictiveness of nicotine. . . .

Please recall that as recently as 1994 the seven top executives of the country's largest tobacco manufacturers stood before a committee of Congress and testified under oath that tobacco does not kill and nicotine is not addictive. While denying that they were marketing to kids and creating a phony controversy over smoking and health, their actions said otherwise. We all know about Joe Camel. . . .

We are dealing with an industry where all of the major tobacco companies knew for longer than did the government, and in greater depth than did the government, the harmful effects of the use of tobacco and the addictiveness of nicotine.

They also knew that their products were lethal to about one-third of their customers. They deliberately marketed to children and minorities. They understood that nicotine was an addictive drug and used that knowledge to alter their products to gain the largest number of steady customers possible.

That was behavior egregious enough, but to deny this knowledge, to lie about the known health effects of their products and to masquerade as an industry functioning within the ethical and moral norms of our society, is unacceptable.

When I refer to the tobacco industry, I am not referring to those who grow tobacco, those who transport it, those who sell its manufactured products in convenience stores—I am referring to the decision-making executive bodies of the various tobacco companies and their lawyers who willfully set about a four-decade course of deceiving the American people. . . .

Although I tried to believe that the so-called "settlement" made available to the public on June [20], 1997, might be what it was advertised to be— a new and improved way of the tobacco industry doing business—after reading it I pronounced it dead on arrival because it was a sell out to the tobacco industry and bought them the security they needed for financial planning for the next twenty-five years, while it did very little for public health. . . .

We [David Kessler and I] assembled a group representing twenty-three distinguished public health organizations . . . and were able to give a report

to Congress and to the White House . . . that . . . was a consensus statement. . . .

. . . [T]he Koop-Kessler report [is] the gold standard against which to
measure any tobacco legislation. [It defines] ten essential public health ele-
ments of . . . legislation. . . :

1. Full authority for the Food and Drug Administration to regulate
   nicotine as a drug and tobacco products as devices.
2. Strong children's smoking-reduction targets, with company-spe-
   cific penalties high enough to stimulate action by manufacturers.
3. Guaranteed and immediate per-pack price increases sufficient to
   reduce children's purchases.
4. Statutory restrictions on advertising and promotion, as well as
   ongoing FDA authority to restrict advertising and promotion in the
   future.
5. Funding for tobacco prevention and treatment programs, including
   counteradvertising, professional and public education, and scientifically sound smoking cessation services.
6. Funding biomedical and behavioral research on prevention and
   treatment, as well as on addiction and tobacco-related illnesses.
7. Elimination of exposure to secondhand smoke in the workplace
   and in public places.
8. No preemption of stronger state and local laws.
9. Full disclosure of all tobacco documents.
10. No special liability protections for the tobacco industry. . . .

The liability portion of S. 1415 is the most egregious to the public health
community. . . .

In view of their behavior, there is no reason in the world why we of the
public health community should agree to, or this Congress should facilitate,
anything which grants this rogue industry immunity or limited liability. . . .

It is this portion of the bill that led to the well-orchestrated departure of
Mr. Goldstone and his friends from what he still erroneously thought were
tobacco settlement talks.

The entire framework of tobacco legislation has changed in the past few
weeks. The companies have walked away from the table. . . . Don't believe
them when they cry these crocodile tears. It's a clever attempt to make the
Commerce Committee bill look strong when it's not.

And many tobacco documents recently have been made public. There
will be a steady drumbeat of news stories now about suppressed science and
perjury.

You never needed tobacco industry permission to act. But both of these
events should free the Congress to get the strongest possible bill to protect
children and limit the damage to the health of the nation.

Source: 13.2 Tobacco Products Litigation Reporter 4.15. Dr. Koop's remarks
have been slightly rearranged.

Republicans seemed less fearful of being caught on the wrong side of the fight, at odds with public opinion. Several developments gave them the protection they needed.

Probably most important was the industry's advertising campaign, which included the purchase of television time in thirty to fifty markets a week. One series of TV spots used "man on the street" interviews of one sentence or less with working-class people who opposed the bill. Another, featuring an exploding cuckoo clock, declared: "Washington has gone cuckoo again. Washington wants to raise the price of cigarettes so high there'll be a black market in cigarettes with an unregulated access to kids." To save money—and also to keep a low profile among the media elite, who would probably have derided the ads—the spots did not run in Washington, New York, and Los Angeles.[22] However, the industry did run discreet print ads inside the Washington Beltway in outlets that decision makers would be likely to see. Thus, a full-page ad in the *National Journal* on May 16, 1998, asked, "What Do Americans Think Supporters of the Tobacco Bill Are Really Interested In?" (see Figure 7–1) and answered that query with a bar chart showing that 20 percent thought supporters were interested in cutting teen smoking by raising cigarette prices, whereas 70 percent thought they were interested in getting additional tax revenue for the federal government. The ad concluded by saying, "It isn't about protecting kids, it's about raising taxes," provided a toll-free number from which the caller could be patched to congressional offices, and carried the signatures of the five major tobacco companies.[23] (For an example of counteradvertising by antitobacco groups, see Figure 7–2.)

In addition to the ads sponsored by the tobacco industry, others from its ally, the U.S. Chamber of Commerce, appeared inside the Beltway and hammered at the theme that trial lawyers stood to profit handsomely from a tobacco settlement. Trial lawyers have been major campaign contributors to the Democratic Party, just as tobacco companies were at the time big contributors to the Republicans.[24]

A second protective factor was the opportunity for Republicans to cast floor votes that at least seemed adverse to the interests of the tobacco companies. The McCain bill reached the floor in mid-May and occupied the Senate, with time out for a lengthy Memorial Day recess, until mid-June. One amendment, coming from Republican senator Judd Gregg of New Hampshire, removed all liability limits from the McCain bill, which had much reduced them in any event. The elimination of what remained, an annual cap on what the industry would have to pay, elicited winning support from an unlikely coalition of left-wing Democrats, who genuinely opposed the limits, and right-wing Republicans,

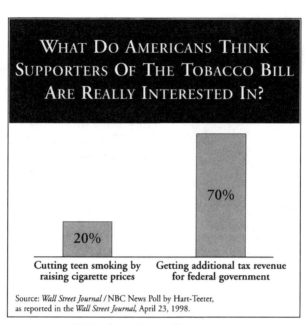

Figure 7-1 Tobacco Industry Ad Opposing the McCain Bill.

Will Big Tobacco Ever Tell the Truth?

They said smoking doesn't cause cancer, that nicotine isn't addictive, and that they don't target kids.

And now they say tobacco legislation won't work.

The tobacco industry has lied for more than 40 years. Now they're pushing the idea that a comprehensive tobacco policy is a big government solution that won't help kids.

That's another lie, and the American people know it.

A new poll* shows that more than 80 percent of the public believe Congress should pass a national tobacco control policy to reduce tobacco use among kids. In fact, a large majority says the tobacco industry's opposition makes them favor legislation even more.

It's time for Congress to pass a tough, effective tobacco bill. No weak imitations.
Don't protect Big Tobacco.

American Cancer Society • Allergy and Asthma Network-Mothers of Asthmatics, Inc.• American Academy of Pediatrics • American Association for Respiratory Care • American Association of Physicians of Indian Origin • American College of Cardiology • American College of Physicians • American College of Preventive Medicine • American Heart Association • American Psychological Association • American School Health Association • American Society of Internal Medicine • Association of American Medical Colleges • Association of Schools of Public Health • Children's Defense Fund • Community Anti-Drug Coalitions of America • Federation of Behavioral, Psychological and Cognitive Sciences • The General Board of Church and Society of The United Methodist Church • The HMO Group • Interreligious Coalition on Smoking or Health • Latino Council on Alcohol & Tobacco • National Association of County and City Health Officials • National Association of Local Boards of Health • National Association of Pediatric Nurse Associates and Practitioners • National Hispanic Medical Association • National Mental Health Association • Oncology Nursing Society • Partnership for Prevention • Society for Research on Nicotine and Tobacco • Society of Behavioral Medicine • Summit Health Coalition

Tobacco vs. Kids. Where America draws the line.

CAMPAIGN for TOBACCO-FREE Kids ™

To learn more, call 202-296-5469 or visit our web site at www.tobaccofreekids.org.
The National Center for Tobacco-Free Kids, 1707 L Street NW, Suite 800, Washington, DC 20036

* Market Facts' TeleNation survey of 1,000 adults, April 13-15, 1998.   © 1998 National Center for Tobacco-Free Kids

Figure 7-2 Antitobacco Ad Supporting National Tobacco Legislation. Reprinted with permission of Campaign for Tobacco-Free Kids.

who were taking cover in an anti-industry vote while, presumably, trying to make the bill so extreme and one-sided as to guarantee that it would die. Democratic senator Robert G. Torricelli of New Jersey remarked in early June that the legislation was "in some trouble because the people who want no legislation at all are trying to make it so good that it becomes bad."[25] Indeed, Matthew Myers believed that passage of the Gregg amendment doomed the bill.[26]

There was protection, too, in the number and diversity of amendments that developed on the floor. Some were extraneous, such as those to reduce taxes on married couples, pay for vouchers for children to attend private and parochial schools, and give grants to the states for child-care programs. There were also new programs to combat drug abuse, apart from antitobacco programs. These changes, which came from the Republicans, cut into the antitobacco programs that could be financed from the bill, but more important, they helped opponents to make the argument that this was not an antitobacco bill at all but a mixed bag. At the last minute the Senate passed by one vote, 49 to 48, an amendment that would have limited the fees that private lawyers could realize from the state governments' tobacco suits.[27] All of this amending and debating took time, under circumstances in which the passage of time favored the opposition.

Finally, Republicans had their backbones stiffened by members of their own party who were bold enough to oppose the bill publicly— Ashcroft, of course, who had been the lone dissenter in the Commerce Committee, and also Phil Gramm of Texas and Don Nickles of Oklahoma, the majority whip. "I want to kill this bill," Nickles said in mid-May. "I think it's a bad bill." Gramm remarked in early June: "This bill has no constituency except people who want to raise a whole lot of money."[28] Sen. Orrin Hatch of Utah, with a record as an opponent of tobacco, called the McCain bill "pitiful" and warned that it could result in bankruptcy for the companies and a black market in cigarettes. Passed over by the party leadership in favor of McCain as the Republicans' point man on tobacco, Hatch had sponsored a bill based on the settlement.[29]

The Senate killed the bill on June 17 by defeating an attempt to invoke cloture—an end to debate, which requires a sixty-vote supermajority—and then voting to send the bill back to the Commerce Committee. In the key vote, forty-three Democrats and fourteen Republicans voted for cloture—in effect, for proceeding to act on the McCain bill—while two Democrats, Wendell Ford of Kentucky and Charles Robb of Virginia—two states that are home to both the cultivation and the manufacture of tobacco—joined forty Republicans in voting against. Senator McCain responded with an angry speech that attacked his party for killing the bill and brought Democrats to their feet in applause.[30]

Understanding Defeat

Two contrasting interpretations of the bill's defeat gained currency. One was that tobacco's opponents had overreached. So blinded were they by hatred of the tobacco companies that they had attached greater importance to punishing them than to achieving legislation. This theory was advanced by the dispassionate Richard Kluger, who was no friend of the industry but was intimately acquainted with the subject of tobacco politics after having written *Ashes to Ashes*.[31] Some tort lawyers, deeply familiar with events and disappointed by the outcome, also espoused this view. "Tobacco did not kill this agreement," tort attorney John Coale would say a year later. "It was the C. Everett Koops and David Kesslers of the world who did. It is almost impossible to work with the advocacy groups. . . . If we gave them $100, they wanted $105."[32]

The other interpretation, advanced by editorial writers of the liberal establishment and by President Clinton, was that the Republicans, as usual, had sold out to the industry, for whom they were stooges. The Republicans in the Senate "simply cannot wean themselves from tobacco money," the *New York Times* said. "Their craven performance . . . will not be forgotten by voters in the election season."[33]

To appraise more objectively what happened, it will help to give extended consideration to two forces that play an important part in legislative politics—public opinion and money.

· Public Opinion on Tobacco Regulation ·

In retrospect, it is mildly puzzling that Republicans seemed so frightened as consideration of the tobacco legislation began. The poll results that were available at that time on the subject of smoking would have provided mixed cues. On one hand, polls for years had shown strong opposition to youth smoking and strong support for prohibitions on sales to minors and on advertising directed at them.[34] Understanding this, and faced with the incontrovertible fact that adult smoking had dropped dramatically since the 1960s, critics of smoking inside and outside the Clinton administration put great emphasis on protecting "kids." Also, polls going all the way back to 1939 revealed public distrust of the tobacco companies.[35] The public had strongly supported bans on smoking in public buildings, workplaces, and airplanes.[36]

Moreover, support for regulation had increased in the 1980s and 1990s.[37]

Public support for higher state and federal excise taxes on cigarettes had also risen, going from 39 percent of poll respondents in 1977 to 67 percent in 1998, a result consistent with actual voting behavior in several states.[38] Between 1988 and 1996, voters in Arizona, California, Massachusetts, Michigan, and Oregon passed initiatives that substantially increased tobacco excise taxes and earmarked some or all of the proceeds for tobacco control programs.

On the other hand, polls also showed with remarkable consistency that respondents were inclined to blame smokers rather than tobacco companies for the consequences of smoking, a finding reinforced by the pattern of jury verdicts in individual cases over the years. These verdicts could not be attributed solely to the indubitably superior litigating resources of the tobacco industry. Polls done in 1997, roughly contemporaneous with the settlement between the industry and the attorneys general, showed that respondents by large margins believed that the cigarette companies should not be held legally or financially responsible for smokers' illnesses. From 64 to 76 percent of respondents in five different polls said that smokers themselves were mainly to blame, suggesting a strong cultural foundation for an ethic of individual responsibility.[39] In late July 1997, immediately after Mississippi had settled its suit against the industry for several billion dollars, more than half of the respondents to a Hart-Teeter poll disagreed "somewhat" or "strongly" with the statement that "tobacco companies should be required to refund states for the cost of medical care for poor people who contract diseases related to smoking."[40]

When the companies backed out and the tobacco legislation began to unravel in April, the public reacted by favoring "voluntary restrictions that the tobacco companies would accept" (33 percent) or leaving things "as they are now" (31 percent), rather than forcing "a settlement on the tobacco companies" (28 percent); 8 percent were "unsure."[41] A majority of respondents to a National Journal/NBC poll said that they thought the government was doing too much (28 percent) or about the right amount (31 percent) to regulate tobacco, while 38 percent thought it was doing too little.[42] As of April 1998, 55 percent of respondents to an Opinion Dynamics poll thought drinking was a bigger problem among teens than smoking, while 25 percent judged the two problems of equal seriousness, and 18 percent thought smoking more serious.[43]

Two specialists in public health who were disappointed by the demise of the McCain bill concluded after reviewing nine public opinion surveys taken between mid-1997 and mid-1998 that "a comprehensive tobacco proposal never garnered strong public support." Of the surveys, only two showed majority support for the legislation, and then by narrow margins. These authors identified five reasons for opposition to the bill:

> . . . the size of the tax increase on cigarettes, the perception that the bill involved too much governmental interference in people's lives, the belief that the government would spend funds raised from the legislation on the wrong things, the fact that the public did not believe that enacting the bill would lead to a reduction in teenage smoking, and lastly, concern that the bill was too favorable to the tobacco companies.[44]

The authors concluded that the public would have been more supportive if it had believed that the companies, rather than tobacco users, would bear the cost of the penalties.

It is possible that poll results are misleading. Because much can depend on sampling techniques and how questions are framed, one would like to confirm polling results with other kinds of evidence. For this purpose, a study of tobacco control enforcement done in the mid-1990s is helpful. The authors interviewed a variety of sources—state and local officials, restaurant owners, tobacco vendors, antitobacco activists, and industry representatives—in seven states, including two large ones, New York and California, that had strong control programs. They excluded the tobacco-growing and -manufacturing states, such as North Carolina and Virginia. Sympathetic to the cause of tobacco control, they were "particularly surprised" to find that "the relative salience of the smoking issue appeared to be low in comparison with other public policy issues. Implicitly or explicitly, respondents indicated that tobacco control often failed to ignite the passions of state legislators or city council members or even of the public at large."[45]

Consider also the philosophic testimony of Mike Synar, who as a member of Congress from Oklahoma was one of the industry's most active opponents until he was defeated in a Democratic primary in 1994. Speaking from sixteen years' experience in office, Synar told a conference of antitobacco activists in the spring of 1995 that they had "confused the public's support on the facts . . . with their lack of support on the values." He summarized the public's attitude as: "'Yes, I don't want to smoke. Yes, I don't want my kids to smoke. Yes, I don't like smoking in a bar and a restaurant, but don't tell me I can't do that.'" He told his friendly audience that "we need to understand that just because we may be right on substance, we may not be right on the values that Americans really respond to."[46]

Why then were Democrats so gleeful and Republicans so anxious in the spring of 1998 when confronted with the McCain bill—assuming the journalistic accounts that portrayed them in this way were correct?[47] There are at least two possible explanations. The main one is that the public's policy preferences or opinions about who is responsible for smoking and what if anything should be done about it are not the most important considerations from a politician's point of view. What the Republicans feared was not being on the wrong side of a policy debate but being tarred with tobacco money. They feared that votes against the bill could be interpreted as evidence that they had sold out to the industry—that they were, in a word, corrupt. This fear was made worse by uncertainty. They had to guess what the public might think and what opposing candidates might say several months later in their campaign ads. Today's poll results are no protection on election day.

Another explanation is that politicians' perceptions are shaped not just by poll data, however eagerly they may consume such data, but also by the pressure of their immediate surroundings. Cues emanate from within the governing community of Washington as well as from physically distant constituencies. As governing has become a full-time job, today's legislators, even though they fly back to their districts frequently, spend much more time in the nation's capital than did their predecessors of previous decades. If Democrats are visibly gleeful and if other Republicans are ducking for cover, and if the media that report on Washington are saying that that is so, it takes fortitude for a Republican member to believe that it need not be true.

In order to summon such fortitude, Republicans needed a reason to believe that opponents would not derive an advantage from their defense of the industry. This was where the industry's apparently effective advertising campaign came in. Since the 1960s voters had developed a strong distrust of American government, and hence were receptive to the claim that Washington had gone "cuckoo" and was engaged in a campaign of aggrandizement through tax increases. The claim, after all, had a solid factual basis in that cigarette excise taxes were to rise so sharply. Likewise, it had an ample basis, surely very much in the minds of congressional Republicans if not in those of the public, in President Clinton's budget-time boast of all that he was going to do with tobacco revenues. The fact that these advertising messages were in the air was reassuring to Republicans. Arguably they, not the public, were the ultimate target. "The message is bounced off the satellite—the satellite being the American people—and comes back to the member," according to the campaign's designer, Carter Eskew.[48] It was the media hit on Washington that mattered in the end, even if, ironically, the messages were not broadcast in Washington TV markets.

Republicans grew more confident as they felt the "bounce." After the bill died, numerous polls indicated that the Republicans were not likely to suffer in November.[49] Democrats still held out hope that they could use the tobacco issue against Republicans who had accepted large contributions from the industry, but privately they conceded that the public did not have much interest in the tobacco legislation.[50] When the November elections came, the results in fact failed to demonstrate public support for the antitobacco crusade. Two Democratic attorneys general who had been among the most vigorous opponents of the industry—Hubert Humphrey III in Minnesota and Scott Harshbarger in Massachusetts—were defeated in campaigns for governor.[51]

· The Power of Industry Money ·

Money has not been the cigarette industry's only resource in politics, but it has been the one most readily available. Probably the industry's greatest political asset, or at least the one in which historically it put most faith, was the popularity of its product. At the outset of the political contest over tobacco use, the industry had confidence that the weakness of the human race would combine with the robustness of American democracy to protect it. Put simply: People wanted to smoke, and American government would do what a majority of the people wanted. The industry proved to be more wrong on both counts than one would have guessed in, say, 1964. By the late 1990s the per capita consumption of cigarettes had been cut roughly in half. And the political system, rather than being ruled simply by majority opinion, was open to influence by intensely motivated minorities in combination with the media.

A second industry resource has been economic importance. This is to be measured not just by the number of manufacturing employees, which is really quite small (fewer than thirty thousand persons in the early 1990s), but also by the number and financial stakes of tobacco growers, stockholders, distributors and retailers, suppliers, advertising agencies and outlets, and consumers. On one hand, gross measures of the economic importance of the cigarette industry were impressively large. In 1985 domestic consumers spent more than $30 billion on cigarettes. After $8.9 billion in federal, state, and local excise taxes was subtracted, distributors received $7.6 billion and manufacturers $13.7 billion. The manufacturers spent $1.7 billion for purchases of domestic tobacco, $2.1 billion on other materials, $1.5 billion on their payrolls, and $2.5 billion on advertising and promotion, among other expenditures. Their net income was $3.4 billion. For growers, tobacco had a high yield of income per acre, more than $3,200 in 1988, a figure far surpassing that for other staple crops such as corn, wheat, cotton, and soybeans.[52] Also, government marketing quotas and price supports enabled the survival of small tobacco farms—"family" farms, as distinct from large corporate enterprises—and the family farm is a beloved American symbol. Here was an industry that one would expect elected politicians to respect.

On the other hand, the hard core of it—growers and major manufacturing plants—has been concentrated in a single region. Senators from Kentucky, North Carolina, and Virginia, and representatives from particular districts within those states as well as South Carolina, Tennessee, and Georgia, have historically been strong partisans of tobacco. Kentucky's agricultural economy, containing many small, family-owned farms, has been especially dependent on it. As of 1997 nearly forty-five thousand of its eighty-two thousand farms grew tobacco, harvesting about 5.7 acres of it per farm. The value of Kentucky's tobacco crop averaged more than $800 million a year between 1990 and 1996, and tobacco accounted for more than 40 percent of the net cash return from agricultural sales in the state.[53] However, the relative economic importance of the tobacco industry diminished over time, both regionally and nationally, even before the attack on tobacco gained political momentum. Tobacco production in the U.S. peaked at 2.34 billion pounds in 1963, fluctuated between 1963 and 1975, and thereafter declined.[54] By 1995 it had fallen to 1.32 billion pounds. Domestic acreage in 1987, at 602,000, was less than half what it had been in the 1950s. Maybe the behemoth was not so big after all.

Constantly under attack for the effects of smoking on health, and unable to get by just on the popularity of its product or importance to the nation's economy, the tobacco industry fought hard to protect itself in politics by means of advertising, lobbyists and political consultants, and campaign contributions and other favors for politicians, such as speaking fees, subsidized travel, and resort vacations. All of these tactics are familiar features of contemporary American politics, by no means peculiar to the tobacco industry, yet they were readily available to it because of its wealth. As the threat to the industry rose in the 1990s, so, of course, did its spending for these purposes. And so did the rage of its critics, who, believing that the industry is per se illegitimate, view any steps it takes to protect itself in politics as illegitimate, too.

Campaign Spending

Citizen watchdog groups documented the campaign spending. A publication of the Center for Public Integrity reported that from 1987 to 1996 the tobacco industry gave $17.7 million to congressional candidates and another $12.7 million to the two major political parties. In addition, the industry paid members of Congress nearly $2 million in speakers' fees and provided them and their staffs with dozens of paid trips for conferences and "fact-finding" in such destinations as Boca Raton, Florida; Las Vegas, Nevada; Palm Springs, California; Scottsdale, Arizona; San Juan, Puerto Rico; and Singapore. On a smaller scale, companies also gave cartons of cigarettes to congressional staff members.[55]

Until the mid-1990s, money was distributed in a bipartisan fashion, but after the Republicans won the House in 1994 and the Clinton administration joined the antitobacco coalition in 1995–1996, donations heavily favored the Republicans. In 1995 tobacco companies gave the Republican Party (as distinct from individual candidates) an unprecedented $2.4 million. Tobacco industry PACs gave $841,120 to Republican members of Congress in 1995, about twice what they had given only two years before ($422,221).[56]

Lobbying

Spending on lobbying is harder to establish than are contributions to political parties. Lobbyists can be directly employed by the companies, which may choose to maintain Washington offices. They also can be employed by the industry as a whole; according to Richard Kluger, the Tobacco Institute had a Washington-based staff of around 75 in the early 1990s and an additional 125 lobbyists under contract in state governments, all at a cost of $5 million to $10 million a year. Although Philip Morris, as industry leader, was increasingly taking charge of political activity, the institute was still host to weekly skull sessions run by lawyers from Covington and Burling, an eminent Washington firm, on how to target the industry's lobbying.[57] The companies can also employ law firms or professional political consultants to represent their interests.

In 1997, the year in which the battle to enact the settlement with the attorneys general began, the industry spent more than $30 million on lobbying and campaign contributions, of which the bulk was for lobbying. Its lobbyists were an "all-star cast" that included a former Democratic majority leader of the Senate, George Mitchell; a former Republican majority leader of the Senate, Howard Baker; and a former Democratic governor of Texas, Ann Richards.[58] For 1998, when the battle to achieve the settlement continued and then metamorphosed into a campaign against the McCain bill, the industry reported an unprecedented $58 million in lobbying expenditures. Much of this spending went to Washington law and lobbying firms, with the biggest share, more than $7.5 million, going to Verner, Liipfert, Bernhard, McPherson and Hand, the acknowledged leader of the Washington lobbying industry. Cigarette manufacturers also got lobbying and consulting services from Charles

Black of Black, Kelly, Scruggs and Healy, a prominent lobbyist with Republican affiliations, and from Haley Barbour, a former chairman of the Republican National Committee. The *Washington Post* reported that virtually every major law firm in Washington with a lobbying practice had a stake in the outcome, on one side or the other.[59] The Campaign for Tobacco-Free Kids, which at first was allied with the industry in the effort to secure approval of the settlement, received an extra $6 million from the Robert Wood Johnson (RWJ) Foundation in 1997 to support its lobbying. This amount was over and above the $9.5 million that it had received from RWJ and other foundations for its normal operations.[60]

Advertising and Promotion

As measured by the Federal Trade Commission, spending on advertising and promotion of cigarettes rose between 1986 and 1991 from $2.4 billion to $4.6 billion per year.[61] Spending for political purposes is hard to trace because it may be done through front groups. In the big referenda campaigns in California, for example, the industry did not act in its own name but helped finance organizations to campaign for its position under such names as San Franciscans Against Government Intrusion, Californians Against Regulatory Excess, Californians Against Unfair Tax Increases, Californians for Common Sense, and Californians for Fair Business Practices.[62]

An organization of smokers, the National Smokers Alliance, was set up in 1993 by Philip Morris with $1 million in seed money. After examining tax records, the Center for Public Integrity concluded that only $73,596 of the alliance's $9 million in revenue in 1996 was attributable to individual dues.[63] In the campaign to defeat the McCain bill, ads were signed with company names. In roughly two months in 1998 the industry spent a reported $40 million on radio and TV ads to defeat that bill.[64]

Return on Investment?

What did the industry buy with all these millions in political spending? According to its critics, it bought Congress. In their eyes, money determines politics. Ripley Forbes, Henry Waxman's legislative aide, told Kluger: "There's no magic in it, it's a very basic issue—their power and influence starts and ends with their money."[65] That was the view as well of the Public Citizen's Health Research Group: "Every year nearly half a million Americans are killed by tobacco products and yet the U.S. Congress does almost nothing because it has been *paid* to do nothing."[66] But if money were so powerful in politics, the industry, with so much of it, would not have been in the weakened position that it was in as of 1997. It had spent a great deal on the state level but had not stemmed the tide of tobacco control legislation there. The industry lost a 1988 tax-increase referendum in California even though it outspent its opponents by $21.4 million to $1.6 million. Four years later, it lost a similar referendum in Massachusetts in which it outspent the opposition by a ratio of almost ten to one ($7.3 million versus $800,000).[67] Kluger reported that it spent $3.3 million in 1994 trying to stave off a tripling of the cigarette tax in Michigan, and an estimated $12.5 million in an attempt to win an industry-initiated referendum in California that would have overridden all three hundred or so local regulations with one statewide regulation. He then added parenthetically, "The industry lost both fights."[68]

In Congress the industry had the considerable advantage of typically trying to stop legislation in a body that poses many obstacles to action. Even its severest critics conceded as much: "The tobacco lobby distributes hush money to the legislators not to buy action but to buy inaction," a Citizen's Public Health Research Group report says.[69] Consider this rather amiable remark from one of the industry's most persistent congressional opponents, the late representative Synar:

> There's a lot of [the tobacco industry's] financial clout up here, and they do their best to reward their friends and punish their enemies. . . . [A]nd they don't pick favorites. . . . They're with the Black Caucus, the Hispanic Caucus, the Democratic Party, the Republican Party. They want [members of Congress] to like 'em so it's uncomfortable to go after them. They're not really trying to accomplish an agenda, they're just trying to stop one from ever being mounted against them.[70]

Reports of the Public Citizen's Health Research Group undertook to show that members who received tobacco money tended to vote in support of the industry's interests. But even assuming a causal link between contributions and votes, it is not easy to establish the direction of causality if only because the money can be given *after* the favorable vote, in appreciation of it—though even then, of course, the donation may anticipate favorable votes yet to come. A further confounding factor is that leading recipients of the tobacco companies' money were members who on partisan and ideological grounds or because of the composition of their constituencies were most likely to vote in support of the industry anyway—or they occupied positions of party leadership or key committee positions.

The group's 1992 report identified "cigarette packs"—that is, groups of top twenty recipients of cigarette money—for the Senate and the House. They consisted disproportionately of members from the tobacco states—North Carolina, Kentucky, and Virginia—along with conservative Republicans and, in the House, selected members of what was then the Democratic leadership. The leader in the Senate between 1987 and 1992 was Robert Kasten of Wisconsin, a free-market Republican whose state was the headquarters of Miller Brewing, which was then a Philip Morris company. Following him were Jesse Helms of North Carolina, Wendell Ford of Kentucky, Majority Leader Robert Dole, and Mitch McConnell of Kentucky, in that order. Of senators running for reelection in 1992, only one, Democrat John Glenn of Ohio, received no tobacco money. The top recipient in the House, with $26,198 in contributions from January 1, 1991, through June 30, 1992, was the Democratic majority leader, Richard Gephardt. He was followed by Tom Bliley of Virginia, whose Richmond district included Philip Morris's research headquarters and a large manufacturing plant.[71]

It becomes difficult to ascertain to what extent the industry was rewarding or reinforcing its "natural" friends and to what extent it may have been making friends among members who otherwise might be indifferent. It was certainly doing a great deal of the former and likely doing some of the latter. Recipients of the money who represented tobacco-producing states declined to be put on the defensive about this subject. When the Center for Public Integrity sent letters to members of Congress in the wake of Waxman's hearings to ask whether they would continue accepting tobacco money, Republican senator McConnell of Kentucky replied yes and said that he would "strive to be, for the first time, the top recipient. I will accept these contributions because I am proud to have the support of a legal industry that is of great importance to my state."[72]

There is no way to know how Congress would have acted in the complete absence of tobacco money. It was not under pressure from the public generally to do more than it had done in regard to tobacco regulation, which was, therefore, a relatively easy matter to leave to the states. The most comprehensive and rigorous scholarly attempt to estimate the influence of tobacco PAC money on congressional voting, based on an analysis of all sixteen tobacco-related votes in the House and Senate between 1980 and 2000, concluded that the "tobacco industry's legislative success is more a function of representatives' regulatory and pro-business ideologies than of tobacco PAC money or a geographically based tobacco voting bloc."[73]

Typically, the industry succeeded in defeating unwanted measures, but a better test of its power came when it *wanted* Congress to act—as in 1997–1998, when it very much wanted legislative endorsement of the 1997 settlement. The industry spent millions of dollars to that end, both in lobbying services and in advertising, and the CEO of Philip Morris traveled to Washington to plead personally with the members. However, the industry was rebuffed by the McCain bill, which gave it practically nothing that it wanted, and then by the McCain bill as amended on the floor, which gave it nothing whatever. Having been rebuffed, it went back to its accustomed task of opposition. Victorious at that strategy, it emerged to be denounced again by editorial writers of the *New York Times* and the *Washington Post* for its manipulation of politics with money. Yet that interpretation is blind to the fact that the industry failed to buy the outcome that it really wanted—and blind also to the ambiguous effects of its lavish spending, which had its Republican allies, recipients of much of the money, at least briefly frightened into hiding. Money in politics cuts both ways. It can help, but in large amounts it can also backfire, becoming a public relations liability for the recipients.

· Obstacles on the Hill ·

Because Congress is broadly representative, with 435 members in the House from a wide variety of districts and another 100 members in the more exclusive Senate, it can be counted on to represent a vast array of interests and opinions. It might have been possible for the negotiators of the 1997 settlement to ignore the interests of tobacco farmers, but it was certainly not possible for Congress to do so—and that was one reason why the settlement became more expensive when it reached Congress: Members added money for the farmers. It might have been possible for the negotiators of the settlement to proceed despite the intensely held and extreme opinions of public health advocates, who thought that any deal with Big Tobacco was a deal with the devil, but it was not possible for Congress to do so because those opinions were well represented in both houses—hence McCain's move to sacrifice the most important liability protections for the industry. Also, the longer the bill stayed in the Senate, the more claimants appeared asking for a piece of the revenue it would generate. Thus, for example, an ad appeared in the *National Journal* on April 25, 1998, asking for benefits for asbestos workers and pregnant women, two "special cases" of victims of smoking. It was signed by the Asbestos Victims of America, the International Association of Heat and Frost Insulators and Asbestos Workers, and the Alliance for a Fair Tobacco Settlement.[74]

For successful legislative coalitions to be formed, political leaders must be willing to argue for the importance of an outcome and to search for the terms on which one can be obtained. Presidents often become coalition leaders; spearheading coalitions is one of their functions in American politics. President Clinton showed no disposition to take the lead on a tobacco settlement, however, although the White House had been involved in the 1997 negotiations, and the leaders of those negotiations thought that they had a promise from the president's deputy counsel, Bruce Lindsey, to endorse the most controversial part of the settlement—the liability protections for the industry. This protection was what the industry most wanted—and what its opponents, including several of the state attorneys general, were most reluctant to give. But when the settlement was announced, the president, after congratulating the attorneys general for achieving it, said he had "not concluded whether it is in the best interests of the public health." Moore and Scruggs felt double-crossed.[75]

In Congress McCain emerged as a coalition leader, having been tapped by the Republican Party leadership for the task.[76] He may have pursued it with more zeal than they intended. A maverick, McCain brought the Democrats along with him but not the members of his own party. But he was in an unenviable position. That no member of Congress had brokered the big tobacco deal—that it had been wholly imported from outside the institution—was a major handicap. It arrived without broad popular appeal, which coalition leaders look for when they select proposals to promote. Although polls showed that the public favored discouraging adolescent tobacco use, the issue was not at the top of its list of concerns. Polls also showed that a majority of the public blamed smokers, not the cigarette companies, for the adverse effects of smoking. Politicians who embraced the antitobacco cause in the hope of gaining popularity—as was true with some of the state attorneys general—were engaged in a speculative venture whose rewards at the polls had yet to be proved.

Mounting Opposition

A failure to bring debate to an end was critical in killing the bill in the Senate. As the tobacco debate dragged on, members grew increasingly impatient to get down to what they saw as the more urgent business of appropriations. The Democrats had thought they had a Republican vote for cloture in Sen. Ted Stevens of Alaska, but he voted with his party, grumbling that "as a practical matter, we spent too much time on this bill. We must get back to our ordinary drudge work of getting the thirteen appropriations bills through the Senate."[77]

It was critical, of course, that a majority of the Republicans, who were the majority party, were opposed to the McCain bill. In their eyes it was, as Senator Nickles had said, a bad bill—and not just because the tobacco industry had given them a lot of money to adopt such a belief. Conservative groups, motivated by free-market ideology or by a commitment to the defense of corporate interests, were mobilized broadly. The Chamber of Commerce was against the bill. At the time the June 1997 settlement was reached, the Cato Institute, a libertarian think tank that is very active in Washington, published a paper arguing that the states' tobacco litigation had snuffed out the rule of law.[78] Opposed also were groups that had organized in opposition to tort actions as a way of making public policy. The Washington Legal Foundation, "an effective advocate of free enterprise," advertised inside the Beltway to protest "a Constitutional Tragedy in the Making." Its ad said,

> Anti-smoking zealots in government seek to simultaneously single out and punish the demonized tobacco industry while continuing to collect billions of dollars in tax revenues from tobacco sales, as they have for decades. . . . By promoting the largest suspension of commercial free speech liberties in history, our leaders are convening a constitutional convention without the rest of us.

Such groups wondered what businesses would be targeted next. Would it be "the Big Caffeine merchants at Coca-Cola and Starbucks"?[79] Then there was the fact that the bill really did produce a large amount of fresh revenue for the government. A party opposed to tax increases could not possibly like this bill—especially if the first administration to benefit from the tax revenues would be that of a Democratic president whom many Republican members despised.

There was much truth in the conservatives' claim that this was a tax measure, but the deeper truth is that its original purpose was *punishment,* and punishment is not Congress's normal business. This measure was a tort action imported into the legislature, which was not comfortable with it. Politics, Speaker of the House Thomas P. Tip O'Neill once remarked, is "sums." Legislative politics typically entails constructing bundles of benefits, which may impose costs—legislative politics is not without losers—but legislatures typically operate by hiding costs and offering compensation to losers. In this case, the tort settlement had offered the industry compensation in the form of liability protections, but Congress did not like that part of the deal, because protecting the tobacco companies and limiting the public's right to collect damages from them had no political appeal. McCain then constructed a bill that responded to the unpopularity of the tobacco companies but was all punishment and no compensation, and Congress did not like that version, either. After their initial perplexity, the Republicans found it possible to apply DDT, as one Democrat put it—"first delay, then destroy, then terminate any action on tobacco."[80]

When the bill died in the Senate, conservatives concluded that the system had worked. As its death approached, Senator Nickles remarked that "a little time is a great disinfectant."[81] A *Wall Street Journal* editorial soon afterward was positively lyrical in its celebration of the American political system:

> What a wonderful system the Founding Fathers gave us. How foresightful of them to know that 210 years later something like John McCain's tobacco bill would come along. And so Madison and company gave us the Senate cloture rule, which . . . would allow 40 Senators plus one . . . to send the tobacco bill back to committee, effectively killing it. . . . The message of the week is that the system works; somehow a deeper wisdom has triumphed.[82]

This editorial was poor history. The cloture rule is a creation of the Senate, not the Founding Fathers. Though consistent with the spirit of the Constitution, it is not to be found in its text. The *Journal's* editorial was flawed, too, as contemporary analysis of the American political system, for it overlooked the fact that there was more to the "system" than Congress. Action would revert now to the state governments and the courts.

• Notes •

1. Jeffrey Taylor, "Big Tobacco's Lawyers Get a Jump in Congress," *Wall Street Journal,* July 10, 1997, A16; and "Brace Yourself For a Tobacco Blitz," *National Journal,* January 17, 1998, 95.
2. Barry Meier and Jill Abramson, "Tobacco War's New Front: Lawyers Fight over Big Fees," *New York Times,* June 9, 1998, A1.
3. Dan Zegart, *Civil Warriors: The Legal Siege on the Tobacco Industry* (New York: Delacorte, 2000), 261–263; Carrick Mollenkamp et al., *The People vs. Big Tobacco* (Princeton, N.J.: Bloomberg, 1998), 187–191; and Michael Pertschuk, *Smoke in Their Eyes: Lessons in Movement Leadership from the Tobacco Wars* (Nashville: Vanderbilt University Press, 2001), chap. 16.
4. John M. Broder and Barry Meier, "High Hurdles Still Confront Tobacco Pact," *New York Times,* June 22, 1997, A1; and John M. Broder, "White House Says Tobacco Proposal Would Hurt F.D.A.," *New York Times,* July 9, 1997, A1. The advisory committee's report, chaired by Koop and Kessler, may be found at http://www.ash.org.report2.html, accessed May 19, 2011. For a more polemical statement of the Koop-Kessler position, see C. Everett Koop, David C. Kessler, and George D. Lundberg, "Reinventing American Tobacco Policy: Sounding the Medical Community's Voice," *Journal of the American Medical Association* 279, no. 7 (18 February 1998): 550.
5. Louis Jacobson, "Trying Time," *National Journal,* April 18, 1998, 862–865.
6. *Competition and the Financial Impact of the Proposed Tobacco Industry Settlement,* prepared by the staff of the Federal Trade Commission (Washington, D.C.: FTC, September 1997).

7. Associated Press, "Tobacco Deal Lacks Support, Poll Finds," *Daily Progress* (Charlottesville, Va.), August 29, 1997, 1. The poll was done for the AP by the ICR Survey Research Group of Media, Penn.

8. John M. Broder and Barry Meier, "Tobacco Accord, Once Applauded, Is All But Buried," *New York Times,* September 14, 1997, A1; and Jackie Calmes, "Clinton to Seek Big Changes in Accord with Tobacco Industry, Delaying Law," *Wall Street Journal,* September 15, 1997, A3.

9. John Schwartz, "U.S. Wants Share of State Tobacco Deals," *Washington Post,* November 5, 1997, A19; Robert Pear, "U.S. Wants a Cut of Tobacco Settlements," *New York Times,* November 19, 1997, A24; and Jeffrey Taylor, "Clinton Plans about Tobacco Dismay States," *Wall Street Journal,* January 9, 1998, A18.

10. Jackie Calmes and David Rogers, "Clinton's Tobacco-Based Budget Puts GOP in Hot Spot," *Wall Street Journal,* January 16, 1998, A16.

11. Jeffrey Taylor, "Tobacco Industry, Congressional Ally Face Rift," *Wall Street Journal,* December 8, 1997, A26; and Peter H. Stone, "Blowing Off Big Tobacco," *National Journal,* April 4, 1998, 760.

12. Pertschuk, *Smoke in Their Eyes,* 105–106.

13. Ibid., chap. 21.

14. Senate Committee on Commerce, Science, and Transportation, *Global Settlement of Tobacco Litigation: Hearing before the Committee on Commerce, Science, and Transportation,* 105th Cong., 1st sess., July 29, 1997 (Washington, D.C.: GPO, 1999), 31–32.

15. Ceci Connolly and John Mintz, "For Big Tobacco, a Future without GOP Support," *Washington Post,* March 29, 1998, A1; and Stone, "Blowing Off Big Tobacco."

16. John Mintz and Saundra Torry, "Secret R. J. Reynolds Documents Appear to Show Cigarette Maker's Marketing Targeted Children," *Washington Post,* January 15, 1998, A1; and Barry Meier, "Files of R.J. Reynolds Tobacco Show Effort on Youths," *New York Times,* January 15, 1998, A12.

17. Peter H. Stone, "Tobacco CEOs Start Working the Hill," *National Journal,* March 21, 1998, 646. McCain's zeal in assailing the tobacco companies came as a welcome surprise to the antitobacco forces, who had not wanted the bill to be referred to the Commerce Committee. See Pertschuk, *Smoke in Their Eyes,* 168, 201–206.

18. Congressional Quarterly, *1998 CQ Almanac,* vol. 54, 105th Cong., 2d sess. (Washington, D.C.: Congressional Quarterly Inc., 1999), 15–4.

19. David E. Rosenbaum, "Cigarette Makers Quit Negotiations on Tobacco Bill," *New York Times,* April 9, 1998, A1.

20. Pertschuk, *Smoke in Their Eyes,* chaps. 30 and 31.

21. *1998 CQ Almanac,* 15–6.

22. Melinda Henneberger, "A Big Ad Campaign Helps Stall the Bill to Reduce Smoking," *New York Times,* May 22, 1998, A1; and Howard Kurtz, "The Democrat Who Switched and Fought: Former Gore Confidant Formulated Tobacco Industry's Effective Ad Blitz," *Washington Post,* June 19, 1998, A1.

23. *National Journal,* May 16, 1998, 1096. The source for the poll data was given as the *Wall Street Journal*/NBC News poll by Hart-Teeter, as reported in the *Wall Street Journal,* April 23, 1998.

24. *1998 CQ Almanac,* 15–13. In the 1996 election cycle, the tobacco industry made $10.5 million in political contributions, 81 percent of which went to Republicans. In the 2008 cycle, its total was $4.2 million, of which 62 percent went to Republicans. Ranked 27th as a contributor among all industries in 1996, it had dropped to 67th place by 2008. "Tobacco: Long-Term Contribution Trends," The Center for Responsive Politics, http://www.opensecrets.org/industries/totals. php?cycle = 2010&ind = A02, accessed August 26, 2010.

25. *1998 CQ Almanac,* 15–10.

26. Pertschuk, *Smoke in Their Eyes,* 230.

27. David E. Rosenbaum, "Senate Approves Limiting Fees Lawyers Get in Tobacco Cases," *New York Times,* June 17, 1998, A1.

28. *1998 CQ Almanac,* 15–7 and 15–10.

29. Kirk Victor, "McCain Gets Hit by Friendly Fire," *National Journal,* May 2, 1998, 994–995.

30. David E. Rosenbaum, "Senate Drops Tobacco Bill with '98 Revival Unlikely: Clinton Lashes Out at G.O.P.," *New York Times,* June 18, 1998, A1.

31. See, for example, Richard Kluger, "The Good Guys Muff It," *New York Times,* June 23, 1998, A25.

32. *Regulation by Litigation: The New Wave of Government-Sponsored Litigation* (New York: Manhattan Institute, 1999), 84. The obstinacy and absolutism of Glantz, Kessler, and others in the public health professions are the central theme also of Pertschuk, *Smoke in Their Eyes.* On the difficulty that Myers had in working with Kessler and Koop, see especially chaps. 25 and 26.

33. "Death of the Tobacco Bill," *New York Times,* June 18, 1998, A34.

34. Lydia Saad, "A Half-Century of Polling on Tobacco: Most Don't Like Smoking but Tolerate It," *Public Perspective* (August/September 1998): 1.

35. In a Roper poll in 1939, respondents judged cigarettes to have the least honest advertising among a series of leading consumer products, including automobiles, insurance, liquor, and drugs. See Roper poll, *Public Perspective* (August/September 1998): 18. See also the numerous poll results that may be found at the data center of the University of North Carolina, http://www.irss.unc.edu/odum/jsp/home.jsp. I am indebted to Paul Freedman for calling this site to my attention.

36. Saad, "Half-Century of Polling," 1–2.

37. Robert J. Blendon and John T. Young, "The Public and the Comprehensive Tobacco Bill," *Journal of the American Medical Association* 280 (14 October 1998): 1280.

38. Ibid.

39. Everett Carll Ladd, "The Tobacco Bill and American Public Opinion," *Public Perspective* (August/September 1998): 6 and 16.

40. Hart-Teeter poll, *Public Perspective* (August/September 1998): 19.

41. *National Journal,* April 25, 1998, 924. The poll was by Yankelovich Partners Inc. for CNN-*Time* magazine.

42. *National Journal,* May 16, 1998, 1116. In contrast, only 8 percent thought the government was doing too much to regulate illegal drugs, and 9 percent, too much to regulate alcohol.

43. Opinion Dynamics poll, *Public Perspective* (August/September 1998): 19.

44. Blendon and Young, "The Public and the Comprehensive Tobacco Bill," 1282–1283.
45. Peter D. Jacobson and Jeffrey Wasserman, *Tobacco Control Laws: Implementation and Enforcement* (Santa Monica, Calif.: Rand Corp., 1997), xvii.
46. Mike Synar, "Political Realities," *Tobacco Control* 4, supplement 2 (Autumn 1995): S80–S81.
47. The sources I mainly relied on for this period were *CQ Weekly, National Journal,* the *New York Times,* and the *Washington Post.* Their accounts are consistent with one another.
48. Kurtz, "Democrat Who Switched and Fought," A1.
49. *Public Perspective* (August/September 1998): 10–11.
50. Jeffrey Taylor, "GOP Lawmakers Say They Don't Fear Voter Reprisals for Killing Tobacco Bill," *Wall Street Journal,* June 23, 1998, A22.
51. Saundra Torry and John Schwartz, "Tobacco Foes Failed to Stoke Voters' Fire," *Washington Post,* November 8, 1998, A2.
52. U.S. Department of Health and Human Services, Office of Smoking and Health, *Smoking, Tobacco & Health: A Fact Book,* pub. no. 87–8397 (CDC) (revised 10/89) (Washington, D.C.: 1989), 22, 34. For an expansive current estimate of the economic importance of the tobacco industry, see Tara Parker-Pope, *Cigarettes: Anatomy of an Industry from Seed to Smoke* (New York: New Press, 2001), 21–26. On the historically privileged position of tobacco in the politics of American agriculture, which helps explain the extreme profitability of the crop, see Anthony J. Badger, *Prosperity Road: The New Deal, Tobacco, and North Carolina* (Chapel Hill: University of North Carolina Press, 1980), chap. 8.
53. See http://www.nass.usda.gov/ky/Pamphlet/tobpam02.pdf, accessed Jan. 12, 2004; and Will Snell and Stephan Goetz, *Overview of Kentucky's Tobacco Economy* (Lexington: University of Kentucky Cooperative Extension Service, AEC-83, 1997).
54. "Tobacco: background," http://www.ers.usda.gov/Briefing/Archive/Tobacco/ accessed May 19, 2011.
55. Charles Lewis and the Center for Public Integrity (CPI), *The Buying of the Congress: How Special Interests Have Stolen Your Right to Life, Liberty, and the Pursuit of Happiness* (New York: Avon, 1998), chap. 6.
56. Peter H. Stone, "Our Good Friend, the Governor," *Mother Jones,* May/June 1996, 38. What the companies gave to political campaigns in the early 1990s was much more than what they had given in the late 1980s. See Sidney Wolfe et al., *The Congressional Addiction to Tobacco: How the Tobacco Lobby Suffocates Federal Health Policy,* a report by the Public Citizen's Health Research Group (Washington, D.C.: October 1992), 3.
57. Richard Kluger, *Ashes to Ashes: America's Hundred-Year Cigarette War, the Public Health, and the Unabashed Triumph of Philip Morris* (New York: Knopf, 1996), 683–684.
58. Jill Abramson and Barry Meier, "Tobacco Braced for Costly Fight," *New York Times,* December 15, 1997, A1.
59. Bill McAllister, "Heavy Hitters in the High-Stakes Tobacco Fight Arena," *Washington Post,* June 4, 1998, A21; and Saundra Torry and Nathan Abse, "Big Tobacco Spends Top Dollar to Lobby," *Washington Post,* April 9, 1999, A37.

60. Abramson and Meier, "Tobacco Braced for Costly Fight," A1.
61. U.S. Department of Health and Human Services, *Smoking, Tobacco & Health*, 27; and Barbara S. Lynch and Richard J. Bonnie, eds., *Growing Up Tobacco Free* (Washington, D.C.: National Academy Press, 1994), 105.
62. Stanton A. Glantz and Edith D. Balbach, *Tobacco War: Inside the California Battles* (Berkeley: University of California Press, 2000), passim.
63. Lewis and the CPI, *Buying of the Congress*, 120.
64. Kurtz, "Democrat Who Switched and Fought," A1.
65. Kluger, *Ashes to Ashes*, 683.
66. Stephen Moore et al., *Contributing to Death: The Influence of Tobacco Money on the U.S. Congress*, a report by the Public Citizen's Health Research Group (Washington, D.C.: Public Citizen's Health Research Group, 1993), 1.
67. Howard K. Koh, "An Analysis of the Successful 1992 Massachusetts Tobacco Tax Initiative," *Tobacco Control* 5, no. 3 (Autumn 1996): 220–225. The figures for spending in the California referendum appear in this article, but the original sources are several journal articles cited by Koh on page 225.
68. Kluger, *Ashes to Ashes*, 683.
69. Moore et al., *Contributing to Death*, 3.
70. Wolfe et al., *Congressional Addiction to Tobacco*, 8. The original source is *ABC News Nightline*, June 24, 1992. This was before the two parties had split on tobacco politics.
71. Wolfe et al., *Congressional Addiction to Tobacco*, 4–6.
72. Lewis and the CPI, *Buying of the Congress*, 110.
73. John R. Wright, "Congressional Voting on Tobacco Policy, 1980–2000," unpublished manuscript, December 2003. An early result of Wright's findings, based on two roll-call votes in the Senate in the 102d Congress (1991–1992), is reported in "Tobacco Industry PACs and the Nation's Health: A Second Opinion," in *The Interest Group Connection: Electioneering, Lobbying, and Policymaking in Washington*, ed. Paul S. Herrnson, Ronald G. Shaiko, and Clyde Wilcox (Chatham, N.J.: Chatham House, 1998), 174–195. Wright is a political scientist on the faculty of Ohio State University.
74. *National Journal*, April 25, 1998, 945.
75. Zegart, *Civil Warriors*, 265–266, 270–271.
76. On the quandary that tobacco posed for the Senate Republican leader, Trent Lott, and the intraparty differences that emerged, see Victor, "McCain Gets Hit by Friendly Fire," 994–995.
77. *1998 CQ Almanac*, 15–13.
78. Robert A. Levy, *Tobacco Medicaid Litigation: Snuffing Out the Rule of Law*, Cato Institute Policy Analysis no. 275 (Washington, D.C.: Cato Institute, June 20, 1997).
79. *National Journal*, May 9, 1998, 1071.
80. *1998 CQ Almanac*, 15–13.
81. Ibid., 15–9.
82. *Wall Street Journal*, June 19, 1998, A14.

CHAPTER EIGHT

The FDA Regulations Die in Court

THE FDA REGULATIONS, IT WILL be recalled, were published in proposed form in August 1995 and in final form a year later. The industry filed a lawsuit challenging them, yet also agreed in June 1997 to incorporate FDA regulatory authority into the settlement with the attorneys general. Thus, the story of the judicial decision on the regulations is to some extent intertwined with the fate of the 1997 settlement.

• The Regulations and the Settlement •

As noted in chapter 5, the settlement incorporated regulatory authority for the FDA but also went beyond the specific regulations that the FDA had produced. For example, the settlement banned all sales through vending machines, all outdoor advertising, and human images as well as cartoon characters in advertising and packaging.

This agreement would have been a momentous breakthrough had Congress enacted it. But the settlement also would have introduced procedural provisions that David Kessler and his collaborator, former surgeon general C. Everett Koop, were unwilling to countenance. There was no more telling sign than this of public health officials' intransigence in 1997.

Limits on FDA Authority

Under the negotiated settlement, for the first twelve years the FDA would have been authorized to gradually reduce, but not eliminate, nicotine yields. The agency would have been required to find that modification of cigarettes (1) would significantly reduce health risks to consumers, (2) was technologically feasible, and (3) would not result in a black market in cigarettes. The FDA itself had given credence to this last danger in its rulemaking in 1995–1996, when it had declined to attempt a nicotine ban partly on the ground that a black market would result. To justify a ban, the FDA would have had to meet a test of "substantial evidence," based on an administrative record developed through a formal rulemaking, which would be subject to judicial review.

After twelve years, the agency would have had authority to require the elimination of nicotine and other harmful constituents but would have been subject to a "preponderance of the evidence" test to ensure that the same three criteria had been met. Again, a formal rulemaking would have been required, and judicial review would have been provided for. The FDA also would have had to establish a scientific advisory committee to "examine and determine the effects of the alteration of nicotine yield levels and to examine and determine whether there is a threshold level below which nicotine yields do not produce drug dependence. . . ."[1] Objecting to this provision, Koop and Kessler argued that the FDA should not be required to do more than prove that its rules were "neither arbitrary nor capricious." It should not be compelled to prove a negative—in other words, that no black market would develop.

Attorney General Christine Gregoire of Washington State, a leader among the attorneys general in negotiating the settlement, defended the more exacting standards for rulemaking as being fair and reasonable:

> I do ask you to look at the fine print; for if you do you will find that in the first 12 years FDA does what it does with every other food product with regard to the regulations and how it holds public comment, notice, rulemaking, in order to reduce the nicotine, tar, or other harmful components. The one place it differs is after 12 years, to ultimately ban nicotine, it requires, at the election of the industry . . . another hearing that is provided under FDA regulations, which is a formal proceeding.
>
> We did not think that was [giving up] too much, in light of what the consequence of that ban would be. . . . If we are going to ban, ultimately ban, nicotine in that product, we felt it deserved a formal rulemaking process by that particular administrative agency.[2]

Unwilling to accept any such qualifications to the FDA's authority, which they thought put too heavy a burden of proof on the agency to defend itself in court, Kessler, Koop, and the Clinton administration singled out for attack the part of the 1997 settlement that included these qualifications. In testimony before Congress, Kessler remarked darkly that it had been crafted by "certain lawyers," meaning, presumably, industry lawyers.[3] The Koop-Kessler Advisory Committee, created by Representative Waxman to offer advice on the settlement, offered the following recommendations in regard to regulatory policy:

- FDA should continue to have authority to regulate all areas of nicotine, as well as other constituents and ingredients, and that authority should be made completely explicit.

- FDA should continue to have the authority to phase out nicotine and remove ingredients that contribute to the initiation of smoking and dependence on cigarettes and other tobacco products . . . , and that authority should be made completely explicit.
- There should be no limitations on or special exceptions to FDA authority to regulate nicotine, other constituents, and ingredients of tobacco products and such a no-limitations policy should be made completely explicit. . . .[4]

In addition to its uncompromising tone, the use of the phrase "continue to" in this document is notable inasmuch as the authority of the FDA to regulate cigarettes at all was still uncertain. The FDA had won an initial victory on that issue in a district court, but as of June 1997 the case was heading into appeal.

Goals of the Public Health Advocates

The goals of Kessler, Koop, and allied public health officials went beyond what the attorneys general had sought in the settlement. Although Kessler and his associates denied that they aimed to prohibit cigarettes, they were forthright about wanting to put the profit-making industry out of business. When the 1997 settlement was announced, Stanton Glantz of California was one of a number of antitobacco activists who disapproved of it because it did not go far enough. It would make the industry a little less profitable while guaranteeing its continued, long-term health. What Glantz had in mind was the following:

> We should consider a settlement when the stock market is driving tobacco stocks down, which would put the cookie, cheese, and beer assets of Philip Morris and the others at risk.
>
> What should we accept in such a settlement? We should take the tobacco business—all of it, including foreign subsidiaries—as part of an agreement to let these companies keep their cookies, cheese, and beer. We should let the government make plain cigarettes available (no fancy brands, no advertising, no nicotine boosting additives, no campaign contributions) for smokers who can't quit. We should take the money from the sales of these cigarettes and use it to help tobacco workers and farmers retool and to run a big, aggressive anti-smoking campaign to reduce smoking as quickly as possible. Since we will own the overseas business, we can simply close it so that America no longer can be accused of exporting death.[5]

In an interview with a *New York Times* reporter in 1998, Kessler spoke in the same spirit: "I don't want to live in peace with these guys. If they cared at all for the public health, they wouldn't be in this business in the first place. All this talk about it being a legal business is euphemism. They sell a deadly, addictive product. There's no reason to allow them to conduct business as usual."[6]

As Gregoire explained to Congress, however, it was not a function of the attorneys general to drive industries into bankruptcy:

> . . . It is not the job nor the role of the attorneys general to put anybody out of business or to force any industry into bankruptcy. Some comments I have heard here today would suggest that we have not taken the toll that we need to take unless and until we either put them out of business as we know it today or force them into bankruptcy.
>
> This is counter to the role of attorneys general. It is obviously the province of this Congress, but it is nothing that we could put down as in any way, shape, or form a goal of us in the settlement negotiations or as part of our lawsuits. Hence we have done everything we can to ensure this industry pays— and pays mightily—to advance the public health of this country, without forcing it into bankruptcy. . . .[7]

· The Regulations in Court ·

The core of the federal judicial branch (special courts aside) consisted in 1997 of ninety trial courts, called district courts; twelve circuit courts of appeal; and the nine members of the Supreme Court. The Constitution created the Supreme Court, and Congress constituted the others under a grant of power contained in the Constitution. Federal courts derive most of their fame from making constitutional rulings, but such rulings are a relatively small part of their workload. Interpretations of statutes, as in this case, are more typical.

The District Court

As soon as the FDA published its proposed regulations in August 1995, the tobacco industry challenged them, selecting for this purpose the Greensboro division of the district court for the middle district of North Carolina, the heart of tobacco country. The judge in this division—one of more than six hundred district judges in the country— was William Osteen Sr., in his mid-sixties, who might have been expected to be sympathetic to the industry's case. When he was growing up, his family had owned a tobacco farm just outside of Greensboro that it leased to tenants. As a private lawyer, he had lobbied in Washington in the 1970s for continuation of the tobacco price support program.[8] But judges are supposed to be unbiased, and if the industry thought that Osteen would lean in its direction, it was destined to be disappointed.

Osteen heard arguments in the case on February 10, 1997. The FDA was represented, as is customary for federal agencies in litigation, by lawyers from the Department of Justice. The industry had a well-qualified lawyer in Richard M. Cooper of the Washington firm of Williams and Connolly, who had been chief counsel at the FDA from 1977 to 1979, in the Carter administration. Osteen asked tough questions of both sides and promised a ruling within ten weeks. When his decision was announced on April 25, it was a shock to the industry. He ruled that Congress had not withheld jurisdiction to regulate tobacco products from the FDA and that the agency could regulate them pursuant to the federal Food, Drug, and Cosmetic Act. He was a bit reluctant about this conclusion: ". . . [A]lthough the court hesitates to agree with FDA that the agency has unfettered discretion to apply the regulatory authority of its choice to combination products, the court finds that the intent of Congress is not clear and, finding FDA's interpretation to be at least reasonable, defers to FDA's interpretation." The ruling was qualified in only one respect: Osteen found that the act did not authorize restrictions on the promotion and advertisement of tobacco products. Thus, only one portion of the FDA's regulation was invalidated.[9]

Pending appeal, Osteen stayed implementation of the regulation except for portions that the FDA had already implemented. The FDA had stipulated that the following two provisions would take effect on February 28, 1997: "No retailer may sell cigarettes or smokeless tobacco to any person younger than 18 years of age" and "each retailer shall verify by means of photographic identification containing the bearer's date of birth that no person purchasing the product is younger than 18 years of age."[10] Simply as a rule, this prohibition against tobacco purchases by persons under eighteen added nothing to the nation's antitobacco armory, for the states already had such laws, and the Synar Amendment of 1992 had instructed them to undertake enforcement or face loss of federal grants for control of substance abuse. In promulgating its rule to govern the age of tobacco purchasers, the FDA intended formally to preempt the laws of the states, one more sign of the boldness of its regulatory enterprise.[11]

The FDA proceeded with an aggressive, $34 million-a-year tobacco control program consisting of two main parts. One was an advertising program to spread knowledge of its rules, and the other a sting operation to test retail vendors' compliance. For the stings, the agency contracted with state regulatory agencies, which in turn employed underage youths to attempt cigarette purchases.[12]

The Circuit Court

Because of the mixed verdict at the district level, both sides appealed. The case came before a three-judge panel of the Fourth Circuit, which has jurisdiction over judicial districts in Maryland, North Carolina, South Carolina, Virginia, and West Virginia. The panel heard oral argument on August 11, 1997, in Warm Springs, Virginia, but before an opinion could be handed down one of the judges died, so the case had to be reargued on June 8, 1998, in Charleston, West Virginia.

On August 14 the Fourth Circuit overruled Osteen. "We begin," the court said, "with the basic proposition that agency power" is not the power to make law but "the power to adopt regulations to carry into effect the will of Congress as expressed by the statute." The court said Osteen had asked the wrong question: "The district court framed the issue as 'whether Congress had evidenced its clear intent to *withhold* from FDA jurisdiction to regulate tobacco products as customarily marketed. . . .' However, we are of [the] opinion that the issue is correctly framed as whether Congress intended to *delegate* such jurisdiction to the FDA." By a 2-to-1 vote, the circuit court decided that Congress had not intended any such delegation. It concluded:

> This is not a case about whether additional or different regulations are needed to address legitimate concerns about the serious health problems related to tobacco use, and particularly youth tobacco use, in this country. At its core, this case is about who has the power to make this type of major policy decision. . . . By its *ultra vires* action, the FDA has exceeded the authority granted to it by Congress, and its rulemaking action cannot stand.[13]

This court's opinion did not address the legal status of the FDA's ongoing program of tobacco control, but in response to petitions from the government, the court issued stays that permitted the FDA to continue enforcing its age of purchase and photo ID rules pending an appeal to the Supreme Court.

The Supreme Court

Soon after the circuit court had ruled, the U.S. solicitor general, the federal government's head litigator, filed a petition for a writ of certiorari before the Supreme Court, which granted the petition on April 26, 1999, and proceeded to hear oral argument on December 1, 1999.

Judging from newspaper accounts of the hearing, the FDA was certain to be defeated. "The Supreme Court was highly skeptical yesterday of the Food and Drug Administration's claim that it can regulate cigarettes . . . ," the *Washington Post* reported. "Justices across the ideological spectrum homed in on weaknesses in the government's case, notably that the FDA had for decades said it lacked the authority to regulate tobacco and that the agency's historical mandate is to oversee items intended to make people healthier. 'It just doesn't fit,' said Justice Sandra Day O'Connor. . . ."[14] Justices' questions do not necessarily indicate their views, however, and they can change their minds in the course of the lawyers' arguments and the court's deliberations. In March 2000 the FDA was defeated but by the narrowest of margins, 5–4.

O'Connor wrote for a majority composed also of Justices Rehnquist, Kennedy, Scalia, and Thomas and repeated in the opinion what she had uttered from the bench: tobacco products "simply do not fit" into the regulatory scheme of the Food, Drug, and Cosmetics Act (FDCA). A fundamental precept of the act is that any product regulated by the FDA must, if approved for sale, be safe for its intended use; if not safe, it must be banned. Before Kessler's arrival, the FDA had taken the position that if cigarettes were under its jurisdiction, they would have to be banned. When Kessler claimed authority to regulate, he did not of course assert that cigarettes *were* safe for their intended use but said that, on balance, a ban would not serve the public health. Suddenly removing from the market products to which millions of people were addicted could be "dangerous." Current tobacco users would suffer withdrawal symptoms for which adequate treatment might not be available, and a black market would likely develop, offering cigarettes even more dangerous than those currently being sold.[15]

The Supreme Court majority thought this argument an unacceptable dodge around the purposes of the act. The FDA would have to either approve cigarettes as safe for their intended use, which was scientifically impossible, or ban them, which the Court said would contradict congressional policy. As evidence that Congress did not intend a ban, the Court cited Congress's construction of its own regulatory scheme. This scheme relied mainly on labeling and advertising restrictions, as well as various statutory provisions that paid tribute to the economic importance of tobacco.

O'Connor's opinion then took up at greater length the argument that Congress did not intend the FDA to have jurisdiction over tobacco. Over the previous thirty-five years, Congress had enacted six separate pieces of legislation, beginning with the Federal Cigarette Labeling and Advertising Act in 1965:

> In adopting each statute, Congress has acted against the backdrop of the FDA's consistent and repeated statements that it lacked authority under the FDCA to regulate tobacco absent claims of therapeutic benefit by the manufacturer. In fact, on

several occasions over this period, and after the health consequences of tobacco use and nicotine's pharmacological effects
had become well known, Congress considered and rejected
bills that would have granted the FDA such jurisdiction. Under
these circumstances, it is evident that Congress' tobacco-specific statutes have effectively ratified the FDA's long-held position that it lacks jurisdiction under the FDCA to regulate
tobacco products. Congress has created a distinct regulatory
scheme to address the problem of tobacco and health, and
that scheme, as presently constructed, precludes any role for
the FDA.

The majority closed by stating that the high importance of the
question before the Court made it reluctant to defer to the agency's
claim of power. Where a statute is ambiguous and an administering
agency construes the ambiguity in its own favor, a court might assume
that Congress's ambiguity "constitutes an implicit delegation from Congress to fill in the statutory gaps." But if the case is extraordinary, "there
may be reason to hesitate before concluding that Congress has intended
such an implicit delegation." (To support this point, the majority here
cleverly—and gratuitously—inserted a citation of a scholarly article by
one of the Court's own members, Stephen Breyer, who was writing in
dissent.) The majority continued:

> This is hardly an ordinary case. . . . Owing to its unique place
> in American history and society, tobacco has its own unique
> political history. Congress, for better or worse, has created a
> distinct regulatory scheme for tobacco products, squarely
> rejected proposals to give the FDA jurisdiction over tobacco,
> and repeatedly acted to preclude any agency from exercising
> significant policymaking authority in the area. Given this his-
> tory and the breadth of the authority that the FDA has asserted,
> we are obliged to defer not to the agency's expansive construc-
> tion of the statute, but to Congress' consistent judgment to
> deny the FDA this power.

The majority did not question the seriousness of the problem that
the FDA sought to address, but it decided that "an administrative agency's power to regulate in the public interest must always be grounded in
a valid grant of authority from Congress."[16]

Justice Breyer, author of the dissent, had taught administrative
law at Harvard before being appointed to the federal bench. Joined by
Justices Ruth Bader Ginsburg, David Souter, and John Paul Stevens,
Breyer reasoned that on the basis of both language and purpose, the
Food, Drug, and Cosmetic Act authorized the FDA to regulate tobacco

products. He concurred with the FDA's claim that tobacco products are "articles (other than food) intended to affect the structure or any function of the body . . . ," and he argued that the statute's purpose, which he said was protecting public health, also supported including cigarettes within the law's scope. Breyer justified this expansive reading of the statute by putting it in historical context: broad delegations were typical of the regulatory laws of the late New Deal, he said.

Breyer rebutted the majority's argument that the law did not fit the case of tobacco because it required the FDA to prohibit dangerous drugs or devices such as cigarettes. "The statute's language," he wrote, ". . . permits the agency to choose remedies consistent with its basic purpose—the overall protection of public health."

He also rebutted the majority's claim that Congress's numerous statutes denying jurisdiction over tobacco to agencies other than the FDA, in combination with Congress's repeated refusal to grant explicit authority to that agency, demonstrated an intention to deny jurisdiction. He pointed out that after Kessler's campaign for regulation began, Congress had failed to act on bills that would have denied FDA jurisdiction.

That the FDA itself had long foresworn jurisdiction was legally insignificant, he said. The agency was entitled to change its position if it could justify doing so. Breyer cited as grounds for the switch the tobacco industry's numerous internal documents describing the effects of nicotine: the FDA had "obtained evidence sufficient to prove the necessary 'intent.'" Establishing this intent was, of course, precisely what Kessler and his task force had set out to accomplish.

Conceding the importance of the case, Breyer would have found the safeguard against agency abuse of power in the political accountability of an elected president:

> Insofar as the decision to regulate tobacco reflects the policy of an administration, it is a decision for which that administration, and those politically elected officials who support it, must (and will) take responsibility. And the very importance of the decision taken here, as well as its attendant publicity, means that the public is likely to be aware of it and to hold those officials politically accountable.
>
> Presidents, just like members of Congress, are elected by the public. Indeed, the president and vice president are the only public officials whom the entire nation elects. I do not believe that an administrative agency decision of this magnitude—one that is important, conspicuous, and controversial—can escape the kind of public scrutiny that is essential in any democracy. And such a review will take place whether it is the Congress or the executive branch that makes the relevant decision.

Breyer's theory of agency accountability would justify the superiority of the presidency to the Congress and would place on the presidential electorate a very heavy burden of responsibility—one that was difficult, as a practical matter, to fulfill. The Eighteenth Amendment's prohibition on serving more than two presidential terms barred President Clinton, whose administration was making this bold new claim of regulatory authority, from running in the next election. His party would, of course, nominate a candidate, but many issues arise in a presidential election. Members of the electorate, to the extent that they vote on issues and policy stands, have to vote on bundles of them rather than making discrete choices. If the FDA's regulations had taken effect, a judgment by the voters after the event, even if such a judgment were feasible, could not be counted on to achieve repeal, if such a repeal were what the public preferred.

David Kessler lamented the outcome:

> The decision that could have saved hundreds of thousands of lives had been lost by a single vote. I thought I had steeled myself for defeat, but the news was painful. . . . The split was not defined by a judgment on the industry's intent, or by the question of whether nicotine was a drug. I have to believe that attitudes toward government regulation determined the vote.[17]

This was undoubtedly true and a revealing comment. In Kessler's eyes the right of his agency to do what he tried to do was not the central issue or even a very important issue. A specialist in public health, single-mindedly committed to tobacco control, he could see the issue only as one of nicotine addiction and industry wrongdoing. It was true, as Kessler said, that "attitudes toward government regulation" determined judicial decisions, especially if one enlarges Kessler's phrase to embrace attitudes toward statutory delegations to administrative agencies. In the Supreme Court as in the circuit court, a narrow conservative majority interpreted Congress's grant of power to the FDA conservatively, whereas a liberal minority construed it expansively. The judges were not at odds over facts about nicotine or the industry's behavior.

· The End of the FDA's Program of Tobacco Control ·

After the Supreme Court ruled, the FDA ended its tobacco control program. State regulatory officials under contract to the agency had conducted 6,464 checks in fiscal year (FY) 1997; 39,439 in FY 1998; and 107,200 in FY 1999. The agency also had begun levying civil penalties on repeat offenders and by January 12, 2000, had collected $820,000 in civil fines from retailers who had violated the agency's rules two or more times. As a federal enforcer of age limitations, the FDA had for at least three years largely displaced its sister agency in HHS, the Substance Abuse and Mental Health Services Administration (SAMHSA), which had authority to administer the Synar Amendment of 1992 (see chapter 2).

Whereas the FDA worked through contracts with state agencies, SAMHSA administered grants-in-aid under regulations that it had issued. According to the FDA, SAMHSA's function was to "withhold substance abuse grants to states that do not achieve required access compliance rates by retailers. . . ."[18] This use of grants-in-aid with conditions, a practice that Congress had authorized, was a less direct and less muscular approach than that designed by the FDA, which Congress had not authorized. Congressional appropriations committees nevertheless approved funds for the FDA's activity, and at least one member of the House Appropriations panel, Rosa L. DeLauro, a Democrat from Connecticut, applauded the agency's program and expressed dismay at a newspaper report that state officials in Virginia were declining to cooperate. The FDA's witness explained in response that although it would be "very important to have state cooperation [it] was by no means essential. It will be a federal law to be enforced by federal officials."[19] The regime that the FDA was seeking to construct had far-reaching institutional consequences, affecting relations between the agency and Congress, the FDA and other federal executive agencies, and the federal government and the states.

* * *

That Congress had failed to enact the 1997 settlement and that the federal courts had refused to validate the FDA's attempt at regulation did not mean that no new regulation of tobacco occurred as a result of the late-1990s assault on tobacco. Instead, these developments made the state governments the main scene of action.

· Notes ·

1. Carrick Mollenkamp et al., *The People vs. Big Tobacco* (Princeton, N.J.: Bloomberg, 1998), 277–279.

2. Senate Committee on Commerce, Science, and Transportation, *Global Settlement of Tobacco Litigation: Hearing before the Committee on Commerce, Science, and Transportation*, 105th Cong., 1st sess., July 29, 1997 (Washington, D.C.: Government Printing Office, 1999), 48.

3. Ibid., 35.

4. *Report of the Koop-Kessler Advisory Committee on Tobacco Policy and Public Health*, released July 9, 1997. Available at http://www.ash.org/report2.html, accessed May 19, 2011.

5. "Firms Got Better End of Bargain," *Daily Progress* (Charlottesville, Va.), June 29, 1997, D4. Glantz's essay appeared originally in the *Los Angeles Times*.
6. Jeffrey Goldberg, "Big Tobacco Won't Quit," *New York Times Magazine*, June 21, 1998, 36ff. The quotation is on page 41.
7. *Global Settlement of Tobacco Litigation*, 64.
8. On Osteen's background, see Mollenkamp et al., *The People vs. Big Tobacco*, 155–156.
9. *Coyne Beahm, Inc., Brown & Williamson Tobacco Corp. et al. v. United States Food and Drug Administration and David A. Kessler*, http://tobaccodocuments .org/lor/89278409-8447.html, accessed May 19, 2011.
10. *Federal Register* 61, no. 168 (28 August 1996): 44616.
11. In November 1996 the FDA published guidelines for state governments that wished to apply for exemption to the preemption of their statutes. 11.8 *Tobacco Products Litigation Reporter* 7.10 (1996).
12. Joseph R. DiFranza, "Reducing Youth Access to Tobacco," *Tobacco Control* 9, no. 2 (June 2000): 235–236. This article was one of several contributions to a symposium on "World's Best Practice in Tobacco Control." DiFranza, a Massachusetts antitobacco activist and a faculty member at the University of Massachusetts Medical School, complimented the FDA in particular on the "lightning speed" with which it had acted and its accomplishment "despite a lack of congressional support in terms of . . . explicit authorization."
13. *Brown & Williamson Tobacco Corp. et al. v. Food and Drug Administration et al.*, http://www.usdoj.gov/civil/cases/tobacco/CtApp.htm, accessed February 26, 2004.
14. Joan Biskupic, "Court Hears Debate in FDA-Tobacco Case," *Washington Post*, December 2, 1999, A4. See also Linda Greenhouse, "Justices Skeptical of U.S. Effort for Jurisdiction over Cigarettes," *New York Times*, December 2, 1999, A1.
15. *Federal Register* 61, no. 168: 44413.
16. *Food and Drug Administration et al. v. Brown & Williamson Tobacco Corp. et al.*, 529 U.S. 120 (2000).
17. David Kessler, *A Question of Intent: A Great American Battle with a Deadly Industry* (New York: Public Affairs, 2001), 384.
18. U.S. Dept. of Health and Human Services, Food and Drug Administration, "Tobacco," http://www.fda.gov/ope/FY00plan/tobacco00.htm and http://www .fda.gov/ope/FY01plan/tobacco.html, both accessed on May 24, 2001. Neither was accessible in 2011.
19. House Appropriations Committee, *Agriculture, Rural Development, Food and Drug Administration, and Related Agencies Appropriations for 1998: Hearings before a Subcommittee of the House Appropriations Committee*, 105th Cong., 1st sess. (1997), part 2, 339.

CHAPTER NINE

The Master Settlement Agreement of 1998

THE UNITED STATES ACQUIRED A STRICT new nationwide regime of tobacco regulation in 1998 despite the failure of Congress to enact the 1997 settlement and despite judicial rejection of the FDA's regulations. The new regime came about in an unusual way—through a settlement of the lawsuits brought by the state attorneys general against the cigarette companies. It was incorporated initially in an agreement between the settling parties and then confirmed by acts of the state legislatures and the courts.

· How Could the States Agree? ·

Perhaps the most perplexing question for a political analyst is how fifty states could have managed to concur in the terms of a legal settlement with Big Tobacco. As political communities, the states vary widely in their social and economic structures, cultures, and prevailing political orientations. Accordingly, they had varied widely in their policies toward cigarette use. Those that are home to the industry, whether as growers or manufacturers of tobacco or both—Georgia, Kentucky, North Carolina, South Carolina, Tennessee, and Virginia—had defended its interests in Congress, imposed light excise taxes, and refrained from burdensome prohibitions on use. When tobacco manufacturers sued to challenge the authority of the FDA to regulate their products, the governments of North Carolina and Kentucky had supported them with amicus briefs.[1]

At the other extreme, states with no direct interest in tobacco products but with populations harboring strong antitobacco movements or prohibitionist cultures—California, Massachusetts, Minnesota, Oregon, and Utah are leading examples—had enacted high excise taxes, adopted early and strict prohibitions on place of use, and contributed leaders to the antismoking movement in Congress. Cigarette excise taxes in 1998 ranged all the way from Virginia's 2.5 cents per pack to $1.00 in Alaska and Hawaii, an extraordinary gap. In 1997 the proportion of adults who smoked ranged from 13.7 percent in Utah to 30.8 percent in Kentucky.

Less than 1 percent of the population chewed tobacco or dipped snuff in the heavily urban northeastern states, whereas 15 percent of the population did so in West Virginia.[2]

A fundamental reason for Congress's historic aversion to tobacco control legislation lay precisely in these sharp differences of culture and interest between regions or states, which made it easy to do nothing and default to the states. But then how could political communities so different come together in support of a common policy in the 1998 settlement?

Part of the answer lies in the fact that with respect to the tobacco litigation, the states did not act as political communities or even as whole governments. As previous chapters have pointed out, the agents of the states in this case were their attorneys general, nearly all of whom were elected officials with strong inducements to seek publicity. Moreover, as a group they possessed broad discretion to act independently. Recall that Attorney General Mike Moore of Mississippi, who was the first to file against the industry and who urged other attorneys general to follow his lead, knew that the Mississippi legislature would not appropriate funds with which to pursue such a suit and had to fight off a suit from his own governor, Kirk Fordice, who claimed that Moore lacked authority to prosecute the case. (When this happened, the attorneys general from thirty-eight other states joined in an amicus brief supporting Moore.)[3] Because the attorneys general hired private attorneys on a contingency basis, most legislatures did not have to appropriate funds to pursue the tobacco cases, and most governors did not actively embrace such suits. Those who embraced the cases most ardently were attorneys general who were trying to become governors, notably Hubert Humphrey III in Minnesota and Scott Harshbarger in Massachusetts.

Nevertheless, a puzzle remained. Surely some of the attorneys general would have operated under a political constraint: one would not expect those from tobacco states to bet their political futures on waging war against the industry. In fact, the attorneys general of Virginia, Kentucky, and Tennessee refrained from filing, while the attorney general of North Carolina was prohibited by his legislature from doing so. Also, the attorney general of business-friendly Delaware, Jane Brady, did not file for what she said was a combination of "practical, legal, and political reasons": she did not expect to win in Delaware's Court of Chancery, which is not receptive to novel theories of tort recovery; she was averse to contingency-fee contracts with outside lawyers; and she detected insufficient support from the governor, legislature, and public for proceeding at the state's own expense. Although the media supported suits against the tobacco companies, the Delaware electorate did not.[4]

Among the attorneys general, there was also one thoroughly out-spoken opponent of the suits—Bill Pryor of Alabama, a conservative Republican and the youngest attorney general in the country. He had been appointed to the office by Governor Fob James in January 1997 to complete the term of Jeff Sessions, who had been elected to the Senate. In essays in the *Wall Street Journal* and the *New York Times* in April 1997, Pryor objected to the circumvention of legislatures and juries, an approach that played "fast and loose with a fundamental civil right." He wrote that "the dirty little secret of these state lawsuits is that many of them have been designed as so-called equity cases to avoid a trial by jury. . . . This wave of lawsuits is about politics, not law, and money, not public health. The overwhelming majority of the lawsuits have been filed by Democratic attorneys general and politically connected, liberal trial lawyers."[5]

There were also dissenters from the political left who agreed with suing but wanted to press on to a greater victory. When settlement negotiations got under way with Moore in the lead, Attorney General Humphrey declined to join, insisting that the industry was not being punished sufficiently; he quickly became a pariah among the attorneys general. Humphrey's neighbor in Wisconsin adopted a similar position.

Given these dissents, the question persists: How did the states arrive at a joint settlement? To answer that question requires taking a closer look at the development of the states' suits and the industry's response. It takes two sides to settle, and the industry continued to have a strong interest in achieving a comprehensive settlement. It will be easier to understand why as one looks at the cases that were settled individually, in advance of the comprehensive settlement of the fall of 1998. Chapter 5 covered the case of Mississippi, which was first to settle. Three others followed: Florida, Texas, and Minnesota.

The Florida Case

The Florida case is significant and instructive because there the separate parts of government did combine to attack the industry. Attorney General Bob Butterworth, though strongly committed, was not acting alone. The Florida legislature passed a law guaranteeing that the industry could not win in the state's courts. Gov. Lawton Chiles signed it and then issued an executive order providing that the law would apply only to the tobacco industry and to sellers of illegal drugs. Finally, a four-man majority of the state's supreme court upheld the law over three dissenters, who protested vainly that cigarette manufacturers "are entitled to just as much constitutional protection as anyone else."[6]

In April 1994, as Mike Moore was getting ready to bring suit against the tobacco companies, the Florida legislature was amending the state's Medicaid Third-Party Liability Act to ensure that any such suit in Florida would end in a victory for the state. Applying only to suits brought by the state government, as distinct from those filed by individuals, the law provided at its core that "assumption of risk and all other affirmative defenses normally available to a liable third party are to be abrogated to the extent necessary to assure full recovery by Medicaid from third-party resources." (Assumption of risk was the defense that the industry had traditionally relied on in individual cases.) Other crucial provisions stated that

1. "causation and damages . . . may be proven by use of statistical analysis" without showing a link between a particular smoker's illness and that person's use of tobacco products;

2. the state "shall not be required to . . . identify the individual recipients for which payment has been made, but rather can proceed to seek recovery based upon payments made on behalf of an entire class of recipients"; and

3. in assigning liability to the individual tobacco companies, the state "shall be allowed to proceed under a market share theory, provided that the products involved are substantially interchangeable among brands."

There would be no need to show, as there had been in individual lawsuits, that a particular smoker had smoked a particular brand. Finally, the law authorized the state to pay "reasonable litigation costs or expenses" to private attorneys, plus a contingency fee not to exceed 30 percent of the amount realized in damages.[7]

Not surprisingly, this law was drafted by a plaintiff's lawyer, Fredric G. Levin of Pensacola, who said that it originated in discussions within the Inner Circle, an exclusive group of one hundred personal injury lawyers who had won judgments of at least $1 million. It was tacked onto an obscure bill in the last week of the legislative session and passed without debate.[8] "We're going to take the Marlboro Man to court," Governor Chiles boasted after he signed the bill.[9]

Big Tobacco's opponents were delighted with this development. "Mississippi filed its suit under existing . . . law, whereas Florida has changed the law to make it easier to bring this sort of case," Jennifer Lew of the Tobacco Products Liability Project explained to a reporter. "It basically tilts the playing field in favor of the state and streamlines the process of getting money from the tobacco companies." Lew's employer,

Richard Daynard, called the new law "the most important legislation ever adopted anywhere in the United States" on the subject of "holding cigarette manufacturers financially responsible for the health care costs their products and conduct produce."[10] He and Lew suggested that other states would want to do the same thing—and quickly.[11]

A year later, after heavy lobbying by business interests, the legislature voted to repeal the law, perhaps anticipating that Governor Chiles would veto the repeal, which he did.[12] Then the law was of course challenged in the courts. After the Florida Supreme Court narrowly upheld it, the tobacco industry sought a reversal from the U.S. Supreme Court, which, however, declined to grant certiorari. The Court accepts only a small fraction of the cases that petitioners seek to bring to it and gives preference to those that involve differences of judgment among lower federal courts. Certainly a powerful case could be made that constitutional questions were at issue here, above all the Fourteenth Amendment protection against deprivation of property without due process of law.[13]

Given this background, the industry elected to settle with Florida even before Moore's suit went to trial. In August 1997 it agreed to pay the state $11.3 billion over twenty-five years and to pay the costs and fees of the private lawyers who had prepared Florida's case. It also agreed to various public health measures, which distinguished the Florida outcome from that of Mississippi, where money only was involved. Here the new regulatory regime began to emerge: the industry agreed (1) to remove all billboard and transit advertisements, beginning with billboards located within one thousand feet of a public or private school; (2) to support efforts in the Florida legislature to pass new laws that would prohibit cigarette vending machines except in locations, such as bars, that are confined to adults, and strengthen penalties against store owners who sold cigarettes to underage buyers; and (3) to spend $200 million in the next two years to finance a pilot program aimed at reducing youth smoking.[14]

In light of the advantages that the plaintiffs enjoyed in Florida, including fresh releases of industry documents, a sympathetic judge, and good chances of a sympathetic jury—"because Palm Beach's well-educated citizenry was hostile to tobacco," according to Dan Zegart in *Civil Warriors*—it is perhaps surprising that Florida's attorney general elected to settle. Ron Motley, whose firm was involved in the case, "would always feel Florida was the one that got away"—that is, would have produced a victory at trial. It was a victory that Motley particularly coveted because in this case the industry's own law firm, Shook, Hardy, and Bacon, was charged with abetting a civil conspiracy. Some of the freshly released documents were from the industry's committee of law-yers, the Committee of Counsel. Thus, a trial in Florida would have tested whether industry lawyers could be held liable for the industry's deceitful conduct.[15]

Cases in Texas and Minnesota

The next case to settle was that of Texas. Filed in a federal district court in Texarkana, it was settled in mid-January 1998 as jury selec-tion was about to begin. The industry agreed to pay $15.3 billion over twenty-five years, including $264 million right away to fund state research and antismoking initiatives directed at youth. The Texas case was notable for fights that it touched off among officeholders within the state over issues of jurisdiction. Two members of the legislature who headed budget committees, Sen. Bill Ratliff, a Republican, and Rep. Rob Junell, a Democrat, petitioned the judge for permission to become parties to the lawsuit, claiming that by earmarking funds for certain purposes the deal had usurped the legislature's authority to set spending priorities. Gov. George W. Bush agreed with their complaint and before long went to court himself to challenge the $2.3 billion in fees (15 percent of the settlement total) that was to be paid to the private lawyers involved; Bush asked that more of the money go to health care and less to lawyers. Also, several Texas legislators filed a mandamus action in state court, challenging the authority of the attor-ney general to bind the state to a contingency-fee agreement. There was a general clamor among public officials for a right to have a say in how the windfall of tobacco money should be spent.[16] In general, these various claims in Texas were resolved when the states collec-tively settled with the industry, in an agreement that left to state leg-islators decisions about how to spend settlement funds and to a board of arbitration the award of attorneys' fees, which were paid by the tobacco companies.

Minnesota's was the last in this series of individually settled cases. Coming to an end in mid-May 1998, as the McCain bill was being debated in the Senate, it yielded $6.1 billion for the state government, an amount half again as much as Minnesota would have received under the settlement of June 1997. Several features of the Minnesota trial were distinctive. Private insurer Blue Cross and Blue Shield of Minnesota participated along with the state government and received an award of $469 million. The grounds for suit included alleged violations of state consumer fraud and antitrust laws. Attorney General Humphrey and his collaborating private attorneys, Mike Ciresi and Roberta Walburn of the tort firm Robins, Kaplan, Miller and Ciresi, attached high priority to obtaining industry documents. They succeeded, with the backing of the presiding judge, in opening up thirty-nine thousand documents that the industry had sought to shield with a claim of attorney-client privilege. In all, the plaintiffs' team gathered approximately thirty million pages of industry documents, which were placed in a depository in Minnesota that would remain open to the public for ten years.

In addition to the usual promises to pay for antismoking programs and to restrict advertising, the industry also agreed to abolish the Council for Tobacco Research, which gave grants for research and which the industry's opponents charged was no more than a propaganda front. The companies entered into a consent decree promising not to misrepresent the health hazards of smoking; the terms of the decree would be enforceable in court. Humphrey announced proudly, "Today the tobacco industry has surrendered, and they have surrendered on our terms."[17] The victory celebration at the Radisson Hotel "resembled a religious revival much more than a postlitigation press conference," according to two local reporters.[18]

More intriguing than the terms of settlement was the fact that Minnesota's case was the only one of the first four to reach trial. The trial consumed eighty days and left the jurors distraught, the women in tears, when a settlement was announced just as they were about to receive the case. According to industry lawyers, it was the judge's instructions to the jury that convinced them they must settle. "We thought the judge had, in effect, prejudged the case against us and was doing everything he could to dictate the outcome of the case," Reynolds's lawyer Arthur Golden said. ". . . When a judge appears to be very strongly against you, you have substantial concern about what the jury will do, because juries are very influenced by what they see the judge do." There was a further concern about what the judge himself might do because he had power to levy fines on the defendants independent of a jury verdict. "The judge could have entered not just fines and penalties," Golden said, "but injunctions that could have effectively destroyed the companies' abilities to do business."[19] The industry had tried without success to have the judge removed.

Because they had no chance to deliberate, no one could say with certainty what the jurors would have done. Five of the twelve talked to reporters immediately afterward. Three said they had not decided on a verdict or damages and were disappointed not to get the chance; the other two doubted that they would have awarded as much in damages. Mostly the jurors expressed frustration at not being able to render a verdict. "Where have the people spoken?" one asked. "I think what's frustrating is you assume it's government of the people, by the people, and for the people. You get here, and you are the people selected to represent Minnesota. So you fulfill your obligation, only to have the carpet pulled out from under you."[20]

The Remaining Forty-Six States

Four states having settled, the forty-six others were left in limbo when the McCain bill failed. If four states were entitled to receive funds from the industry for Medicaid costs—a point on which no jury had ever rendered a decision—presumably the others were entitled as well, for the sake of interstate equity. Yet from a legal standpoint, the question remained problematic because some of the states' cases had failed. In West Virginia, the third state to file (after Mississippi and Minnesota but before Florida), the tobacco companies at trial successfully challenged the authority of the attorney general to bring suit independently of a state agency. A Kanawha County Circuit Court had ruled in their favor in the fall of 1995.[21] The West Virginia Public Employees Insurance Agency and the West Virginia Department of Health and Human Resources then joined the suit as plaintiffs, but early in 1997 the court ruled that they, too, lacked authority to sue.[22]

In late July 1998, Marion County Superior Court Judge Gerald Zore dismissed a seventeen-month-old case filed by Indiana's attorney general, Jeffrey Modisett. In a terse two-page order, Zore said that Indiana could not seek damages from harm to individual smokers because "the injuries are derivative and too remote." He also dismissed allegations of conspiracy, antitrust violations, and "unjust enrichment."[23] In front of TV cameras, Modisett tore the ruling up and threw it in a wastebasket— but that flamboyant gesture did not nullify it.[24]

The case of Washington State, which had been filed relatively early (June 5, 1996) and was scheduled to go to trial in September, had been dismissed in part. The state's effort to recoup Medicaid expenses had been thrown out, so that the case depended entirely on antitrust and fraud claims. Early in September a judge dismissed Idaho's case. In five states with suits pending, the industry's potential liability was limited by a ban on punitive damages in civil cases, and ten other states imposed limits on such damages. Only two states, Maryland and Vermont, had followed the example of Florida and amended their laws so as to undermine the industry's defenses.[25] Given this varied set of circumstances in the states and the legal fragility of the Medicaid recovery claims, the attorneys general had strong incentives to avoid trials and proceed to a settlement.

So did the industry, which had always wanted a comprehensive settlement and did not now want to battle its way through roughly three dozen pending suits. And so, most certainly, did the private tort lawyers, who wanted to be paid as much as possible as quickly as possible without additional investment of effort. Thus, it came as no surprise that one of the initiators of renewed negotiations between the state governments and the industry was Joe Rice, the managing partner in Ron Motley's firm. He sat down with Meyer Koplow, a New York lawyer representing Philip Morris, in early June 1998, even before the denouement had been reached in the Senate's consideration of the McCain bill.[26] Nine attorneys general subsequently joined the negotiations. They represented states that were large (New York, California) or scheduled to go to trial soon (Washington, Oklahoma). The nine also included a range of attitudes toward the industry, from the hostility of Scott Harshbarger of Massachusetts, who dropped out at the end of August complaining of the industry's intransigence and threatening to go to trial, to the moderation of Gale Norton of Colorado ("I'm not an antismoking extremist"), to the solicitousness of Mike Easley of North Carolina, who had never sued. The other two participants were from North Dakota and Pennsylvania.[27] Thus, the group looked like a microcosm of Congress, with members from all regions and types of states, including densely populated states of the two coasts, sparsely populated states of the western plains, and the South. It was as if the group had been constituted to perform legislative acts—policymaking and the allocation of benefits—such as are normally entrusted to representative bodies. Just as Congress in 1997–1998 had been called upon, uncharacteristically, to mete out punishments and grant protections in a tort action, litigants and tort lawyers would now sit down, much as Congress does when it legislates grants-in-aid, to distribute benefits among the states.

Negotiations proceeded fitfully for five months, hampered by differences within the two sides as well as between them. Within the industry, the main source of tension was how to protect against competition from upstarts—small companies, new or existing, that would gain a competitive advantage because they were not covered by the advertising and marketing restrictions of the agreement or burdened by its monetary obligations, which were designed to drive up the price of cigarettes. This issue was of greater concern to R. J. Reynolds and Brown & Williamson than to Philip Morris and Lorillard because they were more directly in competition with renegade brands.[28]

Nationwide, the attorneys general were divided into three groups: hard-liners such as Harshbarger in Massachusetts, Joseph Curran in Maryland, Jim Doyle in Wisconsin, and Richard Blumenthal in Connecticut, whose cases had good prospects and who felt little pressure to settle; those whose chances in court were poorer; and those who had never brought suit at all, such as North Carolina's Easley. The leader of the negotiations for the attorneys general was Washington state's Christine Gregoire, who fell into the second group. Personally a stalwart opponent of the industry, she nevertheless was heading toward trial with a weak case that got still weaker when the presiding judge ruled in July that the industry was entitled to seek to have any damage award offset by the amount of tax revenue that the state had collected from cigarette sales.[29] Even those attorneys general most eager to hold out for strict terms, such as Blumenthal, suffered a setback when the Fourth Circuit Court of Appeals held that the FDA lacked authority to regulate cigarettes. Blumenthal had been determined to demand that the industry submit to FDA regulation, a position hard to maintain in the face of that court's holding.[30]

In the end, a deal was possible because the number of attorneys general with weak cases and the number who had never sued constituted a sizeable majority of the forty-six states that had not settled. When the eight states that had been actively negotiating with the industry signed an agreement on November 13, the remaining states had to decide whether to join, a decision that could be problematic only for that group of perhaps a dozen states—exemplified by Massachusetts and Maryland—that might be tempted to go to court because they thought they could win there.[31] The industry demanded a response within a week. All forty-six did join, despite criticism from public health organizations that the controls on the industry were too weak. James E. Tierney, a former attorney general of Maine who had become an adviser to the attorneys general on the subject of tobacco, told the *Washington Post:* "These are public prosecutors. . . . They have a case. They have an offer on the table. They have to balance whether . . . the people of their state [will] be better off if they accept this settlement." Encouraged, no doubt, by legislators who were eager to see the money, the attorneys general decided yes. "The politicians 'respect the American Lung Association, and they wish them luck as they fight the fight in Congress,'" Tierney said. "But that's not what an attorney general does."[32]

That all of the attorneys general in the end acquiesced should not obscure the fact that some states were coerced by the rest into participating. For example, North Carolina, which had elected not to sue, had the choice of either participating and having its consumers of cigarettes pay higher prices while the state received a share of the new revenue, or not participating, in which case its consumers would still pay the higher prices but the state government would receive nothing. "Some choice," as the director of the Federal Trade Commission's Bureau of Economics commented in a speech on the settlement and antitrust law.[33]

"How to Spend Tobacco Money?" a headline in the *New York Times* asked rhetorically. "New York Counts the Ways." "This is going to be pretty much a feeding frenzy," one legislator said. "I mean, it's free money."[34] It was for most states "their largest revenue windfall ever."[35] Over a twenty-five-year period beginning in 2000, the states would realize amounts estimated to range from a low of $486.5 million for Wyoming, which had not sued, to highs of $25 billion each for California and New York. Settling made the payments certain, whereas going to court would have left them at risk.

· The Agreement ·

The settlement of November 1998, formally known as the Master Settlement Agreement (MSA), was a more moderate version of the June 1997 settlement. It cost the companies less—an estimated $206 billion over twenty-five years, in addition to the more than $40 billion that they had by now promised to the four individually settling states[36]—and also gave them less in return. Although it ended the threat of suits from state governments, it offered no protection from the federal government, which would soon follow the states' example and bring its own suit. Moreover, it provided no protection from private class actions or large punitive damage awards. For its part, the industry promised that it would mount no new challenges to the enforceability or constitutionality of state and local tobacco control laws enacted prior to June 1, 1998, and agreed to dismiss a number of pending legal challenges against the states.

The payments to the states fell into seven categories:

1. Up-front payments ($12.742 billion). The companies would pay $2.4 billion as soon as courts approved the MSA, followed by comparable amounts, with a 3 percent annual increase for inflation, in 2000, 2001, 2002, and 2003.

2. Annual payments ($183.177 billion). These would begin with $4.5 billion on April 15, 2000, and then ramp up gradually to an estimated $9 billion by 2018, where they would remain through 2025. These were allocated among the states according to a formula negotiated by the attorneys general under the leadership of Indiana's Jeffrey Modisett. The formula weighted two variables equally: smoking-related Medicaid expenditures and smoking-related non-Medicaid health care costs (including factors for population and smoking prevalence). However, negotiations led to adjustments to resolve a conflict between New

York and California and to respond to special claims of some of the smaller states.[37]

3. The strategic contribution fund ($8.61 billion). On April 15, 2008, and on April 15 of each year through 2017, the companies would pay $861 million into a fund that would be allocated to "reflect the contribution made by states toward resolution of the state lawsuits against tobacco companies," according to a formula developed by a panel of former state attorneys general. The estimated amounts ranged from $6.5 million per year for states such as Alabama, Delaware, and Virginia, which had not sued, to $49.6 million for Washington, $47.2 million for New York, and $44.5 million for California, which had been aggressively involved.

4. The "national foundation" ($250 million). The companies would make annual payments of $25 million for ten years to support a "charitable foundation," to be established by the executive committee of the National Association of Attorneys General (NAAG), for the study of programs to reduce teen smoking and substance abuse and to prevent diseases associated with tobacco use.

5. The "national public education fund" ($1.45 billion). The companies would make annual payments over five years to carry out a sustained national advertising and education program that would counter youth tobacco use and educate consumers about tobacco-related diseases. Grants from the fund would be administered by the national foundation.

6. The attorney general enforcement fund ($50 million). This was a one-time payment in 1999 to provide funds to individual state attorneys general for the purpose of implementing and enforcing the agreement.

7. Payments to the NAAG ($1.5 million). The industry would pay the association $150,000 annually for ten years beginning on December 31, 1998, to coordinate the implementation and enforcement of the agreement on behalf of the attorneys general and the settling states.[38]

Even these numerous and varied payments did not represent the whole of the industry's financial obligations. As required by the MSA, the companies met with the political leadership of fourteen tobacco-growing states and worked out the National Tobacco Grower Settlement Trust Agreement, known as "Phase II" of the MSA, in which they promised an estimated $5.15 billion over twelve years to compensate growers for an anticipated decline in demand for tobacco. The industry also agreed to pay the lawyers' fees incurred by state governments (of which more will be said in chapter 10).

The companies' shares of the payments were determined in part by their current market value, but the MSA provided for a volume adjustment, such that payments would go up or down depending on the number of cigarettes shipped. There was a provision also for an inflation adjustment, which was set at 3 percent or the actual percentage increase in the Consumer Price Index, whichever was greater.

The agreement imposed numerous advertising and marketing restrictions on the industry but fewer than were in the 1997 settlement. It provided for a qualified ban on transit and outdoor advertising, including billboards and signs or placards larger than a poster in arenas, stadiums, shopping malls, and video game arcades; the earlier settlement would have banned transit and outdoor advertising without exception. It prohibited the use of cartoon characters but not human characters (for example, the Marlboro Man) in advertising, promotion, and packaging; the earlier settlement would have banned both. It forbade the distribution and sale of nontobacco merchandise with brand logos, such as caps, T-shirts, and backpacks, except at tobacco-sponsored events; the earlier settlement would have banned them without exception. It prohibited future brands from being named after celebrities, nationally recognized sports teams, or well-recognized nontobacco brand names, such as Harley-Davidson or Yves Saint-Laurent. It prohibited brand-name sponsorship of concerts, events with a significant youth audience, or team sports (football, basketball, baseball, hockey, or soccer). It did, however, permit one brand-name event per year, thus allowing the Winston Cup to survive, and it contained a special exemption on the concert ban for Brown & Williamson, permitting one concert a year. Formerly B&W had sponsored under its brand names GPC and Kool a country music festival and a jazz festival, respectively, and the MSA would allow it to continue one or the other; the 1997 settlement would have banned brand-name sponsorship of such events altogether—no more Winston Cup, no Kool jazz festival.

The 1997 settlement contained several provisions designed to restrict youth access to tobacco: a requirement of proof of age for tobacco purchases, a ban on all sales of tobacco products through vending machines, a requirement that retailers be licensed, and a plan for enforcing minimum age laws. These restrictions fell within the jurisdiction of legislatures to impose—or of the FDA, if it succeeded with its attempt at regulation—and were omitted from the settlement of 1998.

Unlike the 1997 settlement, which presumed congressional enactment, this one did not provide for FDA regulation, which was not within the power of state governments, let alone state attorneys general, to authorize. Nor did it contain the so-called lookback provisions of the 1997 settlement and the McCain bill—provisions that would have imposed stiff monetary penalties on the companies if youth smoking rates did not fall.

The MSA did, however, contain a number of prohibitions on the industry's political activity, which were some of the least remarked features of the assault on tobacco yet some of the most problematic from the point of view of American political traditions. It disbanded the Tobacco Institute, the industry's lobbying organization, as well as the Council for Tobacco Research. It prohibited the industry from lobbying against eight different categories of state and local legislative proposals, ranging from "limitations on Youth access to vending machines" to "limitations on non-tobacco products which are designed to look like tobacco products, such as bubble gum cigars, candy cigarettes, etc."[39] The settlement also incorporated a promise from the industry to refrain from challenging its constitutionality.

The MSA contained complicated provisions to protect participating manufacturers from new competitors, stipulating that if the participating manufacturers lost market share, a nationally recognized firm of economic consultants would determine whether the agreement had played a significant role in the loss. If so, and if the aggregate market share of participating companies fell by more than 2 percent, their annual payment would be reduced by 3 percent for each percentage point of loss above that threshold. Beyond that, small companies, the potential competitors for market share, were given inducements to join the settlement.

The participating companies initially were the four biggest manufacturers—Philip Morris, R. J. Reynolds, Brown & Williamson, and Lorillard. Liggett, a very small company, had settled independently with the states after promising to make a small payment, admit wrongdoing, and turn industry documents over to the attorneys general (see chapter 5). Small companies that agreed to join the settlement were allowed to keep the proceeds from their sales up to 125 percent of a base-year volume. In effect, they were freed from a threat of liability and given a subsidy in return for accepting a prescribed market share. This arrangement freed the largest companies from a fear that raising prices cooperatively would cause them to lose share to small firms (and, if they did lose share, their payments were more than proportionately reduced). Liggett got a particularly good deal by threatening not to sign and to flood the market with cheap cigarettes. Philip Morris thereupon paid

Liggett $300 million for three dying brands that had combined annual sales of about $40 million. Liggett was also released from its financial obligation under its earlier deals with the states.

But what about small companies that did not want to participate? Such companies, Non-Participating Manufacturers, or NPMs, were compelled by the states to pay large amounts into escrow, where the money would stay for decades, held supposedly against potential future liability judgments. The requirement that small firms contribute to an escrow account constituted a barrier to market entry and could force nonsignatories out of business by depriving them of their profits. The agreement contained the text of a model statute for legislatures to enact to accomplish this purpose. Alternatively, they could pass a "qualifying statute" of their own devising. Technically they were not required to pass such a law, but they risked losing their share of the settlement if they did not. If they enacted a law but it was invalidated by the state's courts—a distinct possibility, given its manifest violation of antitrust laws—the state could, in any given year, potentially lose some or all of its proceeds from the settlement. As the laissez-faire author Walter Olson acidly commented, "The word for this process is *cartelization,* and the irony is that had cigarette executives met privately among themselves to raise prices, freeze market shares, confine small competitors to minor allocations on the fringe of the market, and penalize defectors and new entrants, they could have been sent to prison as antitrust violators. . . ." [40]

Finally, the MSA included a model consent decree for adoption by courts in each of the states. This document contained many of the terms of the settlement, including the restrictions on marketing and advertising. The settlement would go into effect in each state when a court approved the settlement and the consent decree, which would make the terms of the decree judicially enforceable.

This was the largest settlement of civil lawsuits in U.S. history, though economic analysts in particular were quick to point out that it did not have the characteristics of a settlement for damages. It was, rather, a tax increase, given the fact that payments depended so heavily on sales volume. "Every single cigarette tax ever passed has been paid fully by the consumer," said John Gruber, an economist at the Massachusetts Institute of Technology and a former deputy secretary of the Treasury in the federal government. "There's no reason to think this will be any different." [41]

The agreement was to last in perpetuity, although the amounts of industry payments were estimated only through 2025. The attorneys general had agreed not just to drop their pending suits but also to refrain from filing future suits on whatever grounds, be they fraud, antitrust, recovery claims related to health care costs, or anything else.

· Two Kinds of Opposition ·

Public health interests, always the core of opposition to tobacco use, continued to be dissatisfied with what the attorneys general had produced, believing that it did not go far enough and had received too little public discussion. The antitobacco activist John Banzhaf filed amicus briefs in ten to twenty of the most populous states, asking judges to delay approval to give public health groups time to study the agreement. Public health groups filed such briefs in roughly half a dozen states.[42]

An example was New York, where a public health coalition on December 9 asked a state court for delay and revisions. The coalition complained that the MSA had been negotiated without input from public health organizations, that the time between conclusion of the agreement and its submission to the court was too short to permit meaningful public debate or comment, and that it was too vague about marketing and advertising restrictions on the companies and about the size of their financial obligations. The group asked the court to provide for a review period of 90 to 120 days, to appoint a special master to oversee an impartial review, and to condition approval of the MSA on inclusion of a tobacco control program, to be funded from the settlement proceeds.[43] Courts ignored these requests and, in general, moved swiftly to approve the agreement. By December 9, eighteen state courts had already acted affirmatively. The New York court approved the MSA on December 23.[44]

Advocates of market competition also criticized the settlement. The head of the Bureau of Economics at the Federal Trade Commission attacked it, as did publications of the libertarian Cato Institute and op-ed writers who were affiliated with Cato. Two of them, Thomas C. O'Brien and Robert A. Levy, wrote as follows in the *Wall Street Journal:*

> The nasty little secret of the nationwide tobacco settlement is that it violates both the antitrust laws and the Constitution.
>
> The settlement transforms a competitive industry into a cartel, then protects the cartel by erecting barriers to entry that preserve the 99% market dominance of the tobacco giants. Far from being victims, the big four tobacco companies are at the very center of the scheme. In collaboration with state attorneys general and their trial lawyer friends, the four majors have managed to carve out a protected market for themselves—all at the expense of smokers and the tobacco companies that didn't sign the November 1998 Master Settlement Agreement (MSA).
>
> It's a sweetheart deal. . . .[45]

There was no outcry from the nation's opinionmakers, such as editorial writers or policy specialists in other think tanks or on university faculties. This may have been because they were exhausted by the subject of tobacco, or because an action that contained *any* anti-tobacco provisions was sacrosanct, or because the MSA was too lengthy, arcane, and inaccessible to engage much attention. The next chapter will explore the consequences of the MSA.

· Notes ·

1. 11.7 *Tobacco Products Litigation Reporter* (*TPLR*)1.183 (1996).
2. U.S. Department of Health and Human Services, Centers for Disease Control and Prevention, *State Tobacco Control Highlights, 1999,* CDC Publication No. 099-5621 (1999), pp. 116, 118, 124.
3. 11.4 *TPLR* 1.94 (1996). There were other states, too, in which the governor was at odds with the attorney general over the tobacco suit—Arizona, for example. See 11.7 *TPLR* 1.183 (1996).
4. *Regulation by Litigation: The New Wave of Government-Sponsored Litigation* (New York: Manhattan Institute for Policy Research, 1999), 36–39.
5. "Litigators' Smoke Screen," *Wall Street Journal,* April 7, 1997, A14; and "The Law Is at Risk in Tobacco Suits," *New York Times,* April 27, 1997, sec. 4, p. 15. See also Pryor's speech to the Cato Institute, August 5, 1997. Pryor's speeches and articles on the tobacco litigation and related subjects remained accessible as of July 16, 2004, on the Web site of the attorney general of Alabama: http://www.ago.state.al.us. However, he resigned that office on February 20, 2004, upon receiving from President George W. Bush a recess appointment to the U.S. Court of Appeals for the Eleventh Circuit.
6. *Agency for Health Care Administration et al. v. Associated Industries of Florida, Inc.,* Supreme Court of Florida, 678 S. 2d 1239, decided June 27, 1996.
7. For this summary of the act I have relied on Robert A. Levy, "Tobacco Medicaid Litigation: Snuffing Out the Rule of Law," *Cato Institute Policy Analysis* 275 (20 June 1997): 7–8.
8. Junda Woo, "Tobacco Firms Face Greater Health Liability—Florida Seeks to Recover State's Cost of Treating Smoking-Related Illnesses," *Wall Street Journal,* May 3, 1994, A3.
9. Larry Rohter, "Florida Prepares New Basis to Sue Tobacco Industry," *New York Times,* May 27, 1994, A1.
10. Ibid.
11. Ibid.; and Woo, "Tobacco Firms Face Greater Health Liability," A3.
12. Suein L. Hwang, "Florida Judge Upholds Law Allowing State's Suit against Tobacco Industry," *Wall Street Journal,* June 19, 1995, A11.
13. For a discussion of the constitutional issues, see William W. Van Alstyne, "Denying Due Process in the Florida Courts: A Commentary on the 1994 Medicaid Third-Party Liability Act of Florida," *Florida Law Review* 46, no. 4 (September 1994): 563–589.

14. Barry Meier, "Cigarette Makers Agree to Settle Florida Lawsuit," *New York Times,* August 26, 1997, A1.

15. Dan Zegart, *Civil Warriors: The Legal Siege on the Tobacco Industry* (New York: Delacorte, 2000), 281. The Oklahoma suit, filed in June 1996, named three industry law firms as defendants: Shook, Hardy and Bacon of Kansas City; Jacob, Medinger and Finnegan of New York; and Chadbourne and Parke of New York. See Graham E. Kelder Jr. and Richard A. Daynard, "The Role of Litigation in the Effective Control of the Sale and Use of Tobacco," *Stanford Law & Policy Review* 8, no. 1 (winter 1997): 75.

16. Barry Meier, "Tobacco Concerns Settle Texas Case for a Record Sum," *New York Times,* January 16, 1998, A1; Associated Press, "Texas Tobacco Deal Is Approved," *New York Times,* January 17, 1998, A9; Sam Howe Verhovek, "Fat Fees in Tobacco Deals Signal New Foe for States: The Lawyers," *New York Times,* February 9, 1998, A1; and Lester Brickman, "Lawyers' Ethics and Fiduciary Obligation in the Brave New World of Aggregative Litigation," *William & Mary Environmental Law & Policy Review,* 26 (winter 2001), 262–263.

17. Pam Belluck, "Tobacco Companies Settle a Suit with Minnesota for $6.5 Billion," *New York Times,* May 9, 1998, A1.

18. Deborah Caulfield Rybak and David Phelps, *Smoked: The Inside Story of the Minnesota Tobacco Trial* (Minneapolis: MSP, 1998), 430–431.

19. Ibid., 399–400, 410.

20. Ibid., 434–437; and Belluck, "Tobacco Companies Settle a Suit," A1. Later the opposing sides in the suit interviewed the jurors. According to a lawyer for the industry, ". . . their answers suggest they never would have agreed to extract substantial sums from the tobacco industry." See Dan Webb, in *Regulation by Litigation,* 53.

21. I am indebted to Emily Spieler, a professor of law at West Virginia University, for help with this history. She in turn enlisted assistance from a member of the state attorney general's office, Silas Taylor, who supplied a copy of the brief that the attorney general's office filed in its appeal of the first decision.

22. *Darrell V. McGraw Jr. v. The American Tobacco Company, et al.,* 12.1 TPLR 2.43 (1997).

23. Bloomberg News, "Judge Dismisses Indiana's Tobacco Suit," *Los Angeles Times,* July 25, 1998, D2; and Dow Jones Newswires, "Indiana Judge Dismisses State's Tobacco Lawsuit," *Wall Street Journal,* July 27, 1998, B1.

24. Remarks of Bill Pryor, in *Regulation by Litigation,* 18.

25. Tara Parker-Pope and Milo Geyelin, "Tobacco: Without Legislation, Price Rises Could Ease," *Wall Street Journal,* June 19, 1998, B1.

26. Zegart, *Civil Warriors,* 329–330.

27. Suein L. Hwang, "Tobacco Takes New Stab at a Settlement—Companies' Aim in State Talks Is More Modest," *Wall Street Journal,* July 10, 1998, B1; Milo Geyelin, "Tobacco Firms and States Discuss Dollar Figures, but Progress Little," *Wall Street Journal,* July 31, 1998, B10; and Barry Meier, "Talks Stall in Effort to Reach Tobacco Accord," *New York Times,* August 5, 1998, A14. The characterization of Norton and the quotation from her are in Holman W. Jenkins Jr., "At the End of Tobacco Road," *Wall Street Journal,* December 9, 1998, A23. On

Harshbarger, see Frank Phillips, "Bay State Drops Out of Tobacco Pact Talks; Harshbarger Eyes Mass. Settlement," *Boston Globe,* August 30, 1998, A1.

28. Milo Geyelin, "States' Officials Plan to Resume Talks on Tobacco," *Wall Street Journal,* August 26, 1998, B2; and Geyelin, "Tobacco Negotiations to Resume After Massachusetts Walks Out," *Wall Street Journal,* September 1, 1998, B8.

29. Geyelin, "Tobacco Firms and States Discuss Dollar Figures," B10.

30. Ibid.

31. See Daniel LeDuc, "Md. Mulls Joining U.S. Tobacco Settlement or Gambling with Lawsuit," *Washington Post,* November 14, 1998, A9.

32. Saundra Torry and John Schwartz, "Big Tobacco, State Officials Reach $206 Billion Deal," *Washington Post,* November 14, 1998, A1; the quotation is on page A8. At a news conference Harshbarger announced that he had decided to sign but that, independently, using his authority as attorney general to prevent unfair or deceptive practices in trade, he would issue outdoor and point-of-sale advertising regulations for Massachusetts to "close holes" in the MSA. This act led in June 2001 to a ruling of the U.S. Supreme Court, *Lorillard Tobacco Co. v. Thomas F. Reilly, Attorney General of Massachusetts,* that invalidated Harshbarger's regulations and broadly interpreted a 1969 law in which Congress preempted states' regulation of tobacco advertising. That Justice Sandra Day O'Connor's opinion records Harshbarger's conduct at this point makes me suspect that the Court majority may have taken offense at his instantaneous repudiation, in effect, of a legal settlement that he had just put his name on after several years of litigation. See 2001 U.S. Lexis 4911, http://web.lexis-nexis.com/univers, accessed July 6, 2001; no longer accessible in 2011.

33. Jeremy Bulow, "The State Tobacco Settlements and Antitrust," http://www.ftc.gov/speeches/other/abatobacco.htm, accessed May 15, 2011.

34. Richard Perez-Pena, "How to Spend Tobacco Money? New York Counts the Ways," *New York Times,* November 14, 1998, A9.

35. Arturo Pérez, "Alaska Has Oil Settlement Fund," Web site of the National Conference of State Legislatures, http://www.thefreelibrary.com/States + settle + to bacco + suits%3a + so + who + won%3F-a054036511, accessed May 19, 2011. Alaska was an exception, in that it had received $4.8 billion since 1991 from six large oil companies, with which it had reached a settlement in regard to mineral lease bonuses, royalties, and taxes. Alaska would receive only $669 million from the tobacco companies, so it would remain far more oil-rich than tobacco-rich.

36. The $40 million is more than the total of the individual amounts previously given for the four states because some of the early settlements were adjusted upward to make them proportional to Minnesota's award, which was exceptionally high in relation to the 1997 settlement.

37. U.S. General Accounting Office, *Tobacco Settlement: States' Use of Master Settlement Agreement Payments,* GAO-01-851, June 2001, 11-13. For details on how the allocations were determined, see Stephen D. Sugarman's review of W. Kip Viscusi, *Smoke-Filled Rooms: A Postmortem on the Tobacco Deal* (Chicago: University of Chicago Press, 2002) at http://www.bsos.umd.edu/gvpt/lpbr/subpages/reviews/viscusi-kip.htm, accessed May 19, 2011.

38. The settlement is a long and extremely complicated lawyer's document. For a complete version, see http://www.naag.org. I have relied mainly on a summary prepared by a staff member of the National Conference of State Legislatures with the assistance of NAAG. The summary is available at http://www.ncsl .org/statefed/tmsasumm.htm#Glance, accessed February 26, 2004. However, I have also attempted to consult the original document, a complete hard copy of which was supplied to me by the office of the attorney general of Virginia. I would like to acknowledge the assistance of the office of Del. Mitch Van Yahres of Charlottesville in securing it. Information on strategic contribution fund payments is from U.S. General Accounting Office, *Tobacco Settlement: States' Use of Master Settlement Agreement Payments,* GAO-01-851, 57–58.

39. The eight categories were contained in Exhibit F of the MSA, under the heading "Potential Legislation Not To Be Opposed." See http://www.naag.org.

40. Walter Olson, "Puff, the Magic Settlement: The Joy of Enormous Tobacco Fees," *Reason Online,* January 2000, http://reason.com/archives/2000/01/01/puff-the-magic-settlement, accessed May 19, 2011.

41. Sylvia Nasar, "The Ifs and Buts of the Tobacco Settlement," *New York Times,* November 29, 1998, sec. 4, 1.

42. "Questioning That $206 Billion Tobacco Deal," *National Law Journal,* December 14, 1998, A8ff. See http://www.litigationlaw.com/8bac.htm, accessed June 1, 2001; no longer accessible in 2011.

43. Amicus curiae brief filed on behalf of the Ad-Hoc Coalition on the Proposed Tobacco Settlement, in *The State of New York and Dennis C. Vacco v. Philip Morris Inc. et al.,* Supreme Court of the State of New York, County of New York, case no. 40036197, December 9, 1998, 13.8 *TPLR* 3.772 (1998).

44. 13.6 *TPLR* 1.57 (1998) and 13.8 *TPLR* 1.74 (1998).

45. Thomas C. O'Brien and Robert A. Levy, "Rule of Law: A Tobacco Cartel Is Born, Paid For by Smokers," *Wall Street Journal,* May 1, 2000, A35.

CHAPTER TEN

The Aftermath of the MSA

The MSA took effect formally and money began flowing to state treasuries in November 1999. Ten years later, the states had received more than $68 billion. The sailing, however, was not smooth. The MSA's signatories had to beat back challenges to its legality, as well as a market challenge from many small cigarette manufacturers, not bound by the MSA, who saw an opportunity to sell cigarettes more cheaply than the signatories could. Additionally, the short-term success of this market challenge, until the state governments defeated it, led to a dispute between the companies and state governments over how to interpret the MSA.

· Battling the MSA in Court ·

An array of plaintiffs filed suits charging that the MSA violated antitrust laws and the Constitution, including the commerce clause and the compact clause, the latter of which requires that compacts and agreements among the states be approved by Congress.[1]

First to file, about a month after the MSA was concluded, were two individual smokers, Leo Hise and Jack Isch, who tried to mount a class action against the cigarette companies on behalf of all cigarette consumers in the United States. In a federal district court in Oklahoma, they made three claims: (1) that the companies had colluded with the state attorneys general to raise tobacco prices in violation of the Sherman Antitrust Act; (2) that they had deprived tobacco consumers of a property interest without due process of law; and (3) that they were regulating the manufacture, interstate trade, and consumption of tobacco products contrary to the Constitution. The court dismissed the last two complaints as frivolous and ruled on the first that the companies were protected by the Noerr-Pennington doctrine, which shields from antitrust law any concerted effort to influence public officials.[2]

The plaintiffs sought review from a circuit court and then from the Supreme Court, arguing that "national public policy must not be established through negotiated backroom deals between only the most powerful entities within an industry and a select group of state administrative officials." The circuit court rejected their appeal and the Supreme Court declined to hear one.[3]

Later cases pitted wholesale distributors of cigarettes against the tobacco companies and tobacco growers against the companies and a group of fourteen attorneys general. Still later, a case filed in a federal district court in Richmond, Virginia, in December 2000 was brought against the attorney general of Virginia by a small cigarette manufacturer, Star Scientific, Inc. This plaintiff seemed more likely than others to win the sympathy of courts because, as a nonparticipating manufacturer (NPM) required to make escrow payments, it could demonstrate harm from the MSA and because it was seeking to occupy a niche as the manufacturer of a safer cigarette. In 1999 Star had deposited approximately $11.6 million in escrow, an amount that exceeded its after-tax income. In 2000 its deposit was $13.1 million.

Star asked the court to grant an injunction against enforcement of the MSA and to rule that it violated the commerce clause and the compact clause. It further sought a judgment that Virginia's escrow statute violated the equal protection, due process, and takings clauses of the Constitution. In March 2001 Judge James R. Spencer dismissed Star's complaint, ruling that the company lacked standing to challenge the settlement because it was not a party to the MSA. On appeal, the Fourth Circuit ruled in January 2002 that Star did have standing but then rejected its pleas on the merits.[4]

In the Second Circuit, opponents of the MSA for a time had better luck. Here the plaintiffs were cigarette importers who in 2002 moved for a preliminary injunction against the MSA and its complementary legislation in New York. U.S. District Court judge Alvin K. Hellerstein dismissed their complaint, but on appeal the Second Circuit reinstated the suit. A three-judge panel headed by Ralph K. Winter said in January 2004 that the scheme of market control created under the MSA would constitute a violation of the Sherman Act if brought about by agreement among private parties, and although a state-action immunity doctrine might apply in this case, the challengers were entitled to show that the defendant, New York's attorney general, was failing to satisfy the doctrine's test.[5] The case ended early in 2009 when Hellerstein, on remand, ruled that the plaintiffs had failed to show that the MSA or New York's complementary statutes were anticompetitive under the Sherman Act or invalid under the commerce clause.[6]

In 2005 several plaintiffs, including a small manufacturer, a retailer, a distributor, and a smoker, with backing from the Competitive Enterprise Institute in Washington, D.C., filed suit in a federal district court in Shreveport, Louisiana, seeking to invalidate the MSA and Louisiana's complementary legislation. Their petition cited the compact clause, commerce clause, due process clause, and the Federal Cigarette Labeling and Advertising Act, which they claimed preempted state law. The case was argued in February 2009, and in September Judge S. Maurice Hicks Jr. denied all of the plaintiffs' claims. The Fifth Circuit upheld his ruling.[7] The plaintiffs pressed on by filing a petition for certiorari with the Supreme Court, accompanied by amicus briefs from eminent scholars and litigators who argued the MSA's constitutional infirmities.[8] Few such petitions are granted. In the absence of disagreements among lower courts, the prospects for a grant of certiorari are especially poor.

Twelve years after it took effect, the MSA had proved impervious to legal attack.

· Upstart Manufacturers ·

An economic challenge to the MSA from small manufacturers—"upstarts," they were often called—proved more formidable than the legal challenges.

As explained in chapter 9, the MSA was designed collectively to protect the four major manufacturers—Philip Morris, R. J. Reynolds, Brown & Williamson, and Lorillard—from a loss of their U.S. market share. A virtual cartel, they accounted for 98 to 99 percent of the domestic market when the settlement was concluded. Knowing that the tobacco companies would pass the settlement costs along to consumers in higher prices, the authors of the MSA sought to assure that they would not, as a consequence, be undersold by competitors.

In the case of other companies that elected to join, which for a time were called Subsequent Participating Manufacturers (SPMs) to distinguish them from Original Participating Manufacturers (OPMs), the MSA permitted maintenance of a prescribed market share at no cost. Only if the SMPs' share increased beyond the permitted amount did they have to make payments to state governments. As signatories, they gained protection from future liability, and, like the OPMs, they could deduct payments from their taxes. By 2009 there were approximately fifty participating manufacturers.[9] The original four had been reduced to three by the merger of Reynolds and Brown & Williamson, and more than forty had joined.

In the more complicated case of companies that did not sign—called Non-Participating Manufacturers, or NPMs—the MSA induced the states to enact laws requiring them to deposit money in escrow accounts that would be held by the state governments for twenty-five years. These payments were calculated to equal what the NPMs would have had to make if they had been signatories, but they were not tax deductible. Ostensibly, these funds anticipated future liability judgments; meanwhile, by raising the NPMs' costs they would reduce the price difference between their products and those of the participating manufacturers. NPMs were not bound by the advertising and marketing restrictions of the MSA.

By 2003 it was clear that this anticompetitive design was failing to achieve its purpose. The OPMs had lost as much as 10 to 15 percent of the U.S. market to rivals—mainly, of course, the NPMs, whose products were underselling the majors by $1 or more per pack.

The number of NPMs was unknown. They were a varied lot. Some were homegrown operations in tobacco country, run by farmers or former manufacturing employees who decided to try their hand as small proprietors. Such companies had smaller profit margins than the big manufacturers, and they made simpler products, with simpler manufacturing processes. They made a virtue out of selling the pure natural leaf, with no puffed tobacco or any of the chemical additives that critics of tobacco had succeeded in demonizing. Thus, Farmer's Tobacco Company in Cynthiana, Kentucky—a company that was founded by a father and son who had been tobacco farmers—warned on its Web site that "other cigarettes may contain any of more than 500 chemicals, including arsenic, ammonia and chemicals used to make weed and bug killers, car batteries, paint stripper, lighter fluid and mothballs."[10] Yet the new micromanufacturers did not necessarily imply that their cigarettes were safer. There was the notable case of Poison, Inc., owned by Dan Norris, in Castle Hayne, North Carolina, whose brand names included Grim Reapers, Black Death, Go To Hell, and Gravediggers, among others. The logo for Grim Reapers was a black-hooded death's head. No tort lawyer or government agency would ever be able to charge Norris, a former construction worker, with failure to warn. "My product is just telling you the damn truth," he told a reporter.[11]

Other NPMs were found on Native American reservations, and some had domestic addresses but imported the cigarettes they sold. For example, the Carolina Tobacco Company, based in Portland, Oregon, with twenty-five employees, made cigarettes—brand-named Roger—under contract in Latvia. Birdtown Enterprises of Cherokee, North Carolina, imported cigarettes made in Brazil so cheaply that they were retailing in the U.S. in 2003 for as little as $1 a pack. Still others had no domestic address but were foreign manufacturers in such varied locations as India; Indonesia; the Philippines; Cyprus; Macedonia; Mexico; and Prince Edward Island, Canada.[12]

State governments found it very difficult to enforce the settlement's strictures against the NPMs. The National Association of Attorneys General (NAAG) conceded that enforcement was "costly and cumbersome." The model statute that was used to implement the MSA enabled NPMs to sell cigarettes in a state for up to sixteen months before the state could bring an enforcement action. It was difficult and expensive to obtain service of process or to effect judgments against NPMs in foreign countries, and many NPMs were hard to find because they frequently changed names and addresses. Distributors, whose cooperation was needed to enforce the required payments, resisted, partly because they did not regard the MSA as legitimate. "The MSA is a travesty of the American judicial system," one distributor told the economic counsel for NAAG at an industry convention of wholesalers. "This is not a law; it's an agreement. You expect us to do your reporting for you. You are extorting money out of citizens."[13]

The attorneys general began by filing hundreds of lawsuits against the NPMs for failure to make escrow payments, but this was slow work and not very successful in foreign settings. The more promising approach was to reinforce the MSA with stricter state statutes. A typical measure, recommended by NAAG's Tobacco Project and widely adopted, included the following features: (1) prohibiting the affixing of tax stamps to tobacco products not in compliance with a state's escrow statute; (2) requiring certification that a tobacco product manufacturer either was a participating manufacturer under the MSA or, if an NPM, was in full compliance with a state's escrow statute; (3) directing an attorney general or a revenue department to maintain a list of tobacco product manufacturers that were in compliance with state laws; and (4) subjecting violators to civil and criminal penalties and to revocation or suspension of licenses.

With such laws—which, like the MSA itself, have withstood challenges in court—the attorneys general succeeded in bringing roughly fifty NPMs under their supervision. By 2009 the enforcers of the MSA in NAAG and the states were regulating—and driving up the product prices of—approximately one hundred cigarette manufacturers: fifty participating manufacturers and an equal number of NPMs.[14] Nevertheless, the economic effects of the upstarts' early challenge lingered in the politics of tobacco and the implementation of the MSA.

· The Lingering Threat ·

Noncompliance by the NPMs was potentially costly to state governments because the MSA provided the big manufacturers with a relatively generous adjustment for loss of market share. Under the agreement, their payments to the states, though resting on a base, are not fixed but fluctuate with volume; when sales fall, so do payments. And if sales fall because of a loss of market share of more than 2 percent to the NPMs, the downward adjustment is trebled.[15] In the fall of 2003, NAAG warned states to expect a $2.5 billion decrease in the settlement payments due on April 15, 2004—down from a projected $9.3 billion. Roughly one-fourth of the decrease, or $600 million, was due to the NPMs' gain in market share and the rest to declining consumption.[16] This was the beginning of a dispute between the companies and the states that remained active seven years later.

At issue between the states and the major companies as of 2010 was the NPM adjustment for the years 2003–2009. The manufacturers could qualify for a reduction in a given year if they could establish that the following conditions had been met: (1) they had lost more than 2 percent of the market share they possessed collectively in 1997; (2) the MSA was a "significant factor" in producing the loss of market share; and (3) at least some settling states either did not have escrow statutes in effect or did not diligently enforce them. Under the terms of the MSA, the first of these conditions, amount of market share lost, was to be determined by an independent auditor, and the second condition, the significance of the MSA as a factor in such a loss, was to be determined by an economic consulting firm. For the year 2003, the auditor, which was PricewaterhouseCoopers, and the consulting firm, which was the Brattle Group, made determinations favorable to the companies, but the third condition remained at issue. All of the settling states had enacted escrow statutes, but the companies contended that not all states had enforced them diligently.[17]

In July 2010 this issue went into an arbitration proceeding in Chicago, Illinois, overseen by three former federal judges. Although the proceeding technically applies only to 2003, its results may have effects on what the states receive for later years. Claiming that they were entitled to adjustments, companies had already withheld payments that reduced the states' receipts by about 12 percent in 2006, 10 percent in 2007, and 7 percent in 2008.[18]

From the earliest days of the MSA, many state governments and the local governments with which they shared MSA proceeds sought to secure cash quickly and shift risk by issuing tobacco bonds. This was a new type of financial instrument that allowed governments to "monetize" or "securitize" promises of payment from the tobacco companies by using them to back bonds offered in financial markets. New York City was the first jurisdiction to do this. By issuing the bonds through a special-purpose corporation, it was able to escape the state's constitutional debt limit.[19] Other issuers included New York State, California, New Jersey, and Louisiana.

The U.S. General Accounting Office, which monitors states' use of MSA funds, reported early in 2004 that about half of the $34.2 billion that the forty-six MSA states were to receive in fiscal years 2003 and 2004 would come as direct payments from the tobacco companies and the other half as securitized proceeds.[20] As late as 2007, $16 billion of such bonds were issued, despite caustic assessments from some sources of investment advice.[21] By 2010 Standard & Poor reported that ratings on 122 tobacco bonds with a face value of $26.8 billion and graded BBB or lower were under review for a reduction, and all tobacco securities had a negative outlook, the result of both a drop in cigarette sales and the arbitration proceeding getting under way in Chicago.[22]

· Weighing the Benefits ·

The principal victims of the MSA were smokers, roughly one-fourth of the adult population at the time, who had to pay more for cigarettes and were deprived of the advantages of a free market. They had few ways of protesting, being without representation in the process by which the MSA was constructed, and as disproportionately the poorest and least-educated part of the populace, they were not well placed socially to mount a protest. Advocates of free markets such as the Cato Institute and the Competitive Enterprise Institute continued to be critical of the agreement, as did academic economists, notably Jeremy Bulow of Stanford University (formerly of the FTC).[23] Satirists such as columnist Dave Barry observed that the MSA, ostensibly the work of smoking's opponents, ironically made state governments more dependent than ever on the prosperity of the industry. Tort lawyer Richard Scruggs of Mississippi, who launched the adversarial enterprise in collaboration with Attorney General Moore, made the same point: "The perverse result of what we did was essentially put the states in bed with the tobacco companies. . . . I don't like it at all. . . . The tobacco guys are sitting there laughing at us."[24] Early in the decade beginning in 2000, when several juries threatened the cigarette manufacturers with penalties running well into the billions, state legislatures and courts acted to buttress the companies' financial positions by capping the amounts that they were required to post in appeals bonds.[25]

The most ardent defenders of the MSA were naturally its authors. Early in 2006 NAAG issued a report that claimed credit for a sharp drop in smoking. Besides its contribution to a rise in cigarette prices, which were around $1.90 a pack in 1997 but had reached roughly $3.60 a pack by the fall of 2003, the MSA arguably discouraged smoking also by its restrictions on advertising—no more Joe Camel—and the financing it provided for antismoking campaigns. It obliged the big four manufacturers to pay $250 million on March 31, 1999, and an estimated $300 million on March 31 of each of the next four years to finance a national campaign against tobacco use. The money went into a national public education fund and from there to the newly created, obscurely named American Legacy Foundation, which launched a "truth" campaign—for which the word "truth" was a registered trademark—featuring attack ads against the industry.

The NAAG report, issued jointly with the American Legacy Foundation, inspired a lead story in the *Washington Post* headlined, "Smoking in U.S. Declines Sharply, Cigarette Sales At a 54-Year Low."[26] The story said, "Association leaders . . . hailed the decline as a sign that sometimes-controversial developments triggered by the $246 billion settlement have been effective." The fact is that per capita sales of cigarettes, a U.S. Department of Agriculture statistic that NAAG and the *Post* reporter were relying on as an indicator, had been declining steeply at least since 1980.[27] Using a different indicator—smoking prevalence, which is the percentage of the adult population who are current smokers—one can argue that the rate of decline had actually slowed following the MSA. Between 1970 and 1980, smoking prevalence dropped from 37.4 to 33.2 percent, a decline of 4.2 percentage points. In the next decade, 1980 to 1990, it dropped from 33.2 to 25.5 percent, a decline of 7.7 points. Between 1998, when the MSA was signed, and 2008, it dropped from 24.1 to 20.6 percent, a decline of 3.5 points.[28]

Not just because of the MSA, or the manufacturers' attempts to remain profitable through price increases, but also because of repeated tax increases by the states and the federal government, the average price of a pack of cigarettes was around $5.15 by the end of 2009. Between 2002 and 2009, forty-six states, the District of Columbia, and several U.S. territories increased their cigarette tax rates more than ninety-five times. The average state excise tax on a pack at the end of 2009 was $1.34. Fifteen states including D.C. had taxes of $2 per pack or more. Connecticut's tax was $3; Rhode Island's, $3.46; New York's, $2.75.[29] The federal excise tax likewise rose, reaching $1.01 per pack on April 1, 2009, following the highest-ever increase, of 62 cents, as part of a liberalization of the State Children's Health Insurance Program (SCHIP).[30] In June 2010, as "part of an emergency measure to keep the government running," the New York State legislature added $1.60 to its tax, pushing the average price of a pack in the state to about $9.20

and to nearly $11 in New York City, which has its own tax.[31] More or less simultaneously, New York renewed an effort to collect taxes on cigarettes sold on Native American lands. Twice earlier, in 1992 and 1997, it had abandoned the attempt because of violent protests from some of the tribes, whose members blocked upstate highways and fought state police troopers. This time tribal leaders said they would use litigation rather than violence in opposition.[32]

Given the high and steadily rising cost of cigarettes since 1998, it may seem surprising that smoking has not fallen farther and faster. Indeed, the decline has stalled, according to the Centers for Disease Control. One-fifth of the adult population still smokes; the figure reported for smoking prevalence was 20.9 percent in 2005 and 20.6 percent in 2009. Among adults whose income falls below the federal poverty level, the rate is 31.1 percent.[33]

Part of the explanation for the persistence of consumption is that manufacturers' prices are not quite what they seem. With advertising restricted under the MSA, manufacturers have stressed price-reducing promotions. According to reports of the Federal Trade Commission covering 2004, 2005, and 2006, price discounts—that is, payments to cigarette retailers or wholesalers to reduce the price to consumers—constitute the largest single category of promotional expenditures by the five largest cigarette companies, amounting in 2006 to over $9 billion, which was 74 percent of all marketing expenditures.[34]

More fundamentally, the explanation for the stubborn persistence of sales is to be found in both inelasticity of demand, which is attributable to smokers' addiction, and to the availability of cigarettes outside of the usual retail outlets. In particular, Internet and contraband purchases have flourished.

According to the Campaign for Tobacco-Free Kids, in 2006 more than 770 Web sites, about half of them based outside of the United States, were selling cigarettes to U.S. smokers.[35] Those within the country included many that were based on Native American lands, where they enjoyed protections of tribal sovereignty. Internet sellers usually buy cigarettes outside of the United States, in a low-tax state, or on Native American lands, thereby evading all or most of the domestic taxes. State laws that have sought to curb Internet sales of tobacco to teenagers—for example, by requiring tobacco shippers to use a delivery company that provides a recipient-identification service—have been struck down by federal courts, including a unanimous Supreme Court, as a violation of federal law. In this case, which involved laws adopted by Maine, federal preemption, which purports to protect free interstate markets, cut against the state's public health objectives.[36]

Philip Morris USA identifies four categories of contraband:

1. Untaxed and under-taxed cigarettes. These are cigarettes legally manufactured for sale in the United States but on which applicable excise taxes have not been paid. Typically they originate in a low-tax state but then migrate for sales in states and localities with higher taxes.

2. Counterfeit cigarettes. These are packaged to resemble trademarked brands, such as Marlboro or Newport, but are manufactured without the consent of the trademark owner.

3. Illegally imported cigarettes. These are cigarettes manufactured for sale outside the United States but which are sold in the country in violation of federal law. Such cigarettes may fail to comply with U.S. regulations such as the display of warning labels.

4. Stolen cigarettes.[37]

A survey conducted by the New York State Department of Health in 2006 found that 51 percent of smokers in New York purchased cigarettes at least once from a contraband source, and 33 percent purchased cigarettes "sometimes" or "all the time" from such sources.[38] According to the *New York Times,* an underground economy in cigarettes flourishes in New York City. Critics of the industry claim that Lorillard in particular participates in the bootleg trade by supplying cigarettes to Native American tribes in New York State, whose members then peddle them on city streets. A Lorillard spokesman replied that it is not the industry's job, but that of state and local law enforcement officials, to police the trade in untaxed cigarettes.[39]

Finally, smokers have turned to rolling their own cigarettes with loose tobacco, which state governments have taxed less heavily than manufactured cigarettes. Between 2007 and 2008, national sales of cigarettes declined by 4.2 percent while roll-your-own sales of loose tobacco increased by 14.9 percent. The federal tobacco tax increases of 2009 made the tax on roll-your-own tobacco equal to that on cigarettes but continued to tax pipe tobacco at a lower rate. Roll-your-own makers then re-labeled their product as pipe tobacco, with the result that in the first five months after the federal rate increases, nationwide roll-your-own sales dropped by 51 percent whereas "pipe tobacco" sales increased by 167 percent.[40] Tobacco retailers installed high-speed rolling machines that could produce a carton of cigarettes in eight minutes.[41]

It has been a disappointment to tobacco's opponents that state governments have not spent more heavily to combat the persistence of tobacco use. According to the Campaign for Tobacco-Free Kids, in the decade following the signing of the MSA, state governments allocated $6.5 billion to tobacco prevention and cessation programs. This is not a small amount, but it was only 3.2 percent of the states' revenues from tobacco, counting both excise taxes and MSA payments, and allocations fell off sharply with the general economic downturn in 2008–2009.[42]

· The Tort Lawyers ·

The MSA had at least one unambiguous outcome. It made the tort lawyers very rich. Their enormous fees were the most publicized and controversial result of the MSA.

The attorneys general had hired roughly one hundred law firms, most of which worked on contingency-fee contracts that promised them as much as 33 percent of the proceeds. Firms in general expected to realize millions of dollars, while some, such as those of Richard Scruggs and Ron Motley—both of whom had contracts with twenty to thirty states—could realistically aspire to $1 billion dollars or more. However, anticipating that fulfilling the contingency-fee contracts would not sit well with legislatures or voters, the attorneys general had secured from the tobacco companies a promise to pay the fees by having the lawyers' claims go to a three-member board of arbitration or by settling with the lawyers directly if possible. These costs, like others to the companies, would presumably be passed on to smokers in the form of higher prices.

The arbitrators began with Mississippi, Florida, and Texas, states that had settled early and individually. For that reason they decided on large awards, crediting the lawyers in these early suits with being the first to take the risks of suing the tobacco industry to recover Medicaid costs—although how much risk was involved in Florida, given the actions of that state's legislature, is open to question. Florida's lawyers received $3.43 billion; Mississippi's, $1.43 billion; and those of Texas, $3.3 billion. As a percentage of their state's settlement, the largest award went to Mississippi's lawyers, who had been the first to file. The arbitrators had begun by awarding the lawyers 10 percent of a state's settlement, and then they multiplied that figure by a factor ranging from 1.9 to 3.5, depending on what the panel perceived to be the risks and work undertaken in each state. The resulting amounts were to be spread over a period of years not immediately specified, but even up front, in the first year or two, the legal teams in each state would receive hundreds of millions of dollars.[43]

Subsequent awards were smaller, both because the arbitrators thought the lawyers hired by later-filing states merited less and because the industry was freer to challenge the later awards. In its eagerness to settle the early cases—which it had hoped would lead Congress to endorse a comprehensive settlement—the industry had formally agreed not to argue against the claims for legal fees. However, it was bound by no such agreement in subsequent cases.

The arbitrators did not apply a consistent percentage standard but seemed to take idiosyncratic factors into account. Rather than use conventional billing criteria such as time invested—which would have been hard to do since many of the firms, working on contingency-fee contracts, did not keep records of their time—the arbitrators appeared to give weight to the lawyers' contributions to political coalition-building. In the case of Hawaii, they ordered fees of about $90.2 million, about 6.5 percent of Hawaii's settlement. They said that although Hawaii and its lawyers had not played a pioneering role in the litigation, the state had served as a leader for small states and its private lawyers had shouldered "virtually the entire burden" of the case because the attorney general's office was so small.[44] In Illinois the panel awarded $1.21 million to private attorneys, an amount equal to only 1.3 percent of Illinois' settlement proceeds. It conceded that "there was relatively little activity" in Illinois' suit but said the state's outside counsel had contributed to the multistate settlement by helping to persuade states governed by Republicans to join.[45]

No reliable figure for the fee total ever became public. In more than half of the states, usually the smaller ones, the companies and the lawyers reached settlements privately, without going to arbitration. The MSA provided for $1.25 billion to cover this group of awards. One such case was Minnesota, where the industry agreed to pay Robins, Kaplan, Miller & Ciresi $450 million over two years. In general, fee awards in the directly negotiated cases were lower than in those that went to arbitration. Late in 2002 *American Lawyer* published a list of arbitrated awards in seventeen states and Puerto Rico that totaled $12.2 billion; awards in three other jurisdictions were still pending before the panel.[46] It is reasonable to assume that the total for all states was approximately $15 billion.

The ethics of the legal profession prescribe that fees should be reasonable, and courts have rules for the enforcement of ethical standards. The size of these fees, both in total and in individual cases, astounded observers with knowledge of the legal profession.

Professor John Langbein of the Yale Law School put it bluntly and sardonically:

> Mr. Scruggs is a historic figure. His picture is going to go into the legal history books, along with Justinian and Lord Coke. He's going to be there for having had the unbelievable nerve to demand billions upon billions of dollars and then actually to get it, or at least come very close. The idea of charging this kind of money in connection with a legal system is unheard of, not only in our own legal tradition, but anywhere else. When Europeans hear these numbers, their jaws hit their desks. No well-run polity needs to pay $8 billion or $40 billion to facilitate the ordinary functions of government. To pay this kind of money to private entrepreneurs for what is basically a public function is extraordinary, unprecedented, and deeply unprincipled.[47]

Lawyers who were dissatisfied with the awards of the arbitration panel could try to enforce their contracts. Illinois' lawyers claimed that they were owed 10 percent of the state's estimated $9.1 billion in proceeds and sued for an additional $800 million. Maryland's Peter Angelos insisted that the state should honor what he claimed was its promise to pay him 25 percent of the proceeds of litigation, a share that would amount to $1.1 billion. When the state legislature voted to cut that fee in half, the senate president and house speaker said that the cut was justified by the legislature's having passed a law that made Angelos's job easier and the outcome of litigation more certain. According to the speaker, "Mr. Angelos . . . agreed to accept 12.5 percent if we agreed to change tort law, which was no small feat. We changed centuries of precedent to assure a win in this case." This dispute threatened to delay Maryland's receipt of its proceeds, with the result that the state's attorney general brought suit against Angelos. Eventually, Angelos settled his $1.1 billion claim for $150 million.[48]

Lawyers in Massachusetts sued the state government, asking for $1.3 billion more than the $775 million that the arbitration panel had awarded them and claiming that their contract with the state entitled them to the larger amount. Late in 2003 a Suffolk County Superior Court jury decided that they were entitled to an additional $100 million. Attorney General Thomas F. Reilly declared the verdict a victory over "excess and overreaching."[49]

The most byzantine of the postsettlement fee disputes occurred in Texas, where the promising political career of Dan Morales, who had brought the suit as attorney general but chose not to run for the office again in 1999, was derailed by his attempt to profit from it personally. After extensive legal maneuvering, involving investigations by Morales's Republican successor, John Cornyn, and federal prosecutors, Morales was sentenced to four years in federal prison in Texarkana. He had pled guilty to one count of tax evasion—for diverting campaign funds to personal use—and one count of mail fraud—for attempting to secure a share of the contingency fee for his friend Marc Murr, apparently with the expectation that Murr would share the money with him. Murr also pled guilty to mail fraud. The lawyers who had worked on the case, known in Texas as the "Tobacco Five," emerged from the complicated legal fray with their fees intact, although Morales, from his jail cell, claimed that sealed court documents would show no wrongdoing on their part.[50]

A Manhattan Supreme Court judge, Charles E. Ramos, tried in 2002, on his own motion, to freeze payments from the arbitration award to six New York law firms while he reviewed their reasonableness. Ramos was rebuffed by a higher court, which said that he lacked authority to do any such thing.[51] A taxpayer challenge to the fees in Missouri failed for lack of standing.[52] The one state in which a penalty was imposed on the tort lawyers was Louisiana, where the issue was not the size of the fees but the fact that government services had been paid from private sources—the tobacco companies. The Louisiana Board of Ethics found this to be a violation of the state's code of ethics, and it fined the lawyers $650,000.[53] In 2003 the U.S. Senate turned aside an attempt by two Republican members, Arizona's Jon Kyl and Texas's John Cornyn, to compel the tort lawyers to surrender roughly $9 billion of the present value of their fees to their clients, the state governments. The Kyl-Cornyn bill, S. 887 of the 108th Congress, was framed to limit contingency fee contracts generally, in addition to its specific applicability to the tobacco awards.[54] In response to what took place with tobacco, several state legislatures have since acted to regulate contingency-fee contracts, for example with "sunshine" provisions that require disclosure, certain practices with regard to competitive bidding, or caps on contract amounts.[55]

The tort lawyers, like the state governments, sought to maximize their up-front return by securitizing the promised stream of revenue. They issued "litigation bonds" that were marketed to institutional investors. The first such deal, concluded in February 2001, converted nearly $1 billion in legal fees due to be paid over twelve years into $308.1 million in cash. Eleven law firms in four states participated.[56] Unlike the state governments, the lawyers did not experience losses in anticipated revenue due to the OPMs' decline in volume or market share. If their contingency-fee contracts had been strictly executed as such, that would have happened, but instead they got fixed awards in lieu of contingency fees. On the other hand, because the MSA put an annual $500 million cap on industry payments to lawyers under the arbitration awards, they had to wait for much of the money. That gave them an incentive to convert to litigation bonds.

The tobacco tort lawyers used their huge new fortunes in various ways—in addition, of course, to personal consumption. Much was invested speculatively in fresh lawsuits. Just as the profits from the asbestos cases were invested in tobacco suits, some of the tobacco profits were invested in suits against gun manufacturers, lead paint manufacturers, and health maintenance organizations. Some was invested in running for office. One of the leading tobacco lawyers, Minnesota's Michael Ciresi, campaigned for the Democratic nomination for the Senate in 2000. Ciresi had reported receiving more than $14 million from his law firm in 1999 and 2000 as a "preliminary" share of tobacco and other settlements.[57]

More often than they finance campaigns of their own, tort lawyers contribute to the campaigns of others. Especially in the South, they are a major source of campaign contributions to Democratic candidates. In the first half of 2000, the Texas tobacco lawyers alone donated at least $2.2 million to Democrats at the national level, compared with $1.4 million that Philip Morris had given to Republican Party committees.[58] In the tobacco litigation, attorneys general often selected as private lawyers those who had contributed previously to their campaigns and would, one could safely assume, contribute again. Joseph J. Jamail, a Texan and one of the country's richest trial lawyers, claimed that Attorney General Morales had asked him for $1 million in 1996 to discuss the possibility of his hiring Jamail to head the state's legal team.[59]

The financial links between the private lawyers and the attorneys general were an especially troubling feature of the tobacco litigation. "I think we need plaintiffs' attorneys," Professor John Coffee of the Columbia Law School told the *New York Times.* "But we need the process in which they represent the public to be purged of political overtones. This was probably the biggest pay-to-play issue of all time."[60]

· Notes ·

1. For critiques of the MSA from authors affiliated with think tanks, see Thomas C. O'Brien and Robert A. Levy, "Rule of Law: A Tobacco Cartel Is Born, Paid For by Smokers," *Wall Street Journal,* May 1, 2000, A35; Thomas C. O'Brien, "Constitutional and Antitrust Violations of the Multistate Tobacco Settlement," *Cato Institute Policy Analysis* 371 (May 18, 2000); and Michael S. Greve, "Compacts,

Cartels and Congressional Consent," *Missouri Law Review* 38 (Spring 2003): 285–387.

2. *Hise & Isch* v. *Philip Morris et al.*, 208 F. 3d 226 and 2000 U.S. App. LEXIS 2497. The opinion appears also at 14.3 *Tobacco Products Litigation Reporter* (*TPLR*) 2.112.

3. Robert S. Greenberger, "Justices Decline to Hear Bid to Overturn Pact between Tobacco Firms and States," *Wall Street Journal,* October 31, 2000, B16.

4. Gordon Fairclough, "Judge Throws out Star Scientific's Suit Seeking to Overturn Tobacco Settlement," *Wall Street Journal,* March 27, 2002, B7; and *Star Scientific, Inc.* v. *Beales,* 278 F. 3d 339, 2002WL 80620 (4th Cir. 2002).

5. *Freedom Holdings* v. *Spitzer,* 2004 U.S. App. LEXIS 5600 (2nd Cir. 2004).

6. *Freedom Holdings, Inc.* v. *Cuomo,* 2009 U.S. Dist. LEXIS 1788 (S. D. N. Y., Jan. 12, 2009).

7. In the trial court, the case was *A. B. Coker* v. *Foti,* but at the appellate stage it became *S&M Brands* v. *Caldwell.* See www.ca5.uscourts.gov, case number 09–30985. For help with this case, I am indebted to Hans Bader of the Competitive Enterprise Institute.

8. Todd Zywicki, "Amicus Brief in Support of Cert. in Tobacco Master Settlement Case," *The Volokh Conspiracy,* December 20, 2010, http://volokh.com/2010/12/20.

9. Patricia Molteni, "NAAG Tobacco Project: 11 Years of MSA Coordination," *NAAGazette,* May 29, 2009, www.naag.org/naag-tobacco-project-11-years-of-msa-coordination.php.

10. Farmer's Tobacco, www.farmerstobacco.com/products/index.html, accessed January 8, 2004. Link no longer active but a hard copy of the information exists in the author's notes.

11. Associated Press, "Playing with the Big Boys," *Daily Progress* (Charlottesville, Va.), January 20, 2004, B3.

12. Pat Stith, "Upstart Brands Hurt Big Tobacco," *Raleigh News & Observer,* January 4, 2004, http://www.mooregop.org/nando_1-4-2004_upstart_brands_hurt_big_tobacco.html, accessed March 18, 2011; Neil Buckley, "Is Big Tobacco Headed for Another Round of Trouble?" *Financial Times,* May 7, 2003, 13; and Brandy Fisher, "Outlaws," *Tobacco Reporter,* September 2001, 48ff.

13. National Association of Attorneys General, Tobacco Project, "Model Complementary Legislation: Introduction and Analysis," January 2003, www.naag.org, accessed July 26, 2004; and Fisher, "Outlaws," 52.

14. Molteni, "NAAG Tobacco Project: 11 Years of MSA Coordination."

15. On the threat of declining revenues, see James B. Carroll and David A. Moss, *Tobacco Settlement and Declining State Revenues* (Lexington, Ky.: Council of State Governments, March 2002).

16. Associated Press, "Playing with the Big Boys," B3.

17. "Tobacco Arbitration Begins with Chicago Hearing," *NAAGazette,* www.naag.org/tobacco-arbitration-begins-with-chicago-hearing.php, accessed August 2, 2010.

18. *Ibid.*; Campaign for Tobacco-Free Kids, "Cigarette Company MSA Payment Withholdings—The NPM Adjustment Threat & How the States Can Fight Back,"

April 24, 2008, www.tobaccofreekids.org/research/factsheets/pdf/0293.pdf, accessed March 18, 2011.

19. U.S. General Accounting Office, "Tobacco Settlement: States' Use of Master Settlement Agreement Payments," GAO-01–851, June 2001, 43.

20. U.S. General Accounting Office, "Tobacco Settlement: States' Allocations of Fiscal Year 2003 and Expected Fiscal Year 2004 Payments," GAO-04–518, March 19, 2004, www.gao.gov/new.items/d04518.pdf, accessed March 18, 2011.

21. Richard Lehmann, "The Great Tobacco Bond Scam," *Forbes.com*, www.forbes.com/2003/04/09/cz_rl_0408soapbox.html, April 9, 2003, accessed March 18, 2011.

22. Michael Quint, "Cigarette Sales Drop Points to $12 Billion Tobacco Bond Defaults," *Bloomberg.com*, www.bloomberg.com/news/2010-08–06/cigarette-sales-decline-points-to-tobacco-bond-defaults-sims-report-says.html, August 6, 2010, accessed August 7, 2010.

23. Jeremy Bulow and Paul Klemperer, "The Tobacco Deal," *Brookings Papers on Economic Activity: Microeconomics, 1998* (Washington, D.C.: Brookings Institution, 1999), 332. For a more recent academic critique, see Andrew P. Morriss, Bruce Yandle, and Andrew Dorchak, *Regulation by Litigation* (New Haven, Ct. Yale University Press, 2009), chap. 6.

24. Allan M. Brandt, *The Cigarette Century* (New York: Basic Books, 2007), 437. The original source is Thomas Farragher, "Up in Smoke/First of Two Parts: Little of $246b Deal Fights Tobacco," *Boston Globe*, August 9, 2001.

25. Vanessa O'Connell, "New Laws Help Tobacco Makers with Big Judgments," *Wall Street Journal*, July 19, 2004, A1.

26. Marc Kaufman, "Smoking in U.S. Declines Sharply," *Washington Post*, March 9, 2006, A1.

27. "Cigarette Consumption, United States, 1900–2007," www.infoplease.com/ipa/A0908700.html, accessed August 8, 2010. The Department of Agriculture data set, which ends with 2007, can be found at http://usda.mannlib.cornell.edu.

28. "Smoking Prevalence among U.S. Adults, 1955–2007 (as a percent of population, eighteen years of age and older)," www.infoplease.com/ipa/A0762370.html, accessed August 8, 2010; Centers for Disease Control, "Cigarette Smoking among Adults and Trends in Smoking Cessation—United States, 2008," *MMWR Weekly*, November 13, 2009/58 (44): 1227–1232, www.cdc.gov/mmwr/preview/mmwrhtml/mm5844a2.htm, accessed November 30, 2009.

29. Campaign for Tobacco-Free Kids, "State Cigarette Excise Tax Rates & Rankings," www.tobaccofreekids.org/research/factsheets/pdf/0097.pdf, accessed December 6, 2009; Kevin Sack, "States Look to Tobacco Tax to Fill Their Budget Holes," *New York Times*, April 21, 2008, A14; Shaila Dewan, "States Look at Tobacco to Balance the Budget," *New York Times*, March 21, 2009, A8.

30. Wendy Koch, "Biggest U.S. Tax Hike on Tobacco Takes Effect," www.usatoday.com/money/perfi/taxes/2009-03-31-cigarettetax_N.htm, accessed August 1, 2009; David Brown, "Cigarette Tax Rises—And So Does Incentive to Quit," *Washington Post*, April 3, 2009, A1.

31. Nicholas Confessore, "Cigarette Tax Is Increased to Keep New York Running," *New York Times*, June 22, 2010, A19.

32. Fernanda Santos, "New York Will Try Again to Tax Indians' Sale of Cigarettes," *New York Times,* September 1, 2010, A17; and "Court Blocks State Tax on Tribal Cigarette Sales," *New York Times,* September 2, 2010, A24.

33. Centers for Disease Control and Prevention, "Vital Signs: Current Cigarette Smoking among Adults Aged [Over] 18 Years—United States, 2009," September 10, 2010/59 (35) 1135–1140, www.cdc.gov/mmwr/preview/mmwrhtml/mm5935a3 .htm, accessed on March 18, 2011.

34. Federal Trade Commission, "FTC Releases Reports on Cigarettes and Smokeless Tobacco," April 26, 2007, www.ftc.gov/opa/2007/04/cigaretterpt.shtm, and Federal Trade Commission, "FTC Releases Reports on Cigarette and Smokeless Tobacco Sales and Marketing Expenditures," August 12, 2009, www.ftc.gov/ opa/2009/08/tobacco.shtm, both accessed on May 19, 2011.

35. "Internet Sales of Tobacco Products," April 28, 2008, www.tobaccofreekids.org/ research/factsheets/pdf/0213.pdf, accessed on May 19, 2011.

36. Robert Barnes, "Supreme Court Strikes Down State's Law to Diminish Internet Tobacco Sales to Teens," *Washington Post,* February 21, 2008, A2; the case is *Rowe* v. *New Hampshire Motor Transportation Association,* 128 S. Ct. 989.

37. Philip Morris, USA, "Contraband Trade," www.philipmorrisusa.com/en/cms/ Responsibility/Government_Affairs/Legislative_Issues/Contraband_Trade .aspx, accessed on March 18, 2011.

38. Philip Morris, USA, Legislative Issue Book 2008, *Philipmorrisusa.com.* Link no longer active but a hard copy of the information exists in the author's notes.

39. Stephanie Saul, "Lawsuits Shine a Light on Indian Tribes' Sales of Untaxed Cigarettes," *New York Times,* October 2, 2008, A29.

40. Campaign for Tobacco-Free Kids, "The Problem with Roll-Your-Own (RYO) Tobacco," November 17, 2009, www.tobaccofreekids.org/research/factsheets/ pdf/0336.pdf, accessed March 18, 2011.

41. David Kesmodel, "Roll-Your-Own Cigarette Machines Help Evade Steep Tax," *Wall Street Journal,* August 30, 2010, B1.

42. Campaign for Tobacco-Free Kids, "A Decade of Broken Promises: The 1998 State Tobacco Settlement Ten Years Later," www.tobaccofreekids.org/reports/settle ments, accessed May 19, 2011.

43. Barry Meier, "Lawyers in Early Tobacco Suits to Get $8 Billion," *New York Times,* December 12, 1998, A1; Barry Meier, "The Spoils of Tobacco Wars," *New York Times,* December 22, 1998, C1; and Ann Davis, "Cashing in on a Tobacco Bonanza," *Wall Street Journal,* December 15, 1998, B1.

44. Gordon Fairclough, "Tobacco Lawyers for Hawaii to Get Fee of $90.2 Million," *Wall Street Journal,* September 9, 1999, B10.

45. Dow Jones & Co., "Illinois Lawyers to Get $1.21 Million in Fees from Cigarette Makers," *Wall Street Journal,* October 8, 1999, A6. For a detailed account of how the panel was formed and how it worked, see Susan Beck, "Trophy Fees," *American Lawyer,* December 2, 2002, www.law.com, accessed May 19, 2011.

46. "And the Winners Are . . . ," *American Lawyer,* December 2002, www.law.com/ special/professionals/amlaw/2002/and _the_winners_are.shtml, accessed May 19, 2011.

47. *Regulation by Litigation: The New Wave of Government-Sponsored Litigation* (New York: Manhattan Institute for Policy Research, 1999), 41–42. As of 2010, Scruggs was not well positioned to enjoy his wealth. In 2008 he was found guilty of attempting to bribe a judge, fined $250,000, sentenced to five years in prison, and deprived of his license to practice law. There was no overt connection with tobacco litigation, but the federal judge who imposed the sentence said that reviewing secretly recorded conversations "made me think perhaps this was not the first time you did this, because you did it so easily. And there is evidence before the court that you have done it before." Scruggs asked to be sent to a minimum-security federal prison in Pensacola, Florida, where another Mississippi attorney and former Scruggs associate was serving an eleven-year sentence for bribing two state court judges. Holbrook Mohr, "Famed Litigator Gets 5-Year Term for Conspiracy to Bribe Judge," *Washington Post*, June 28, 2008, A3. The success of the states' assault on the tobacco industry would be entitled to deeper respect if it were not traceable to a suit brought by Scruggs in a Mississippi court.

48. Daniel LeDuc, "Angelos, Md. Feud Over Tobacco Fee," *Washington Post*, October 15, 1999, B1; LeDuc, "Angelos Says Md. Reneged on Tobacco Contract," *Washington Post*, December 22, 1999, B1; LeDuc, "Angelos Tells Md. He'll Cut His Fee," *Washington Post*, January 10, 2002, A1; and LeDuc, "Md. To Pay $150 Million to Angelos," *Washington Post*, March 23, 2002, A1.

49. Frank Phillips, "Jury Caps Fees Owed Tobacco Law Firms; Attorney General Cites a Victory," *Boston Globe*, December 20, 2003, Metro Section, A1.

50. Several Texas legislators in 1998 had filed a mandamus action in Texas state court challenging the authority of Morales to bind the state to a contingency-fee agreement. Private counsel removed that action to the federal court in which the tobacco case had been brought, and the challenge was found moot as a result of the arbitration panel's award to the lawyers. For an account of this part of the action in Texas, see footnote 58 in Lester Brickman, "Lawyers' Ethics and Fiduciary Obligation in the Brave New World of Aggregative Litigation," *William & Mary Environmental Law and Policy Review* 26 (winter 2001), 243 and 262–263. On the case against Morales and his accusations regarding the Texas Tobacco Five, see Associated Press State and Local Wire, "Ex-Attorney General Dan Morales to Serve Time in Texarkana Prison," November 18, 2003, www .freerepublic.com/focus/f-news/1024031/posts, accessed March 18, 2011; and Janet Elliott, "Morales Urges Probe of Tobacco Attorneys," *Houston Chronicle*, December 20, 2003, A37, www.chron.com/disp/story.mpl/metropolitan/ 2309735.html, accessed March 18, 2011.

51. Andrew Tilghman, "Court Cuts Short Scrutiny of Fees in Tobacco Suit," *Times Union* (Albany, New York), August 1, 2003, A1, http://writer.zoho.com/public/ tdchi/big-tobacco/noband, accessed March 18, 2011; and Daniel Wise, "Panel Rejects Review of Tobacco Fee Award," *New York Law Journal*, August 1, 2003, 1.

52. Personal communication from Margaret A. Little, January 28, 2004.

53. Louisiana Board of Ethics, Opinion No. 2000–381, May 17, 2001. The opinion may be found on the board's Web site, http://domino.ethics.state.la.us, accessed May 19, 2011.

54. For the remarks of Kyl and Cornyn upon introduction of the bill, see *Congressional Record*, 108th Cong., 1st sess., 2003, S5237–S5248.
55. "Progress on Pay to Play," *Wall Street Journal*, February 12, 2010, A22.
56. Thomas B. Edsall, "Lawyers Get Tobacco Fees Early," *Washington Post*, February 14, 2001, A14.
57. Dan Morgan, "From Courtroom to Campaign Trail: Huge Corporate Settlements Provide Fuel for Trial Lawyers Running as Democrats," *Washington Post*, June 25, 2000, A6.
58. Rick Anderson, "Tobacco Money Flows Both Ways," *Mother Jones.com*, July 6, 2000, http://motherjones.com/politics/2000/07/tobacco-money-flows-both-ways, accessed March 18, 2011.
59. Barry Meier and Jill Abramson, "Tobacco War's New Front: Lawyers Fight over Big Fees," *New York Times*, June 9, 1998, A1.
60. Meier, "Lawyers in Early Tobacco Suits to Get $8 Billion," A1.

CHAPTER ELEVEN

After Litigation, a Return to Legislation

ACTIONS OF STATE GOVERNMENTS in the American federal system are often precursors to action by the federal government. This proved true of the state lawsuits against the tobacco manufacturers. In his State of the Union message to Congress in 1999, President Clinton at the last minute inserted a surprise promise that the federal government was preparing its own suit. "Democrats began jumping up and down, cheering, as if they were at a basketball game," the president's speech-writer recalled. "It was a powerful moment—a reminder, in terms as stark as the Constitution allowed . . . that he didn't need Congress for everything."[1]

The incentive for the White House to act lay not just in the states' demonstration of what could be done, but also in the fact that the Clinton administration had been thwarted in attempts both to extend FDA regulation to the cigarette industry and to recoup a portion of the states' settlement. The budget that President Clinton presented early in 1999 presumed that the federal government would secure a share of the states' proceeds, but the governors resisted and were supported by Congress. The administration then tried to get Congress at least to compel the states to spend a prescribed portion of their tobacco money on anti-smoking and other health-related programs, but the Senate defeated a bill for that purpose by a large bipartisan majority, 71–29. On the initiative of senators Kay Bailey Hutchison (R-Texas) and Bob Graham (D-Fla.), representing two of the states with large and early settlements, Congress permanently amended the Social Security Act to protect the states against having to share the proceeds of the tobacco settlement.[2]

Criminal prosecutors in the Justice Department had been investigating the tobacco companies since 1994. After the Waxman hearings, they had opened an inquiry to determine whether the tobacco company CEOs had committed perjury by testifying to a belief that nicotine was not addictive. In addition to perjury, the potential criminal charges included fraud, conspiracy, racketeering, and obstruction of justice. By 1996 federal prosecutors had convened grand jury inquiries in Brooklyn,

NY; the District of Columbia; Manhattan, NY; New Orleans, Louisiana; and Alexandria, Virginia. They got as far as sending "target letters," which are usually final warnings to plead guilty or be prosecuted, to executives of Brown & Williamson. Eventually, however, the prosecutors concluded that they did not have a case, and the department swallowed the target letters—an unusual move. No indictments were brought.[3]

The possibility of a civil case remained, which would be easier to pursue because the burden of proof is less demanding. In a criminal case, the government would have to prove guilt beyond a reasonable doubt, whereas in a civil case it had only to meet the standard of a "preponderance of the evidence." In 1997, when the first state settlements were reached, the Clinton White House had shown an interest in a civil suit that would recoup costs for medical care. Career officials in the civil division of the Justice Department were dubious, and Attorney General Janet Reno testified to a Senate committee that "the federal government does not have an independent cause of action."[4]

Despite the reluctance of the Department of Justice to proceed, the Clinton White House persisted and was joined by Richard Scruggs, who began lobbying the federal government to sue after the McCain bill collapsed. Some of the tort lawyers—all of whom were eager to collect their fees from the state-level litigation—believed that the industry would be more likely to settle if it faced the combined weight of the state and federal governments.

Pressure on the Justice Department to bring suit came also from Democratic senators who opposed the tobacco industry—Richard Durbin of Illinois, Kent Conrad of North Dakota, and Edward M. Kennedy of Massachusetts. Senator Durbin sent Attorney General Reno a lengthy memorandum prepared by antitobacco activist Clifford Douglas, making the case for a federal suit.[5] These senators may have been motivated by a desire to punish the industry and compel it to submit to regulation, to retaliate against Republicans for defeat of the McCain bill in the Senate, or to hasten a settlement so the interested parties—state governments, lawyers—would realize the proceeds. It is noteworthy that these members of Congress were active in seeking litigation as an alternative to legislation. Whatever was uppermost in their minds, it was not a concern for congressional prerogative—nor, one might add, was it a concern for the integrity of the Justice Department.[6]

With the Justice Department still dragging its heels, the president elected to proceed with the suit, which was filed in a district court in the District of Columbia in September 1999. It charged that the companies had conspired since the 1950s to defraud and mislead the public and to conceal information about the effects of smoking. The filing relied on two statutes that authorized the government to recover medical costs and a third, the Racketeer Influenced and Corrupt Organizations Act (RICO), which was passed in 1970 to combat organized crime. Federal prosecutors have since employed RICO much more widely, but this was the first time that it had been used against an entire industry.[7] In September 2000 Judge Gladys Kessler dismissed the government's claims for recovery of medical-care costs but allowed the RICO count to go forward, finding that the government had "adequately alleged" that in concealing the health risks of cigarettes and deceiving smokers, the industry had engaged in "a pattern of racketeering activity."[8]

Opponents of tobacco feared that the George W. Bush administration would not pursue its Democratic predecessor's suit, and a disillusioned career official in the Department of Justice, the lead prosecutor in the case, eventually resigned and complained of political interference.[9] Nevertheless, the suit did go forward after the change of administrations. In a massive filing early in 2003, the Bush administration's Justice Department argued that the industry should forfeit $289 billion in profits that it had earned since 1971—the year in which RICO took effect—from 33 million people who had become addicted to cigarettes as minors. It was preparing to argue that the major cigarette companies were running what amounted to a criminal enterprise by manipulating nicotine levels, lying about the dangers of tobacco, and directing multibillion-dollar advertising campaigns at children. Judge Kessler scheduled the trial to begin on September 15, 2004.[10]

It soon became clear that the federal case was likely to have an anticlimactic outcome. In February 2005 an appellate court ruled that the RICO statute was forward-looking only, and that while the trial judge could constrain future conduct she could not compel disgorgement of past profits even if she found the companies guilty.[11] The Supreme Court declined to review this decision.[12]

Judge Kessler tried to get the parties to settle, but they would not, and the case crept along until the summer of 2006, when she found the companies guilty and issued an opinion of nearly 1,700 pages, which the *Washington Post* welcomed as "a kind of official legal recognition of what this industry has done."[13] She wrote that it had sold "a highly addictive product which causes diseases that lead to a staggering number of deaths per year, an immeasurable amount of human suffering and economic loss, and a profound burden on our national health care system." She found that although it had knowledge of the harm of its product, it denied the facts to the public. The judge singled out the industry's lawyers for particular condemnation:

A word must be said about the role of lawyers in this fifty-year history of deceiving smokers, potential smokers, and the American public about the hazards of smoking and second hand smoke, and the addictiveness of nicotine. At every stage, lawyers played an absolutely central role in the creation and perpetuation of the Enterprise and the implementation of its fraudulent schemes. They devised and coordinated both national and international strategy; they directed scientists as to what research they should and should not undertake; they vetted scientific research papers and reports as well as public relations materials to ensure that the interests of the Enterprise would be protected; they identified "friendly" scientific witnesses, subsidized them with grants from the Center for Tobacco Research and the Center for Indoor Air Research, paid them enormous fees, and often hid the relationship between these witnesses and the industry; and they devised and carried out document destruction policies and took shelter behind baseless assertions of the attorney client privilege. What a sad and disquieting chapter in the history of an honorable and often courageous profession.[14]

Disillusioned with the legal profession, the judge had also developed doubts about the efficacy of litigation as a way of dealing with the industry or the public health problems associated with smoking. In a footnote, she wrote:

One cannot help wondering whether this litigation was the best vehicle for attempting to hold Defendants accountable for their indifference to the health of American citizens. In a democracy, it is the body elected by the people, namely Congress, that should step up to the plate and address national issues with such enormous economic, public health, commercial, and social ramifications, rather than the courts which are limited to deciding only the particular case presented to them in litigation.

· Congress Acts: Ordinary Politics at Work ·

In 2009 Congress did step up to the plate and pass the Family Smoking Prevention and Tobacco Control Act, which gave the FDA broad authority to regulate both the manufacture and marketing of tobacco products. The law passed by wide margins—307–97 in the House, 79–17 in the Senate—with little debate.[15] North Carolina's two senators briefly fought a rearguard action. One of them, Richard Burr, hinted at a filibuster but did not carry out the threat.[16] The other, Kay Hagan, was the only Democrat in the Senate to vote against the bill.

The new law creates a section of the Food, Drug, and Cosmetic Act solely for the regulation of tobacco products. Although it draws extensively on the act's provisions for regulating pharmaceutical products and medical devices, tobacco products are to be regulated on the basis of a public health standard rather than the safety and effectiveness standard by which the FDA regulates drugs and devices. Under the new language, the FDA must demonstrate that any proposed tobacco product regulation is appropriate for protection of the public health, taking into consideration the risks and benefits to the population as a whole.

Most significantly, the FDA can require changes in the design and characteristics of current and future tobacco products, including the reduction or elimination of harmful ingredients and additives, although it cannot reduce nicotine yields to zero. Manufacturers have to obtain FDA approval in order to market a new tobacco product unless the FDA determines that it is substantially equivalent to, or a minor modification of, a product already on the market. The law restricts youth marketing and sales; requires detailed disclosure of ingredients; prohibits use of terms such as "light," "mild," and "low" that might be taken to imply safety; and requires bigger, graphic warnings on both sides of packs and in advertising. The cost of FDA regulation is to be paid from fees imposed on manufacturers.[17]

Antitobacco activists had made a regulatory statute a major objective ever since the Supreme Court's ruling in 2000 that the Food, Drug, and Cosmetic Act precluded regulation of tobacco products, thus ending the regulatory demarche launched by the zealous David Kessler as FDA commissioner. For ordinary politics to produce what they sought required above all that tobacco politics become partisan and that the partisan opposition, now located in the Democratic Party, achieve control of the government. By 2009 this had occurred. A second condition, facilitating change but not so clearly necessary, was that tobacco's agricultural and industrial defenders needed to divide. Divisions occurred prior to 2009 along two dimensions and helped put regulation on a path to success in Congress even before the Democrats' capture of the government was complete. One division was between manufacturers, a majority of whom opposed regulation, and tobacco growers, who were prepared to accept it if that became the political price of preserving their markets. The other division was between Philip Morris, the biggest manufacturer, which endorsed regulation in 2000–2001, and the rest of the manufacturing industry, which persisted in opposing it.

Tobacco Turns Partisan

Historically, tobacco control was not a partisan issue in American politics. Neither major party favored it. Republicans were sympathetic to corporate interests, and Democrats were dominant in states where tobacco was grown and manufactured. However, beginning in the 1960s, Republicans began replacing Democrats in the South, a change that was largely completed in the 1990s and that liberated Democrats to be the party of tobacco opposition.[18] They had had a leader of the opposition since 1979 when Henry Waxman of Beverly Hills, California, defeated L. Richardson Preyer of Greensboro, North Carolina, as chair of the Subcommittee on Health and the Environment of the House Commerce Committee. Waxman fought tobacco unrelentingly for the next thirty years; by his own account, the fight defined his career. He thought he was on the brink of a legislative breakthrough in 1994, following hearings in which the industry was pilloried on television, but electoral politics intervened when Republicans captured control of the House in November of that year—and then kept it for the next twelve years.[19]

The Republican House victory, together with rising Democratic opposition to tobacco both in Congress and the Clinton White House, sharpened partisan cleavage on the issue and altered the industry's pattern of campaign donations. Traditionally, it had sought to reward friends and punish enemies without regard to party, but after 1994 its contributions in national politics heavily favored the Republicans. In the first six months of 1995, the largest cigarette companies contributed $1.5 million to the Republican Party, ten times what they had given it in 1993. The top two contributors to the party in 1995 were the cigarette makers Philip Morris and RJR Nabisco. Five of the top ten recipients of tobacco PAC contributions to the House of Representatives in 1995 were Republican freshmen.[20] The pattern of heavy favoritism for Republicans would persist until 2008, although the volume of contributions dropped after 2002. In the 2008 election cycle contributions were $4.2 million, less than half of what they had been six years earlier.[21]

Along with staunch Republican opponents of regulation in Congress, George W. Bush as president stood athwart enactment after 2000. The Bush administration's FDA commissioner, Andrew von Eschenbach, opposed regulation.[22] Bush did not send an international agreement, the Framework Convention on Tobacco Control, to the Senate for ratification even though the United States under his presidency had voted for it in the World Health Assembly; administration critics charged that Bush appointees had undermined the treaty during negotiations.[23] Bush twice vetoed liberalization of the State Children's Health Insurance Program, which included a big increase in the cigarette tax.

The Tobacco Buyout: A Marriage of Convenience

Notwithstanding the partisan cleavage, a bill for regulation ironically passed the Republican-controlled Senate in 2004, an important step toward ultimate adoption. In a classic example of legislative logrolling, it was combined with a multibillion-dollar buyout of the nation's tobacco growers and owners of tobacco "quota," which was the right to grow tobacco under the federal government's price support program. A buyout would end that program.

By 2003 American tobacco farmers were deeply anxious, with their markets shrinking, their production costs rising, and their income falling. The origins of this situation lay in the agricultural price-support programs of the New Deal. The federal government's program of tobacco price supports, which combined quotas that limited the size of the crop with a guaranteed minimum price, had perversely driven the cost of domestic tobacco far above the world price. "My company can go to Brazil and buy tobacco for 40 cents on the dollar," a witness from Brown & Williamson told the House Committee on Agriculture.[24] The percentage of U.S. leaf contained in domestically manufactured cigarettes had fallen from 90 percent in the mid-1960s to half as much by 2002, and there was a comparable drop in exports of U.S. leaf, from 25 percent to less than 10 percent of world tobacco exports.[25] In addition, manufacturing was moving overseas—U.S. cigarette exports, which peaked at 243.9 billion units in 1996, were half that amount by 2003—while in their offshore locations, U.S. manufacturers used even more foreign leaf.

Antitobacco activists started cultivating an alliance with tobacco farmers as early as the mid-1990s, shrewdly seeing an opportunity to divide them from the manufacturers and gain support in Congress, whose tobacco-state members were acutely sensitive to the farmers' plight. These activists had been careful to demonstrate similar sensitivity themselves, in sharp contrast to their demonization of the manufacturers. Though suspicious of federal regulation via the FDA, the farmers were increasingly willing to pay whatever political price was necessary to get a buyout. A presidential commission appointed late in the Clinton administration—with Matthew Myers of the Campaign for Tobacco-Free Kids and the president of the Burley Tobacco Growers Cooperative Association as cochairs—had formalized this alliance with recommendations for simultaneously fortifying both the farmers and smoking prevention programs.[26]

Reaching agreement on precise terms of the separate parts of the buyout-plus-regulation package proved difficult, as Philip Morris and tobacco's opponents quarreled over the details of regulation and fiscal conservatives inside and outside of Congress objected to the buyout, the cost of which was estimated at $15 billion. Opponents said that parties who had benefited for decades from government protection were not entitled now to be paid generously for relinquishing it. The buyout could not get through Congress independently, as Senator Elizabeth Dole of North Carolina and Representative Jack Kingston of Georgia learned when they tried and failed to attach a relatively modest version of it to an end-of-the-session appropriations bill in 2003.

Midway through the presidential election year of 2004, the prospects for a buyout suddenly surged. In June the House Ways and Means Committee added a buyout to a corporate tax relief bill that was considered "must" legislation because it included relief from a ruling of the World Trade Organization that penalized American corporations for an export subsidy embedded in domestic law. The House passed the amended bill 251–178. Meanwhile, Senate Republican whip Mitch McConnell of the tobacco state of Kentucky was urging fellow Republicans to resolve their differences with Democrats over FDA regulation. The future of the tobacco industry in the United States would depend heavily, he said, on whether the "marriage of convenience" was adopted. In July the Senate added both FDA regulation and a buyout to its version of the tax relief bill.[27]

It proved impossible to bring House Republicans—and arguably also the Bush White House—along with the regulatory part of the package.[28] Only the buyout passed Congress in 2004, but it had the effect of quickly reducing the number and presumably the influence of tobacco growers.

The government's price support program ended with the 2004 crop year. During the first uncontrolled year, tobacco acreage decreased by 25 percent to 298,020 acres, the lowest level since before the Civil War.[29] Whereas North Carolina had eight thousand tobacco farmers in 2002, by 2009 it had only three thousand.[30] Kentucky's remaining eight thousand farms represented a 72 percent reduction from the era of price supports.[31] Nevertheless, tobacco farmers and their partisans in Congress retained enough influence to leave footprints on the new law, which denied the FDA authority over tobacco growers and warehouses and also over tobacco leaf unless it were in the possession of a manufacturer. It prohibited FDA employees from entering a tobacco farm without written consent of the producer. It also required that the FDA's published notices of proposed rulemaking invite the secretary of agriculture to provide relevant analysis and information. The farmers' backers in Congress, located in the House Agriculture Committee, would have preferred to avoid regulation by the FDA. At the eleventh hour, they sponsored a rival bill, the Youth Prevention and Tobacco Harm Reduction Act, which, if it had passed, would have authorized the Department of Health and Human Services to set up a new unit "to realistically address tobacco harm reduction with scientifically based programs instead of bureaucratic mandates."[32]

The Defection of Philip Morris

The growers' split from the manufacturing industry in 2004 was less significant than a deepening division among manufacturers themselves. Philip Morris, the leader in sales, had broken with the rest in 2000–2001 by announcing support for FDA regulation and thereafter encouraging tobacco farmers to support it as well.[33] Further proving that it was serious, the company endorsed the bill of 2004 and expressed disappointment at the "lost opportunity" when it failed in the House.[34]

In supporting regulation, Philip Morris was making several wagers:

1. that it was more prudent, after years of merciless battering in legislatures, courts, and other venues, to seek peace and stability rather than invite incessant charges of criminality and even, at the imaginable extreme, calls for prohibition of tobacco use or nationalization of the companies

2. that regulation might facilitate introduction of new and putatively safer products with official approval

3. that Philip Morris, with the largest market share and greatest technical sophistication of the tobacco manufacturing companies, could survive in a regulated environment more successfully than its competitors, who liked to call the various regulatory proposals "Philip Morris protection acts"

4. that the FDA would use its powers conservatively, calculating that extreme measures of nicotine reduction would encourage black markets to flourish and deprive governments of needed revenue from tobacco taxes.

A key concession to Philip Morris was to give up use of the drug and device provisions of the Food, Drug, and Cosmetic Act, the FDA's statutory charter. When the FDA undertook regulation under David Kessler's leadership, it proposed to treat nicotine as a drug and cigarettes as a delivery device. Public health advocates preferred this approach, but Philip Morris objected that it gave the FDA no alternative but to ban tobacco as unsafe. The company sought addition of a new section addressed specifically to tobacco, and this was done. Although the developing legislation endorsed most of the FDA's 1996 tobacco rule, it did not endorse labeling cigarettes as a "nicotine delivery device for persons 18 and older." The company also objected successfully to giving the FDA authority to eliminate nicotine or ban tobacco products.[35]

After 2004 a bill still had to pass the House and be signed by the president. For the next four years, party politics continued to stand in the way. That a Republican Senate voted for regulation was an anomaly, attributable both to the "marriage of convenience" that ended price supports and to the presence of a few strong Republican opponents of tobacco, such as Ohio's Mike DeWine and Arizona's John McCain. After 2008, when Barack Obama, who had backed regulation as a member of the Senate, was elected to succeed Bush, along with large Democratic majorities in both the House and Senate, tobacco regulation moved swiftly to the conclusion that partisan politics determined. The House, which had turned Democratic in the election of 2006, passed a bill in July 2008, even before the election. The vote was 326–102.[36]

As the partisan composition of the government changed, and with it the ordinary politics of tobacco control, Philip Morris USA continued to collaborate in the campaign for regulation. In October 2007 Mike Szymanczyk, chair and chief executive officer, expressed "strong support" for the bill being considered by Waxman, newly returned to committee leadership following the Democrats' recapture of the House in 2006. "Almost five years after we announced our full support for FDA regulation PM USA remains committed to passage of comprehensive regulation of tobacco products," Szymanczyk testified.[37] Early in March 2009 he wrote to Waxman urging him to report his bill out of committee and thanking him for his leadership. In June he wrote a similar letter to the president, applauding the impending achievement of historic legislation that would shortly be presented for the president's signature. Philip Morris spent more than $4 million in the first quarter of 2009 lobbying for the bill.[38]

After enactment, Philip Morris declined to join other tobacco companies, including Reynolds American, Lorillard, and Commonwealth Brands, in challenging various provisions of the law on the grounds that they violated the companies' First Amendment rights, a challenge that was mostly rejected by a federal judge in Kentucky.[39] If this preeminent party-at-interest had not entered into negotiations with its opponents, there would likely have been more debate and closer votes, but if the law after nearly a decade of negotiation was good enough for Philip Morris, why should it not be good enough for business-friendly Republicans?

The conspicuous defection of Philip Morris meant that the tobacco industry was not an influential opponent of regulation, and, with the industry divided, no other such opponents existed. Presumably smokers had been thought an important, if latent and unorganized, source of opposition in the middle of the twentieth century, when smoking was widely practiced throughout the adult population, but that time had long passed. At roughly 20 percent of the population, their number still was not small, but they were concentrated among the least influential strata of society. The stubborn persistence of tobacco use sustained the opponents' sense of urgency without legitimating the practice of smoking or empowering smokers in politics.

· Regulation in the New Era ·

The new statutory regime in no way supersedes the Master Settlement Agreement. In response to a general invitation from the FDA, published on July 1, 2009, to comment on implementation of the new law, the National Association of Attorneys General called particular attention to Internet sales and tribal sales as problems in tobacco enforcement and promised to share lessons from its own experience.[40]

A readily foreseeable challenge of which NAAG said little is smokeless tobacco products. Though cigarette smoking persists in the United States and the manufacturers remain profitable, domestic sales volumes have been dropping by around 1 to 3 percent a year. In response, the industry searches for other products, of which the most promising appears to be smokeless tobacco.

Sometimes referred to as "spit" tobacco, smokeless tobacco has traditionally taken four forms: moist snuff, the most popular, which is a finely cut processed tobacco that the user places between the cheek and the gum; dry snuff, a fine powder that is inhaled into the nostrils; loose-leaf chewing tobacco, a processed cigar-type that is loosely packed to form small strips and typically sold in a foil-lined pouch; and plug or plug/twist chewing tobacco, which is formed as small, oblong, semisoft blocks. No statistics exist to show that cigarette smokers have been switching to smokeless tobacco, but the sales volume has been rising. According to the Federal Trade Commission, the five largest domestic manufacturers had $2.61 billion in sales in 2005 compared to $2.13 billion in 2001. And—a source of alarm to tobacco's opponents—since 1970 smokeless tobacco has gone from a product used primarily by older men to one used predominantly by young men and boys. According to CDC data, 13.4 percent of U.S. high school boys and 2.3 percent of high school girls were using smokeless tobacco products in 2007, and in some states the rate was much higher—more than 20 percent for high school boys in Kentucky, Montana, Oklahoma, Tennessee, West Virginia, and Wyoming.[41]

Sensing opportunity in these facts, cigarette manufacturers have bought the manufacturers of smokeless tobacco. Philip Morris in 2009 bought the biggest of them, U.S. Smokeless Tobacco Company (UST), maker of the Skoal and Copenhagen brands, for $20.4 billion plus the assumption of $1.3 billion in debt.[42] Earlier, Reynolds American had bought Conwood, producer of the brands Grizzly and Kodiak. In addition, cigarette manufacturers have begun testing smokeless products of their own, principally snus, a tobacco product borrowed from Sweden, where it has a long history. Snus are now appearing with American brand names—Camel Snus, Marlboro Snus, Liggett Group's Grand Prix Snus, Lorillard's Triumph Snus. They are small pouches, like tea bags but containing tobacco instead, that users place between the upper gum and the lip. They do not require spitting, can easily be concealed, and can be consumed in places where smoking is prohibited. This is true also of another new product, nicotine lozenges, made by Star Scientific.[43]

An early task of the FDA will be to evaluate evidence about the effects of smokeless tobacco. The industry has made clear an intention to promote it as a less risky alternative to cigarette smoking. In response to the FDA's invitation to comment on implementation of the new act, Philip Morris and U.S. Smokeless Tobacco, now joined as units of Altria Group, Inc., wrote that a regulatory framework that takes into account the "continuum of risk" of different tobacco products could "have a significant public health benefit." They argued that regulations permitting the industry to convey to consumers the lower dangers of smokeless tobacco products could complement efforts to get people to stop using tobacco or keep them from starting. Reynolds American had submitted similar comments.[44] The industry would like to claim, or at least imply, that its products are safer because of FDA approval. The law contained a provision prohibiting such statements, but a federal judge struck that provision down, along with a provision banning the use of color and graphics—as distinct from black-and-white text only—in publications with a significant youth readership.[45]

A contest has already been under way over the effects of smokeless tobacco, which research in Britain and Sweden has shown to be, if not free of harm, at least substantially less harmful than cigarette smoking.[46] Tobacco opponents in the U.S. public health community, such as the office of the surgeon general and the National Cancer Institute, along with private lobbies led by the Campaign for Tobacco-Free Kids, have insisted that smokeless tobacco also causes cancer.[47] High on the agenda of the FDA's tobacco unit will be the task of evaluating the science in this matter, weighing the arguments and implications for public health, and interpreting the law. This is the next battleground of America's long-running war over tobacco.

The new era of regulation could result in a larger role for judges in tobacco policymaking because it will draw courts into the familiar task of reviewing the decisions of a regulatory agency. Interpreting regulatory statutes is a function that administrative agencies and courts share in the United States.

An early example of such involvement in tobacco came in January 2010 in the decision of a federal district judge in Washington, D.C., to issue a preliminary injunction ordering the FDA to cease blocking the importation of electronic cigarettes from China. The cigarette at issue—an "e-cigarette"—consists of a battery-powered tube that heats liquid nicotine, turning it into an inhalable vapor. The plaintiff in the case was a distributor in Florida called Smoking Everywhere. The company was joined by the Electronic Cigarette Association, whose chair claimed that electronic cigarettes are a $100 million business nationwide. He also told the *New York Times* that the FDA had impounded thousands of e-cigarettes and millions of nicotine cartridges at the border.

For his part, the judge wrote, "This case appears to be yet another example of FDA's aggressive efforts to regulate recreational tobacco products as drugs or devices," for which it lacks authority. He pointed out that with the passage of regulatory legislation, the FDA's new tobacco division could regulate e-cigarettes along with other tobacco products, but said that in the meantime its drug division could not ban them as devices.[48] Late in 2010 a panel of the U.S. Court of Appeals for the District of Columbia Circuit upheld this decision.[49]

Public health advocates are divided over the likely impact of e-cigarettes, some believing that they will contribute to the cessation of conventional smoking, others believing that they will lead to more of it. The FDA began intercepting imports in June 2008 but did not immediately move against the developing manufacture of e-cigarette liquids and other equipment in the United States. However, in 2010 it sent letters to five domestic distributors of e-cigarettes warning that they were violating federal law by claiming that these devices could help smokers of conventional cigarettes to cut back or quit.[50]

· Notes ·

1. Michael Waldman, *POTUS Speaks: Finding the Words That Defined the Clinton Presidency* (New York: Simon & Schuster, 2000), 257, 260.
2. James Bennet, "Tobacco Fund Is Ours, States Tell President," *New York Times,* February 23, 1999, A17; Saundra Torry, "Tobacco Firms Win Suit Filed by Unions; Health Funds Sought to Recover Costs," *Washington Post,* March 19, A2; and John Schwartz, "GOP Snuffs Out White House Hopes for Tobacco Settlement Money," *Washington Post,* May 14, 1999, A5. The Post's headline errs in identifying the Republican Party as the sole source of opposition to the White House on this question.

3. Barry Meier and David Johnston, "How Inquiry into Tobacco Lost Its Steam," *New York Times,* September 26, 1999, A1; Edward Walsh, "Final Decisions Near on Tobacco Probe," *Washington Post,* March 12, 1999, A2; and Ann Davis, "How a Lawyer Turned Tables in Tobacco Case," *Wall Street Journal,* October 4, 1999, B1. Davis's story tells how William C. Hendricks III, formerly a Justice Department prosecutor but now working for the Atlanta law firm of King and Spaulding as head of Brown & Williamson's defense, let it be known that he would argue that FDA officials had attempted to sandbag B&W by first asking vague questions about nicotine manipulation and then citing the company's incomplete answers as proof that it was trying to hide its use of enriched tobacco. Hendricks also suggested that the FDA may have destroyed evidence after the agency told him that it had misplaced an official's notes of a crucial meeting.

4. David S. Cloud, "U.S. Faces Hurdles to Recovering Tobacco Health Costs," *Wall Street Journal,* May 27, 1999, A28.

5. "Why the Federal Government Should Sue the Tobacco Industry," 14.2 *TPLR* 4.1 (1999).

6. My account of how the Justice Department was brought around depends primarily on a *Wall Street Journal* story, "Justice Reverses: Lobbying Effort Wins Turnabout on Tobacco Suit," September 24, 1999, B1. The story does not carry a byline, but the reporters are identified as David S. Cloud, Gordon Fairclough, and Ann Davis.

7. "United States Sues Cigarette Companies to Recover Federal Health Care Costs," U.S. Department of Justice press release, September 22, 1999, www.justice.gov/opa/pr/1999/September/428civ.htm, accessed March 18, 2011. There was abundant press coverage. See, for example, Marc Lacey, "Tobacco Industry Accused of Fraud in Lawsuit by U.S.," *New York Times,* September 23, 1999, A1. On the expanded use of RICO, see Jim McGee and Brian Duffy, *Main Justice* (New York: Simon and Schuster, Touchstone ed., 1997), chap. 9.

8. Gary Fields and Gordon Fairclough, "U.S. to Pursue Tobacco Case under RICO," *Wall Street Journal,* September 29, 2000, A3; and Bill Miller, "Judge Carves a Chunk Out of Tobacco Suit," *Washington Post,* September 29, 2000, A1.

9. Wall Street Journal Abstracts, "Government Lawyer in Tobacco Case Quits," December 2, 2005, www.lexisnexis.com, accessed on March 28, 2011; Carol D. Leonnig, "Prosecutor Says Bush Appointees Interfered with Tobacco Case," *Washington Post,* March 22, 2007, A1.

10. Eric Lichtblau, "U.S. Lawsuit Seeks Tobacco Profits," *New York Times,* March 18, 2003, A1; John R. Wilke and Vanessa O'Connell, "U.S. Asks Judge for $289 Billion in Tobacco Suit," *Wall Street Journal,* March 19, 2003, B2; and Neely Tucker, "In Major Case, U.S. Alleges Tobacco Firms' Conspiracy," *Washington Post,* March 19, 2003, A29.

11. Carol D. Leonnig, "Court Rejects Tobacco Penalty; U.S. Sought $280 Billion in Past Profits," washingtonpost.com, February 5, 2005, www.washingtonpost.com/wp-dyn/articles/A63833–2005Feb4.html, accessed March 18, 2011; Michael Janofsky, "Appellate Court Backs Companies in Tobacco Case," *New York Times,* February 5, 2005, A1.

12. Linda Greenhouse, "Justices Reject Appeal in Tobacco Case," *New York Times,* October 18, 2005, A16; Vanessa O'Connell and Jess Bravin, "Justices Won't Hear Tobacco Case," *Wall Street Journal,* October 18, 2005, A12.

13. Carol D. Leonnig, "Judge in Tobacco Case Urges Settlement," *Washington Post,* June 21, 2005, A12; "Smoke but No Fire," *Washington Post,* August 19, 2006, A16.

14. Final Opinion, *U.S. v. Philip Morris USA, Inc., et al.,* Civil Action No. 99–2496 (GK), United States District Court for the District of Columbia, August 17, 2006.

15. Duff Wilson, "Congress Passes Measure On Tobacco Regulation," *New York Times,* June 13, 2009, B3.

16. Duff Wilson, "Foe Throws in the Towel on Tobacco Regulation Bill," *New York Times,* June 6, 2009, B4.

17. C. Stephen Redhead and Vanessa K. Burrows, *FDA Tobacco Regulation: The Family Smoking Prevention and Tobacco Control Act of 2009,* May 28, 2009, www.fda.gov/downloads/AdvisoryCommittees/CommitteesMeetingMater ials/TobaccoProductsScientificAdvisoryCommittee/UCM204344.pdf, accessed March 18, 2011.

18. Alexander P. Lamis, ed., *Southern Politics in the 1990s* (Baton Rouge: Louisiana State University Press, 1999), chap. 1; Earl Black and Merle Black, *The Rise of Southern Republicans* (Cambridge, Ma. Harvard University Press, 2002).

19. Henry Waxman with Joshua Green, *The Waxman Report: How Congress Really Works* (New York: Twelve, an imprint of Grand Central Publishing, 2009), ix–xv, 177ff. This is a detailed account of all that Waxman did, up until 2009, to defeat the tobacco industry in legislative politics.

20. Peter H. Stone, "Our Good Friend, the Governor," *Mother Jones,* May/June 1996, 38; Sidney Wolfe et al., *The Congressional Addiction to Tobacco: How the Tobacco Lobby Suffocates Federal Health Policy,* a report by the Public Citizen's Health Research Group (Washington, D.C.: October 1992), 3; Linda Killian, *The Freshmen* (Boulder, Colo.: Westview Press, 1998), 118–119.

21. Center for Responsive Politics, "Tobacco: Background," OpenSecrets.org, www .opensecrets.org/industries/background.php?cycle = 2010&ind = A02, accessed August 26, 2010.

22. Peter Hardin, "FDA Chief Assails Tobacco Bill," *Richmond Times-Dispatch,* October 4, 2007, B7.

23. Allan M. Brandt, *The Cigarette Century* (New York: Basic Books, 2007), 475–476.

24. U.S. Congress, House of Representatives, The Tobacco Quota Buyout, Hearing before the Committee on Agriculture, 108th Cong., 1 sess. (July 24, 2003), serial 108–15, 43.

25. "Tobacco at a Crossroad: Final Report of the President's Commission on Improving Economic Opportunity in Communities Dependent on Tobacco Production While Protecting Public Health," May 14, 2001, 5–6; and Jasper Womach, "Tobacco Price Support: An Overview of the Program," Congressional Research Service Report for Congress, November 3, 2003.

26. The commission's report, Tobacco at a Crossroad, could be found as of February 10, 2004, at www.fsa.usda.gov/tobcom/reports.htm. Appendix B is "A Brief History of Tobacco Farmers and Public Health Representatives Working Together."

27. David Rogers, "Thomas Engineers Showdown over Tobacco," *Wall Street Journal,* June 25, 2004, A4; Josephine Hearn, "Sens. Gregg and DeWine Reignite

Tobacco Debate," *The Hill*, April 20, 2004, 22; and Carl Hulse, "Senate Approves Tobacco Buyout and New Curbs," *New York Times*, July 16, 2004, A1.

28. Dan Morgan and Helen Dewar, "House Blocks FDA Oversight of Tobacco," *Washington Post*, October 12, 2004, A4; "Mr. Bush and Tobacco," *Washington Post*, September 23, 2004, A28.

29. Thomas Capehart, "U.S. Tobacco Sector Regroups," www.ers/usda.gov/Amber Waves/February06/Findings/findings_mt1.htm, accessed March 11, 2011.

30. Testimony of Steve Troxler, North Carolina agricultural commissioner, March 26, 2009, http://agriculture.house.gov/hearings/statements.html, accessed on October 20, 2009.

31. Testimony of William M. Snell, agricultural economist, University of Kentucky, March 26, 2009, http://agriculture.house.gov/hearings/statements.html, accessed on October 20, 2009.

32. Testimony of J. T. Bunn, president of U.S. Tobacco Cooperative, Inc., March 26, 2009, http://agriculture.house.gov/hearings/statements.html, accessed on October 20, 2009.

33. Barry Meier, "Executive Says Philip Morris Is Open to Some Regulation," *New York Times*, February 29, 2000, A12; Gordon Fairclough, "Philip Morris Pushes for FDA Tobacco Regulation," *Wall Street Journal*, April 11, 2001, A2; Vanessa O'Connell, "Why Philip Morris Decided to Make Friends with FDA," *Wall Street Journal*, September 25, 2003, A1.

34. Warren Vieth, "Senate Passes Big Tax Breaks," *Los Angeles Times*, October 12, 2004, http://articles.latimes.com/2004/oct/12/nation/na-tax12, accessed on March 18, 2011.

35. C. Stephen Redhead and Vanessa K. Burrows, *FDA Tobacco Regulation: The Family Smoking Prevention and Tobacco Control Act of 2009*, May 28, 2009, www.fda.gov/downloads/AdvisoryCommittees/CommitteesMeetingMaterials/ TobaccoProductsScientificAdvisoryCommittee/UCM204344.pdf, accessed March 18, 2011.

36. Stephanie Saul, "House Votes to Regulate Tobacco as a Drug," *New York Times*, July 31, 2008, C2.

37. "Written Statement of Mike Szymanczyk, Chairman and Chief Executive Officer, Philip Morris USA," www.philipmorrisusa.com/en/cms/Responsibility/ Government_Affairs/pdfs/Written_Statement_of_Mike_Szymanczyk_for_ House_Hearing_on_10_3_07.pdf.aspx, accessed on March 18, 2011.

38. Lyndsey Layton, "Chances Bright for Legislation Seeking FDA Regulation of Tobacco," *Washington Post*, May 11, 2009, A11.

39. David Kesmodel, Lauren Etter, and Alicia Mundy, "Tobacco Giants Challenge Law," *Wall Street Journal*, September 1, 2009, B3; Duff Wilson, "Judge Lifts Some Limits On Tobacco Advertising," *New York Times*, January 6, 2010, B3; David Kesmodel and Suzanne Vranica, "Mixed Tobacco Ruling," *Wall Street Journal*, January 6, 2010, B2.

40. "Attorneys General Offer Comments on Federal Tobacco Law," National Association of Attorneys General, www.naag.org/attorneys-general-offer-comments-on-federal-tobacco-law.php, accessed on January 2, 2010.

41. "FTC Releases Reports on Cigarettes and Smokeless Tobacco," www.ftc.gov/ opa/2007/04/cigaretterpt.shtm, accessed on December 19, 2009; Campaign for

Tobacco-Free Kids, "Smokeless Tobacco and Kids," www.tobaccofreekids.org/research/factsheets/pdf/0003.pdf, accessed on December 6, 2009.

42. Associated Press State & Local Wire, "Altria Closes Buy of Smokeless Tobacco Company," January 6, 2009, http://lexisnexis.com, accessed on December 20, 2009.

43. Campaign for Tobacco-Free Kids, "Smokeless Tobacco and Kids," www.tobaccofreekids.org/research/factsheets/pdf/0003.pdf, accessed December 6, 2009.

44. David Kesmodel, "Philip Morris Pushes Smokeless," *Wall Street Journal,* January 6, 2010, B2.

45. David Kesmodel and Suzanne Vranica, "Mixed Tobacco Ruling," *Wall Street Journal,* January 6, 2010, B2; "New Tobacco Regulation Law Clears Legal Hurdle," www.lungusa.org/about-us/our-impact/top-stories/new-tobacco-regulation-law-1.html, accessed on March 18, 2011.

46. Kevin Harlin, "Don't Chew on This: Snus Offer Safer Fix," *Investor's Business Daily,* January 22, 2008, A11; Kevin Helliker, "Tobacco Road Takes a Turn to the Smokeless," *Wall Street Journal,* January 27, 2009, D1.

47. Campaign for Tobacco-Free Kids, "Smokeless Tobacco in the United States," July 9, 2008, www.tobaccofreekids.org/research/factsheets/pdf/0231.pdf; Campaign for Tobacco-Free Kids, "The United States Isn't Sweden," July 9, 2008, www.tobaccofreekids.org/research/factsheets/pdf/0283.pdf. Both accessed on December 6, 2009.

48. Duff Wilson, "Judge Orders F. D. A. to Stop Blocking Imports of E-Cigarettes from China," *New York Times,* January 15, 2010, B3.

49. David Kesmodel, "Court Limits FDA's E-Cigarette Role," *Wall Street Journal,* December 8, 2010, B7.

50. David Kesmodel and Danny Yadron, "E-Cigarettes Spark New Smoking War," *Wall Street Journal,* August 23, 2010, A1; John Reid Blackwell, "FDA Gives Warning on E-cigarette Marketing; 5 Distributors Get Letters that Efficacy of Devices Has Not Been Approved," *Richmond Times-Dispatch,* September 10, 2010, http://lexisnexis.com, accessed March 29, 2011.

CHAPTER TWELVE

Ordinary Politics versus Adversarial Legalism

IN THE THREE DECADES AFTER THE SURGEON general's advisory committee warned in 1964 of the hazards of smoking, ordinary politics served well to reduce smoking in the United States.

In 1999 the Centers for Disease Control hailed the late-twentieth-century drop in tobacco use as one of the century's ten greatest achievements in public health.[1] After rising with few interruptions through most of the century, per capita consumption of cigarettes in the United States declined steadily after the official campaign against tobacco use began. By 1999 it had fallen to pre–World War II levels. In addition to the decline in per capita consumption of cigarettes (from 4,345 in 1963 to 2,136 in 1999) and in smoking prevalence among adults (from 42.4 percent in 1965 to 24.7 percent in 1997), the CDC cited the numerous clean indoor air laws enacted by state governments.

Country statistics compiled by the World Health Organization help put the change in U.S. smoking habits in perspective. Whereas the United States ranked second in per capita consumption of cigarettes in 1980–1982, it had dropped to eleventh place a decade later. Ranked according to smoking prevalence by gender—that is, the proportion of the male and female populations fifteen and over who smoke—the United States ranked seventy-eighth among eighty-seven nations for males and thirty-third for females. (Female smoking rates are generally higher in developed nations than in the less-developed ones.)[2]

Of course, how much of the dramatic drop in smoking is attributable to actions of government is impossible to say. In this period, social norms changed, and perhaps government should not be credited with the pressures that Americans exerted on one another. Yet governments played a critical role in shaping the new norms, and it cannot be an accident that the drop started at about the time that the landmark report to the surgeon general appeared. Everett Koop, a prominent opponent of smoking when he was surgeon general in the administration of President George H. W. Bush, was right when he spread the credit broadly: "The anti-smoking achievements in the United States—the most successful of any country's—reflect the combined efforts of private citizens, private organizations, health professionals, and the government."[3]

Not everyone agreed with this assessment. Tobacco's opponents were dissatisfied because smoking rates did not drop faster and further, because underage smoking persisted, and because regulation did not reach tobacco products per se. Libertarians disapproved of even the modest amount of coercion that governments employed.[4] But if one grants that protecting the public health is a legitimate end of government, then discouraging tobacco use is a legitimate means to that end, and the question becomes one of weighing the benefits and costs of government measures. Many benefits were realized in the years 1964–1993 with a relatively low cost in coercion—and coercion should always be reckoned as a cost. Smoking was very much reduced, and with measures far more consensual than not.

From the perspective of mid-2011, in the third year of the Barack Obama presidency and the twelfth year of the Master Settlement Agreement, it is hard to see why anyone ever thought that elected legislatures in the United States could not take action against tobacco. In the closing decade of the twentieth century, just before the wave of lawsuits began, the states were a hotbed of such activity, producing many restrictions on where smoking was permitted, restrictions on youth access such as retail licensing for cigarette vendors, and frequent increases in excise taxes. Most tobacco control advocates in the early and mid-1990s were not designing end runs around legislatures but were busily trying, as in the past, to use state and local legislatures to construct a society-wide norm against tobacco use.[5] Under the impact of the Synar Amendment, state governments were beginning to gain traction on enforcement of laws against youth purchases of cigarettes, a historic weakness of tobacco control.[6]

Nor did such efforts flag as the country moved into the next century and took the turn toward litigation. Between 2000 and 2010, the number of states that had in place comprehensive smoke-free policies (no smoking allowed in workplaces, restaurants, and bars) rose from none to twenty-six. Almost half of U. S. residents are reached by such laws.[7] Late in 2009 the tobacco state of Virginia banned smoking in public restaurants and bars.[8] North Carolina, with an economy more dependent on tobacco than that of Virginia, imposed a similar ban at the beginning of 2010.[9] New York City banned smoking at public parks, beaches, plazas, and boardwalks early in 2011.[10] Between 2002 and

2009, state legislatures repeatedly increased cigarette tax rates. The federal excise tax likewise rose, reaching $1.01 per pack on April 1, 2009, following the highest-ever increase of 62 cents as part of a liberalization of the State Children's Health Insurance Program that was enacted by the newly installed Democratic government.[11]

So why was there a plunge in the late 1990s into adversarial legalism, if there was much to applaud in the record of ordinary politics?

· The Roots of Adversarial Legalism ·

Legislative politics tested the patience of tobacco's opponents with its gradualism and compromises, but that is not the fundamental explanation for the turn to the courts. Crucially, some of tobacco's most zealous opponents wanted to achieve what legislatures could not deliver. They wished to attack tobacco at its commercial source, the manufacturers of cigarettes. They wanted to punish the manufacturers—to brand their executives as criminals, compel disclosure of internal documents, burden them with damage costs, or possibly drive them into bankruptcy—as had happened with asbestos manufacturers. Lawsuits were seen as the way to do this.

The key practitioners of the strategy, powerful because they held high government offices, turned out to be the state attorneys general. As chief law enforcement officers of their governments, they were well positioned to test the reach of litigant activism in the making of public policy. They saw in lawsuits a way to enrich their governments and their political supporters among tort lawyers, whom they engaged as collaborators.

They took their work, a settlement negotiated with the major manufacturers, to Congress, asking the national legislature to approve it. That adversarial legalism has important differences from ordinary politics was demonstrated when the legislature refused. The negotiated settlement failed in Congress because elected politicians could not satisfy the many interests and ideological positions that were involved when the policy process was open to them. Ordinary politics, with elected legislatures at its core, is representative. That is its distinctive virtue, the source of its legitimacy. As Congress deliberated, more and more claimants for a piece of the action emerged, and the two main opposing forces—health advocates on one side, the companies on the other—had positions as of 1997–1998 that were extreme and irreconcilable.

When the opposing litigants returned to the bargaining table with no interests other than their own to attend to, they crafted an extremely complicated, self-serving document that gave the state governments money and the companies protection against further lawsuits from the states. The companies were also protected from the competition of rival tobacco manufacturers who were not party to the agreement. There were enough restrictions on the marketing and advertising practices of the companies and enough money committed to a campaign against smoking to clothe the settlement with the appearance of tobacco control in the public interest, but such control was not the main purpose. The MSA was the state governments' instrument for taking more money from commerce in tobacco than they were already taking in excise taxes—and taking it without the trouble of having legislators do it.

· What Happened to Checks and Balances? ·

The tobacco settlement was public policy of a kind that the Framers of the Constitution tried to protect Americans against. At worst it was "state terrorism," as Lester Brickman of the Cardozo Law School called it. "Contingency fee lawyers and the attorneys general used bare, brute force to bludgeon the tobacco companies into submission. Even though there were filings in state courts and one in federal district court, the object was not to litigate. The object was to raise the threat level high enough to coerce tobacco companies into suing for peace. The lawsuits had no basis in law." Moreover, they were corrupting: "Partnerships between state governments and private attorneys amount to a corruption of both legal ethics and the legal process. . . . [C]ontingency fee agreements . . . were wildly excessive and utterly incompatible with fiduciary principles and rules of legal ethics. . . . Much of the money being paid to the lawyers rightfully belongs to state taxpayers."[12] At the very least—putting it as mildly as possible and ignoring abuses of the legal system—one can say that a policy result was arrived at without public deliberation and by serving private interests disproportionately, albeit with an overlay of public interest justification in the removal of billboards, reduced cigarette promotions, and higher cigarette prices.

Some of the state-level events, particularly the actions of the Florida legislature in depriving the industry of its defense in court, remind one of nothing so much as what brought James Madison to Philadelphia in 1787. Madison was concerned about the mutability of the laws of the states and about extreme attacks on private property in several state legislatures, Rhode Island's especially.[13] The Framers constructed an elaborately complicated and moderately nationalized system of government, in order to ensure that national policies were adopted only after prolonged deliberation in a system of separated and checked powers that would guarantee against abuses of power by governments or popular majorities.

The national tobacco policy of 1998 was not the creature of a popular majority. On the contrary, polls showed that the public did not support the lawsuits, even if it generally supported measures to discourage youth smoking. The MSA was distinctly the creation of officeholders—the state attorneys general (mainly Democratic ones)— in combination with private tort lawyers who were or would become their political allies and campaign contributors. It was an unusual event in American political experience, and it is worth asking why it succeeded, given a constitutional system designed to promote deliberative lawmaking by the people's elected representatives and to inhibit the use of power either for private ends or for public ends not enjoying broad public support. Why did checks and balances, in the well-known textbook phrase, not work?

Above all in this case, the federalism check failed. Indeed, federalism had perverse consequences, driving policy in the direction of uniformity rather than diversity. Federalism divides power among governments, and this division, in theory, limits the effects of action by any one government. However, the initial lawsuits and settlements imposed costs on smokers outside the settling states. The settlements reached in Mississippi, Florida, Texas, and Minnesota drove up the prices of cigarettes everywhere, not just in those four places. Four states in effect imposed a tax on cigarettes in all fifty states, contrary to constitutional norms. If it had actually been called a tax, they could not have done it. When attorneys general elsewhere saw from the early cases that revenue could be obtained for their state governments by suing, many quickly followed the example of the leaders. Even the few long-term holdouts, states such as Delaware, North Carolina, and Virginia, eventually faced the choice of joining the others and getting their share of a settlement or getting nothing. How many of the suing attorneys general would have eventually prevailed in court and what individual settlements they might have reached had things gone that far, no one can say. Nor can one say, even, that a majority of states prevailed over a minority; were that so, it would have improved the legitimacy of the outcome. Instead, a small minority of states created a situation in which the other states and the cigarette makers had powerful incentives to reach a comprehensive settlement.

· The Results of Adversarial Legalism ·

Whereas the states' suits ended with a financial and policy bang—the extremely complicated regime of compensation and regulation embodied in the MSA—the federal government's lawsuit ended with a whimper, at least from a financial point of view. Given that RICO could not be used to compel disgorgement of past profits, an industry analyst at Morgan Stanley pronounced the outcome a "complete win" from a business perspective.[14] That held true even as the verdict was upheld by a circuit court and rejected for review by the Supreme Court, at which point tobacco stocks surged.[15]

The detour into the courts did not seriously harm the companies commercially. Even though they are under duress from declining domestic consumption, they have remained profitable. Gordon Silverstein in his book *Law's Allure* reports that for the five years between May 2002 and May 2007, tobacco outperformed the Dow Jones Industrial Average (DJIA) by more than 2 to 1, with the DJIA rising about 30 percent and tobacco stocks rising 70 percent.[16] When consulted in August 2010, Silverstein's source, a Web-based investment advisor, urged buying tobacco stocks because they were paying good dividends (6.4 percent for Reynolds American and 6.2 percent for Altria, the parent of Philip Morris).[17] A mutual fund specializing in "vice" industries—it is actually called the Vice Fund—whose three biggest holdings are Philip Morris International, Lorillard, and Altria Group—rose 4 to 5 percent in 2010 and thus ranked in the top 3 percent of large-blend funds, according to Morningstar.[18]

Tobacco's commercial success is attributable in part to inelasticity of demand. Even after years of declining consumption, U.S. consumers spent $77 billion on cigarettes in 2009.[19] But the success is attributable also to the MSA, with its suppression of price competition. This intricate and largely invisible product of adversarial legalism has enabled major manufacturers to keep raising their prices without fear of being undercut.[20]

Yet if the manufacturers more than survived the onslaught of litigation commercially—even benefited from it—it is less clear how they have fared politically. Lawsuits both public and private moved toward harsher condemnation. Judge Kessler's lengthy and damning opinion put her squarely where tobacco's opponents wanted judges to be, even if she expressed doubt that courts were the proper venue for making tobacco policy. Likewise, in the wake of the states' suits, juries proved more willing than before to find the companies guilty and to award huge punitive damages ($28 billion in one case), as well as compensatory damages. This was true particularly of juries on the West Coast.[21]

Among scholars, those most receptive to the states' lawsuits have been political scientists who study judicial policymaking. More concerned with process than with the tangible outcome, which in this case was the MSA, they have found much to admire. Silverstein, in a comprehensive study of "juridification," as he calls the institutionalized resort to courts, says, "At their best, litigation and judicial orders can break through profound political and institutional barriers that can be broken in no other way short of violent or massive systemic, institutional or constitutional change. Properly used, law can and should be the battering ram that opens the way for genuine and lasting political change."[22] Studying a series of important policy areas in which courts have acted, he found litigation promising in the case of tobacco—a battering ram that nearly worked—but its promise failed to be realized when the settlement of 1997 capsized in Congress. That was due, he concluded, to the fatally exaggerated expectations of public health partisans. Litigation had achieved so much that they incorrectly thought it could achieve everything they wanted.

In 2009 political scientists Michael McCann, William Haltom, and Shauna Fisher approvingly analyzed the way in which prosecutions over a long period had taken a turn toward what are labeled "crimtorts." Tobacco companies were increasingly portrayed in court as white collar criminals, guilty of fraud, conspiracy, and misrepresentation of their products.[23] Using content analysis of the *New York Times* coverage of tobacco in the twenty-two years from 1984–2005, McCann and his co-authors demonstrate that the coverage was abundant (a total of 7,830 items), that it increased in the 1990s, and that the volume of "litigation-heavy" articles surpassed that of "litigation-light" articles. It seems doubtful, however, that the reframing of tobacco politics through litigation reshaped mass public opinion, as they claim. Judging from the authors' own recounting of poll results, the public dislikes and distrusts Big Tobacco but continues to adhere to an ethic of individual responsibility and to blame smokers more than cigarette manufacturers for effects on smokers' health. As late as 2008, a Rasmussen poll reported that 71 percent of those questioned thought that the industry should not be held liable for smoking-related illnesses. This had been the lesson as well from years of jury verdicts in private lawsuits against cigarette manufacturers.

In any case, tobacco politics in legislatures was never driven by mass opinion. It was interest group politics. It pitted antitobacco activists, who were intensely motivated and effective in a number of states— California and Massachusetts were leading examples—against the industry. Lawsuits altered the shape of interest group politics by encouraging conversion of the leading manufacturer, Philip Morris, to support of national regulation.

It is hard to know exactly what motivated Philip Morris to make its switch. The company has always been more concerned than others to appear statesmanlike and altruistic despite the nature of its product. It has contributed to civic, cultural, and artistic causes and educational institutions. Undoubtedly, its CEOs did not like being called criminals. Beyond that, and more fundamentally, Philip Morris surely noticed that it is very hard to beat governments in the governments' courts and that it was under threat from uniquely powerful entities—several of which, in the case of the state governments, had changed their laws in order to guarantee a win in court.

Political scientist Lynn Mather, who like McCann and his co-authors is sympathetic to the use of litigation, assessed its effects both in terms of the "framing" of tobacco issues and of the impact on industry welfare and behavior. She wrote in 1998 that the wave of state suits had expanded the range of policy alternatives, constructed a new reality and a new problem definition and normative frame, created new policy actors and alliances, and devised new rules of the game. Moreover, the suits had caused the tobacco companies to reinforce "the narrative of blame placed upon them" by agreeing to pay billions of dollars to the states to drop their litigation. The legal uncertainty created by lawsuits had "hurt the tobacco industry."[24] The uncertainty increased as President Clinton announced the federal government's intention to sue, causing Democrats in Congress to jump up and down with excitement at the prospect.

It is not surprising that Philip Morris, under these circumstances, undertook a serious examination of its options and came to the conclusion—not unusual for American business corporations—that it would be prudent to submit to government regulation rather than resist so threatening a force, one uniting sovereign power with intense emotion and a hunger for revenue. As Congress approached completion of a statute in the spring of 2009, a company official said, "We recognize that we create a product that is harmful and causes serious disease. For the betterment of even our business, it is best to have a set of regulations in place to provide stability and predictability."[25] Presumably, Philip Morris calculated that cooperating with the federal government in creating a regime of regulation would create an opportunity to influence what the regime contained. It did, in fact, secure some concessions in the negotiations over the bill of 2004, including the guarantee that nicotine would not be prohibited in cigarettes and that tobacco regulation would be severed in law from the regulation of devices and pharmaceuticals.

· The Bottom Line ·

In its fifteen years of predominance (1993–2008) as a method of making public policy for tobacco, adversarial legalism did not prove more effective than ordinary politics in reducing the incidence of smoking, nor was it notably effective even in taking a toll on the companies' commerce. It was possible to assail the makers of cigarettes, but it was quite another thing to halt commerce in their product. The industry stood condemned in a federal court as of 2006, but by then condemnation was old news. The judge herself, evidently a frustrated foe of tobacco, pronounced ordinary politics preferable to litigation as a way to address issues of harm from smoking.

Yet to compare the two modes of policymaking as rivals, conceiving of them as distinct alternatives, overlooks the extent to which they have come to overlap—and are used by plaintiffs with the intention that they *should* overlap.[26] In this case of tobacco, adversarial legalism penetrated ordinary politics by turning Philip Morris, the industry leader, into an advocate of government regulation through the use of threats and legal uncertainty.

Whether one deplores this, and, like Professor Brickman, considers it state terrorism with which the companies were lawlessly bludgeoned into submission, or admires it along with Professor Silverstein, viewing it as a battering ram that could open the way for lasting political change, depends very much on one's estimate of the merits of the country's political institutions, which by original design move slowly. Though intended to produce government much stronger than that provided under the Articles of Confederation, the institutions were also intended to protect against abuses from government. It depends also on one's estimate of whether the politicizing of legal processes—their deliberate use, even, as instruments of propaganda—does harm by fostering doubt about the fairness and impartiality of such processes. In the particular case of tobacco, it depends also on whether one judges the success of public policy by a pragmatic test—the decline in smoking—or by a more ideological criterion such as the volume and intensity of condemnation cast upon the manufacturers of cigarettes. That the defendants in this case had become phenomenally rich by making a harmful product tended to color judgments of the litigation. Civil libertarians and editorial writers who would have exploded in outrage if more admirable organizations had had their political speech curtailed, their lobbies abolished, or their legal defenses wiped out, either averted their eyes or thrilled to the chase.

The argument advanced in this book has been that political institutions worked well, if gradually, in the tobacco case. Neither a critic nor a defender of cigarette manufacturers, I have sought to "think institutionally," to borrow a phrase from Hugh Heclo, and to argue the merit of ordinary politics as compared to adversarial legalism.[27] Ordinary politics did not flout public opinion and produced increasing restraints on cigarette smoking as both governments and private activists vigorously publicized the threat to public health. Even before litigation began to have an impact, Henry Waxman succeeded in shaming the companies with congressional hearings, one form of ordinary politics. His years of determined work reached a culmination when party competition, which is the engine of ordinary politics, restored him to leadership of the House Committee on Energy and Commerce. A major act of regulation followed from partisan change. Ordinary politics requires great patience and persistence, which Waxman exhibited, but did not on that account justify resort to the use of a "bludgeon" or "battering ram"—instruments that are subject to abuse (Silverstein's very choice of the name would seem to suggest as much) and are hard to deploy without risks of collateral damage.

Legislatures were supplanted by litigation in this case not because they were unresponsive to the populace but because they were only moderately and intermittently responsive to antitobacco activists. Worse, the mostly self-serving attorney general–tort lawyer alliance rendered legislatures irrelevant, except for demanding at the end that they legitimate what had been done by enacting "qualifying statutes."

· A New Era ·

Under Congress's law of 2009, the effort to eradicate smoking has become the responsibility mainly of a federal government regulator, the FDA. How effective it will be only time will tell. It will be complemented by other federal executive agencies, principally the Centers for Disease Control (CDC) and the office of the surgeon general, both of which have long been at the forefront of the effort to publicize the dangers of smoking and which can be counted on to persist in that work.[28]

These agencies may function henceforth in a political setting less marked than that of the past half century by pervid opposition to tobacco. In the efforts of governments, public health professionals, and social critics to get ordinary people to refrain from harming themselves, tobacco is falling behind obesity.[29] The health-oriented Robert Wood Johnson Foundation, which once lavished money on antitobacco activity, spent only $4 million for that purpose in 2009 as compared to $58 million to combat obesity. Within the federal government, the Obama administration and a Democratic Congress committed $1.15 billion to fighting obesity, a cause championed by the president's wife, compared to $200 million in the same period to prevent tobacco use.[30] It could be argued that ordinary politics is handicapped by dependence on the attention span of society's activists. If so, the commitment of a permanent regulator, able to function independently of fluctuations in activism, will take on particular importance.

· Notes ·

1. Centers for Disease Control and Prevention, "Achievements in Public Health, 1900–1999," *Morbidity and Mortality Weekly Report* 48 (November 5, 1999): 986–993.
2. World Health Organization, *Tobacco or Health: A Global Status Report* (Geneva, 1997): 14–17, 25–27.
3. C. Everett Koop, *Koop: The Memoirs of America's Family Doctor* (New York: Random House, 1991), 164.
4. Jacob Sullum, *For Your Own Good: The Anti-Smoking Crusade and the Tyranny of Public Health* (New York: Free Press, 1998).
5. For analyses of the processes of policy diffusion among state and local governments, see Charles R. Shipan and Craig Volden, "Bottom-Up Federalism: The Diffusion of Antismoking Policies from U.S. Cities to States," *American Journal of Political Science* 50 (October 2006), 825–843, and Shipan and Volden, "The Mechanisms of Policy Diffusion," *American Journal of Political Science* 52 (October 2008), 840–857.
6. For a meticulous review of Synar Amendment enforcement, conducted at the request of Representative Henry Waxman, see U.S. General Accounting Office, "Synar Amendment Implementation: Quality of State Data on Reducing Youth Access to Tobacco Could Be Improved," GAO-02-74, November 2001.
7. Centers for Disease Control and Prevention, "State Smoke-Free Laws for Worksites, Restaurants, and Bars—United States, 2000–2010," *Morbidity and Mortality Weekly Report* 60, no. 15 (22 April 2011): 472–475. http://www.cdc.gov/mmwr/preview/mmwrhtml/mm6015a2.htm, accessed June 13, 2011.
8. Brian McNeill, "Restaurant Smoking Snuffed out Across Va.," *Daily Progress,* Charlottesville, Va., December 2, 2009, A2.
9. Chris Herring, "North Carolina Sets Curbs on Smoking," *Wall Street Journal,* January 2–3, 2010, A3.
10. Associated Press, "Smoking Ban Signed Into Law," *Washington Post,* February 23, 2011, A3.
11. Wendy Koch, "Biggest U.S. Tax Hike on Tobacco Takes Effect," www.usatoday.com/money/perfi/taxes/2009-03-31-cigarettetax_N.htm, accessed August 1, 2009; David Brown, "Cigarette Tax Rises—And So Does Incentive to Quit," *Washington Post,* April 3, 2009, A1.
12. *Regulation by Litigation: The New Wave of Government-Sponsored Litigation* (New York: Manhattan Institute for Policy Research, 1999), 27–31.
13. James Madison, "Vices of the Political System of the United States," April 1787, in *The Papers of James Madison* 9 (Chicago: University of Chicago Press, 1975), 345–358.
14. Nell Henderson, "Tobacco Ruling Seen as a Win for Shareholders," *Washington Post,* August 19, 2006, D1.
15. Del Quentin Wilber, "Big Tobacco Loses in Appeals Court," *Washington Post,* May 23, 2009, A5; Duff Wilson, "Supreme Court Rejects Appeals of Tobacco Ruling," *New York Times,* June 30, 2010, B4.
16. Gordon Silverstein, *Law's Allure: How Law Shapes, Constrains, Saves, and Kills Politics* (Cambridge, Mass.: Cambridge University Press, 2009), 246.

17. Russ Britt, "A Roster of Dividend-paying Stocks to Consider," *Market Watch,* August 20, 2010, www.marketwatch.com/story/a-roster-of-dividend-paying-stocks-to-consider-2010–08–20, accessed August 22, 2010.
18. Andrew Ross Sorkin, ed., "Vice Fund Reaps the Wages of, Well, Sin," *The New York Times Deal Book,* http://dealbook.nytimes.com/2010/08/20/vice-fund-reaps-the-wages-of-well-sin, accessed October 16, 2010.
19. "Market Information—Philip Morris USA," www.philipmorrisusa.com/en/cms/Company/Market_Information/default.aspx?, accessed October 16, 2010.
20. Federico Ciliberto and Nicolai V. Kuminoff, "Public Policy and Market Competition: How the Master Settlement Agreement Changed the Cigarette Industry," www.bepress.com/bejeap/vol110/iss1/art63, accessed March 22, 2011. An indirect illustration of the MSA's effects comes from Florida, which, because it settled separately, is not a party to the MSA. Florida is home to DTC—the Dorsal Tobacco Company—which was selling as of 2011 nearly as many cigarettes as Reynolds American, and at a price lower by 50 cents to $2 a pack. The major manufacturers were lobbying the Florida legislature to impose fees on Dorsal and about thirty other small manufacturers in order to close the price gap. David Kesmodel, "Florida Cigarette Maker Says Fees Will Send Low Prices Up in Smoke," *Wall Street Journal,* March 15, 2011, B1.
21. The punitive damages were, however, invariably much reduced on appeal; the $28 billion, for example, turned into $13.8 million. Courts proved resistant both to extravagant punitive awards and to class actions. In the landmark Florida case of *Engle* v. *R. J. Reynolds Tobacco Company,* in which a Miami-Dade County jury in 2000 awarded $145 billion in punitive damages to Florida smokers, the state's appellate courts decertified the class action. As of 2010, individual suits, called "Engle progeny," were proceeding with mixed results. For a summary of major private suits after 2000, see W. Kip Viscusi and Joni Hersch, "Tobacco Regulation through Litigation: The Master Settlement Agreement," in *Regulation versus Litigation: Perspectives from Economics and Law,* ed. Daniel P. Kessler (Chicago: University of Chicago Press, 2011), 71–101. For a report on the Engle progeny, see Corey Stephenson, "Ending Defense Streak, Tobacco Plaintiff Wins $80 Million," *All Business,* November 19, 2010, http://www.allbusiness.com/legal/torts-punitive-damages/15322377–1.html, accessed March 18, 2011.
22. Silverstein, *Law's Allure,* 245.
23. Michael McCann, William Haltom, and Shauna Fisher, "Criminalizing Big Tobacco: Legal Mobilization and the Politics of Responsibility for Health Risks in the United States" (paper presented at the meeting of the Western Political Science Association, 2009). I am indebted to Paul J. Quirk for calling attention to this paper and to its authors for sending me a copy.
24. Lynn Mather, "Theorizing about Trial Courts: Lawyers, Policymaking, and Tobacco Litigation," *Law and Social Inquiry* 23, no. 4 (Fall 1998): 897–940.
25. Duff Wilson, "Philip Morris's Support Casts Shadow over a Bill to Limit Tobacco," *New York Times,* April 1, 2009, B3.
26. For arguments that legislation and litigation are often overlapping, and often usefully so, see Mark C. Miller and Jeb Barnes, eds., *Making Policy, Making Law: An Interbranch Perspective* (Washington, D.C.: Georgetown University

Press, 2004), and Barnes, "In Defense of Asbestos Tort Litigation: Rethinking Legal Process Analysis in a World of Uncertainty, Second Bests, and Shared Policy-making Responsibility," *Law and Social Inquiry* 34, no. 1 (Winter 2009): 5–29.

27. See Hugh Heclo, *On Thinking Institutionally* (Boulder: Paradigm Publishers, 2008).

28. For example, the surgeon general late in 2010 issued a report claiming that even occasional or secondhand exposure to cigarette smoke causes immediate damage to a person's lungs and DNA that can lead to serious illness or death. This was in the 30th tobacco-related surgeon general's report issued since 1964.

29. For analysis of the politics of obesity, see Rogan Kersh and James A. Morone, "Obesity, Courts, and the New Politics of Public Health," *Journal of Health Politics, Policy and Law* 30 (October 2005): 839–868, and Kersh, "The Politics of Obesity: A Current Assessment and Look Ahead," *The Milbank Quarterly* 87 (2009): 296–316.

30. Duff Wilson, "A Shift Toward Fighting Fat," *New York Times*, July 28, 2010, B1.

Chronology of Cigarette Regulation in the United States

January 1964—An advisory committee to the U.S. surgeon general issues a report on the link between smoking and health. It says that "cigarette smoking is a health hazard of sufficient importance to warrant appropriate remedial action."

July 1965—Congress enacts the Federal Cigarette Labeling and Advertising Act (P.L. 89–92, 79 Stat. 282), which requires that cigarette packs bear this warning: "Caution: Cigarette Smoking May Be Hazardous to Your Health." The act preempts further regulation of cigarette labeling or advertising by federal agencies or state governments and requires an annual report from the secretary of Health, Education, and Welfare (HEW) on the health consequences of smoking, along with "such recommendations for legislation as he may deem appropriate." The law also requires an annual report from the Federal Trade Commission (FTC) on the effectiveness of cigarette labeling and the industry's advertising and promotion practices, along with legislative recommendations.

April 1970—The Public Health Cigarette Smoking Act of 1969 (P.L. 91–222, 84 Stat. 87) becomes law. It requires the following language on cigarette packs: "Warning: The Surgeon General Has Determined That Cigarette Smoking Is Dangerous to Your Health." This message is to be located in a "conspicuous place" and to appear in "conspicuous and legible type." The law preempts any other government or government agency from requiring any other statement on smoking and health on cigarette packs, and it provides that "no requirement or prohibition based on smoking and health shall be imposed under State law with respect to the advertising or promotion of any cigarettes the packages of which are labeled in conformity with the provisions of this Act." The act prohibits cigarette advertising on radio and TV after January 1, 1971, and bars the FTC from acting on a pending rule for cigarette advertising prior to July 1, 1971. It also instructs the FTC to give Congress six months' notice of trade regulations dealing with cigarette advertising "in order that the Congress may act if it so desires." It continues the requirement of annual reports on smoking and health by the secretary of HEW and on cigarette advertising and promotion by the FTC.

April 1977—The Berkeley, California, city council passes an ordinance restricting smoking in public indoor spaces and requiring separate sections for smokers and nonsmokers in restaurants.

1982—The annual report of the surgeon general identifies cigarette smoking as the "chief preventable cause of death."

June 1983—San Francisco adopts a clean indoor air ordinance, making that city the twenty-second locality in California—and the first big American city—to do so. Such ordinances spread in the 1980s and 1990s in California and elsewhere, surging after the Environmental Protection Agency in 1990 tentatively calls environmental tobacco smoke a human carcinogen.

October 1984—Congress enacts the Comprehensive Smoking Education tion Act (P.L. 98–474, 98 Stat. 2200), which proclaims "a new strategy for making Americans more aware of any adverse health effects of smoking." The act requires the secretary of Health and Human Services (HHS—formerly HEW) to carry out a program of smoking research, education, and information, including the compilation of state and local laws relating to the use and consumption of cigarettes. It also mandates the use of four different warnings on cigarette packs and in advertisements, including billboards. These warnings are to be rotated quarterly, and each is to be preceded by the phrase "SURGEON GENERAL'S WARNING." The warnings are "Smoking Causes Lung Cancer, Heart Disease, Emphysema, And May Complicate Pregnancy"; "Quitting Smoking Now Greatly Reduces Serious Risks to Your Health"; "Smoking By Pregnant Women May Result in Fetal Injury, Premature Birth, And Low Birth Weight"; and "Cigarette Smoke Contains Carbon Monoxide." The law also requires cigarette manufacturers annually to provide the secretary with a list of ingredients added to tobacco in the manufacture of cigarettes, and removes restraints on the FTC contained in previous laws. Opponents of tobacco regard this act as their first victory in Congress.

October 1987—The Centers for Disease Control and Prevention (CDC) publishes an estimate that 315,120 deaths resulted from cigarette smoking in 1984. In 1997 the CDC revises this estimate to 437,000 deaths per year as an average for 1990–1994. Thereafter, 430,000 deaths per year becomes a commonly used figure.

December 1987—Congress includes in a transportation appropriations bill a ban on smoking on domestic airline flights of two hours or less, to take effect in 1988. This ban covers an estimated 80 percent of all domestic flights.

November 1988—California voters approve Proposition 99, which increases the tobacco excise tax from 10 cents to 35 cents a pack and devotes 20 percent of the resulting revenues to a tobacco control program. By the late 1990s, according to the federal Office on Smoking and Health, Maine, Oregon, Massachusetts, and Arizona join California in establishing well-funded state tobacco control programs through earmarked increases in their excise taxes on tobacco.

November 1989—In a transportation appropriations bill, Congress enacts a permanent ban on smoking on almost all domestic commercial airline flights, to take effect in 1990. The only exceptions are for flights beginning or ending in Alaska or Hawaii and lasting more than six hours.

February 1990—A national status report on smoking and health, issued by the federal Office on Smoking and Health, reports that all but seven states impose limits on smoking in public places.

July 1992—Congress enacts the Synar Amendment (a provision of P.L. 102–321, 106 Stat. 394), which requires as a condition of federal grants for control of alcohol and substance abuse that state governments have a law prohibiting sale of tobacco products to persons under eighteen years of age. States are required to enforce such laws "in a manner that can reasonably be expected to reduce the extent to which tobacco products are available to individuals under the age of 18," to "annually conduct random, unannounced inspections to ensure compliance with the law," and to make an annual report to the secretary of HHS regarding progress and enforcement strategies.

February 1994—In a letter to the chairman of the Coalition on Smoking OR Health, Commissioner David A. Kessler of the Food and Drug Administration (FDA) announces an intention to regulate cigarettes because they contain the drug nicotine, which cigarette manufacturers design to satisfy an addiction. This stance breaks with the position of previous FDA commissioners, who interpreted the Food, Drug, and Cosmetic Act (FDCA) to mean that the FDA lacked authority to regulate cigarettes.

March–June 1994—Hearings of the Subcommittee on Health and the Environment of the House Committee on Energy and Commerce, with Henry Waxman as chairman, provide a platform for Commissioner Kessler to attack nicotine as an addictive drug and cigarette companies for manipulating the nicotine content of cigarettes. Cigarette company executives testify that nicotine is not addictive in a televised event that is a high point in the propaganda war against tobacco.

May 1994—Mike Moore, attorney general of Mississippi, sues the major cigarette manufacturers to recover the costs of Medicaid that the state claims are attributable to smoking. Dozens of other states also sue, the largest single group in 1997 as it becomes clear that Moore's suit will end in a financially rewarding settlement.

August 1995—The FDA publishes proposed regulations designed to discourage youth consumption of tobacco. Among other things, they prohibit sales of cigarettes to persons under eighteen; require vendors of cigarettes to verify the age of purchasers with a photo ID; prohibit vending machine sales or self-service displays except where persons under eighteen are not permitted; ban the use of billboards and advertising posters near schools and public playgrounds; limit advertising and labeling to a black-and-white, text-only format; prohibit the sale and distribution of promotional items such as hats and T-shirts bearing cigarette brand names; and prohibit sponsorship of sporting and musical events and of sports teams using brand names.

August 1996—FDA regulations are published in final form, to take effect for the most part a year later. However, the prohibition on sales to persons under eighteen and the requirement of a photo ID are to take effect in February 1997. The regulations are designed to preempt state laws governing age of purchase.

April 1997—In response to a suit filed by the industry, a federal district judge in North Carolina rules that Congress has not withheld authority to regulate cigarettes from the FDA. However, he also rules that the FDCA does not authorize the FDA to regulate the promotion and advertisement of tobacco products. Both sides appeal. Regulations already implemented, which govern age of purchase and requirement of a photo ID, are allowed to remain in effect pending appeal.

June 1997—The state attorneys general and the cigarette manufacturers announce a comprehensive settlement of the states' lawsuits. The companies agree to pay $368.5 billion over twenty-five years and submit to FDA regulation and many onerous restrictions on their marketing and advertising. They are to be relieved of class-action suits and punitive damage claims for past misconduct, and their payment of judgments or settlements in lawsuits will be subject to an annual cap. This agreement is contingent on enactment by Congress as well as consent decrees, but Congress does not approve it. In 1998 the Senate considers but fails to enact a substitute—called the McCain bill for its sponsor, Sen. John McCain of Arizona—that is far more punitive to the industry.

June 1997—Mississippi and the cigarette industry settle the state attorney general's lawsuit, with an industry agreement to pay the state more than $3 billion. Individual settlements follow also in Florida (August 1997, for $11.3 billion); Texas (January 1998, for $15.3 billion); and Minnesota (May 1998, for $6.1 billion, along with $469 million for Blue Cross–Blue Shield of Minnesota).

August 1998—Reversing the judgment of the district court, the U.S. Court of Appeals for the Fourth Circuit rules that the FDA lacks jurisdiction to regulate tobacco products and that all of the FDA's regulations of August 1996 are invalid. However, in response to requests from the government, the circuit court issues stays that permit the FDA to continue enforcing its age-of-purchase and photo ID rules pending appeal to the Supreme Court.

November 1998—The major cigarette manufacturers and the attorneys general of the forty-six states that have not previously settled individually with the industry conclude a "master settlement agreement" that is a much-modified version of the settlement of June 1997. This agreement will cost the industry an estimated $206 billion over twenty-five years; drive up the cost of cigarettes; and restrict the industry's marketing and advertising (for example, by eliminating billboards, transit ads, and the use of cartoon characters, and by limiting the number of event sponsorships). The industry receives no protection from liability in private lawsuits or from class actions. This agreement does not provide for FDA regulation and does not depend on congressional enactment. State legislatures and courts approve it, and it withstands legal challenges. States begin receiving money in November 1999.

January 1999—The outgoing attorney general of Massachusetts issues regulations that he says are designed to "close holes" in the Master

Settlement Agreement. Among other things, they prohibit "outdoor advertising, including advertising in enclosed stadiums and advertising from within a retail establishment that is directed toward or visible from the outside of the establishment, in any location that is within a 1,000 foot radius of any public playground, playground area in a public park, elementary school or secondary school," as well as "point-of-sale advertising . . . any portion of which is placed lower than five feet from the floor of any retail establishment which is located within a one thousand foot radius. . . ." The Massachusetts rules are for the most part upheld by federal district and circuit courts, but the industry in January 2001 secures a grant of certiorari from the Supreme Court. Circuit courts around the country have divided on the question of whether federal law preempts advertising regulations enacted by state and local governments.

September 1999—The U.S. Department of Justice, following the example of state governments and instructions from the Clinton White House, files a civil lawsuit against the largest cigarette manufacturers, charging that they have conspired since the 1950s to defraud the public and conceal information about the effects of smoking. Relying on three statutes—the Medical Care Recovery Act, the Medicare Secondary Payer Act, and the Racketeer Influenced and Corrupt Organizations (RICO) Act—the government seeks to recover billions of dollars in medical care costs. A year later, a federal judge dismisses the counts brought under the first two statutes but allows the case to proceed under RICO.

March 2000—By a 5 to 4 majority, the Supreme Court rules that Congress "has clearly precluded the FDA from asserting jurisdiction to regulate tobacco products. Such authority is inconsistent with the intent that Congress has expressed in the [Food, Drug and Cosmetic Act's] overall regulatory scheme and in the tobacco-specific legislation that it has enacted subsequent to the FDCA." The FDA's regulatory regime ends.

June 2001—The Supreme Court rules in *Lorillard Tobacco Co. v. Reilly, Attorney General of Massachusetts,* that the Federal Cigarette Labeling and Advertising Act, as enacted in 1965 and as amended in 1969, preempts Massachusetts's regulations governing outdoor and point-of-sale cigarette advertising. This decision appears likely to invalidate the advertising regulations of other states and their local subdivisions but does not affect advertising restrictions contained in the Master Settlement Agreement.

2001—Philip Morris begins to seek FDA regulation of cigarettes, improving prospects of action by Congress.

2002–2003—New York City enacts a strict antismoking ordinance that applies to all indoor workplaces; restaurants, no matter how small; and bars. The New York legislature follows with a similar statewide law. Antismoking ordinances spread even in Tobacco Country. As of 2003, all fifty states and the District of Columbia restrict smoking in public places, variously defined. California, Delaware, New York, Maine, and Connecticut prohibit smoking in virtually all public places and enclosed places of employment. Forty-five states and the District of Columbia restrict smoking in government workplaces, and twenty-six states and the District of Columbia restrict smoking in private workplaces.

July 2004—The Senate approves FDA regulation of tobacco.

August 2006—U. S. District Judge Gladys Kessler finds the major cigarette companies guilty of violating the civil provisions of RICO. In an opinion of nearly 1,700 pages, she writes that they have sold "a highly addictive product which causes diseases that lead to a staggering number of deaths per year, an immeasurable amount of human suffering and economic loss, and a profound burden on our national health care system." The ruling asserts that although the cigarette companies had knowledge of the harm of their products, they denied the facts to the public. An appellate court upholds her verdict in 2009, and the Supreme Court in 2010 declines review. The financial impact of the decision is limited by a federal appellate court ruling of 2005 that the RICO statute is forward-looking only and cannot be used to compel disgorgement of past profits.

July 2008—The House of Representatives enacts tobacco regulation.

February 2009—The General Assembly of Virginia, a state that is home to Philip Morris, the country's leading cigarette manufacturer, and that has a long and proud tradition of producing tobacco, approves a ban on smoking in most of its bars and restaurants, to take effect in December.

June 2009—President Barack Obama signs the Family Smoking Prevention and Tobacco Control Act (P. L. 111-31, 123 Stat. 1776), which gives the Food and Drug Administration broad authority to regulate both the manufacture and marketing of tobacco products, following passage by wide margins in both the House and Senate. The FDA is authorized to require changes in the design and characteristics of current and future tobacco products, including the reduction or elimination of harmful ingredients and additives, although it cannot reduce nicotine yields to zero. Manufacturers must obtain FDA approval to market a new tobacco product unless the FDA determines that it is substantially equivalent to, or a minor modification of, a product already on the market. The law prohibits use of terms such as "light," "mild," and "low" that might be taken to imply safety, and requires bigger, graphic warnings on both sides of cigarette packs and in advertising.

January 2010—A ban on smoking in bars and restaurants goes into effect in North Carolina, which produces nearly half of the tobacco grown in the United States.

February 2011—The New York City Council, following a recommendation of Mayor Michael R. Bloomberg, votes to extend a prohibition on smoking to all 1,700 of the city's parks and to 14 miles of public beaches.

Index